IF MEN WERE ANGELS
A View from the Senate

IF MEN WERE ANGELS

A View from the Senate

by JAMES L. BUCKLEY

G. P. Putnam's Sons
New York

SBN: 399-11589-7
Library of Congress Catalog Card Number: 75-27407   1-21 76

PRINTED IN THE UNITED STATES OF AMERICA

To the women in my life (in chronological order):

To my mother, Aloïse Steiner Buckley, for—along with so very much more—having instilled in me a knowledge and love of country

To my sisters, Aloïse, Priscilla, Jane, Patricia, Maureen, and Carol, whose accomplishments have never allowed me any illusions as to which is the more equal sex

To my wife, Ann, for her love and good-natured tolerance of the impulse that led me into public life, and

To my daughter, Priscilla, for providing me (along with her five brothers) with incentive enough to work for the preservation of the American heritage.

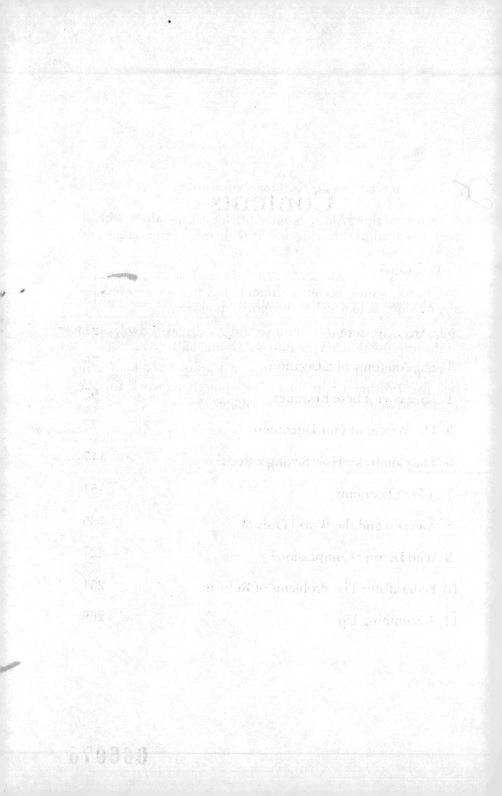

Contents

Foreword

When my friends ask me what sort of a book I have been working on these past many months, I have been hard put to describe it. As I look over the final draft, I see that I have produced a mixed bag of narrative, observations, and reflections based on my first four years in office.

However it will be described, I hope this volume will prove informative on how the Senate of the United States operates in practice and what the life of a Senator is like. But of far greater importance, I hope it will stimulate a little reflection on the insights into the nature of man and liberty on which the American Republic was structured.

I believe that in the last analysis the most important thing in social and political life is freedom, and I believe that it is because of the safeguards written into the Constitution, and the character of the American people, that we have enjoyed it in so great a measure. But I also believe that our freedom is now in clear and present danger for the reasons I have attempted to describe in the chapters that follow.

I hope this book will remind the reader of some of the premises on which our society has been built, and of the distance we have strayed from too many of them. If so, it will have contributed to my first goal in political life, which is to defend, preserve, and expand the realm of freedom.

JAMES L. BUCKLEY

WASHINGTON, D. C.
JUNE, 1975

If men were angels, no government would be necessary. . . . In forming a government which is to be administered by men over men, the great difficulty lies in this: You must first enable the government to control the governed; and in the next place, oblige it to control itself.

—*The Federalist Papers*

1
Why Me?

ON JANUARY 21, 1971, Jacob Javits, pursuant to custom, escorted me down the center aisle of the United States Senate Chamber. Vice President Agnew swore me in and I was handed a pen with which I entered my name on the books of the Senate. I then walked a few steps to my desk on the Republican side of the aisle. I had become the junior Senator from the State of New York. Or, as Senatorial courtesy has it, the distinguished and honorable Senator from the great State of New York. Rarely had anyone, distinguished and honorable—or otherwise—entered the United States Senate so innocent of the mechanisms of a legislative body or of the political influences that shape the legislative process.

Eventually, however, through the courtesy and patience of my colleagues and the expert knowledge of parliamentarians and committee staffs, I managed to learn, if not entirely master, the intricacies of Senatorial duties. Yet the more I learned, the more I became convinced that what ultimately mattered in the Senate was not possession of a photographic memory capable of storing the entire *Rules and Manuals of the United States Senate*, but rather an understanding of the role of government in a free society and the ability to translate that understanding into an effective analysis of the programs and policies before me.

My entry onto the political stage had come at a particularly opportune time for one who believed that ideas do have relevance to the practical world, and that those ideas that illuminated the political understanding of the founders of the American Republic continue to be as fresh and pertinent today as they ever were.

13

These are ideas that in a very real sense are now being rediscovered, after years of neglect, as part of a coherent understanding of the nature and needs of a free society. And I believe they contain today, as they did so long ago, the seeds of true reform—if the protection of freedom, the advancement of justice, and the improvement of the condition of life of the American people are considered the proper objectives for reform.

A little more than ten years before my election, in January, 1960, the Victor Publishing House of Shepherdsville, Kentucky, had published a slim 123-page volume with the then-intriguing title *The Conscience of a Conservative*. In those days it was a kind of heresy to suggest conservatives had minds, let alone consciences. But Barry Goldwater changed all that.

The reception given his book was, to put it mildly, mixed. On the one hand the public eventually purchased over 1,000,000 copies in all editions. On the other hand, like some other best-selling authors, Senator Goldwater suffered the fate of a bad review from the New York *Times*.

The *Times'* reviewer—who also happened to be a member of the *Times'* editorial board—began his review by warning Senator Goldwater that he would not receive the Vice Presidential nomination at the 1960 Republican convention unless he "suppressed" this book. In the *Times'* tradition of damning with faint praise those books of whose message they disapproved, their reviewer described Goldwater as "pleasant," and as being as true a conservative as a "stagecoach" or "buffalo." But the *Times'* man wasn't sure if Goldwater's conservatism would be approved either by "Alexander Hamilton or the Almighty."

The condescending tone of the reviewer, his barely disguised irritation at the presumption of this conservative Republican Senator—of all people—from Arizona—of all places—to dare to speak out on matters of political philosophy were certainly typical of the Eastern establishment smugness of 1960.

But that book, and its plain-spoken author, and the issues he raised in his subsequent Presidential campaign, planted and nourished seeds that within a decade had transformed the American political landscape. In so doing, he prepared the way for my own election. But of more fundamental importance, he launched a movement that has caused students and writers and even politicians to reexamine the premises of our political institutions: to stand back and see how far we have managed to move away from them in recent years.

In part, it is the purpose of this book to continue this examination, applying those premises, as I understand them, to my own experiences and to the problems that have faced our nation during my first four years in the United States Senate.

It was in March of 1970 that I made a decision that would abruptly change the whole course of my life. That was the decision to seek election to the United States Senate.

My initiation into politics had been largely accidental. I had always lived an intensely private life. Following my graduation from the Yale Law School in 1949, I practiced law for four years in New Haven. In 1953 I married and moved to New York City where, for the next seventeen years, I worked as vice-president of the Catawba Corporation, a firm owned by members of my family. The firm provides a variety of services to small independent companies engaged in oil and gas exploration, primarily outside the United States. Because this work involved a great deal of foreign travel, I had little time for active political involvement.

But in 1965 I received a wholly unexpected telephone call from brother Bill, confirming (a) that he had yielded to an impulse and now found himself the New York Conservative Party's candidate for Mayor of New York City and (b) that he wanted me to be his campaign manager. It was clear that he knew he couldn't win, because he was proposing that the blind lead the blind. I had never had any experience with a political campaign, let alone the management of one.

When I protested my total ignorance of the art, he assured me that there were plenty of able men and women within the ranks of the Conservative Party who were capable of handling such matters as scheduling and strategy. What he needed was somebody who understood the limitations under which he would have to operate, and who would protect him from the excessive zeal of the party brethren. When I then protested that I was far too busy to worry about his adventures into politics, he assured me that he too was busy and that he had agreed to run on the understanding that he would not be required to spend more than two or three days a week campaigning. For my part, all that would be required would be two or three hours in the morning every other day or so. Bill can be enormously persuasive, and I found myself, against my better judgment, agreeing to become a campaign manager.

Needless to say, we were no sooner into the campaign than both of us found it was demanding from eight to twelve hours a day and more of our time. There is simply no way to do less than your best in such a venture, even when you know there is no possibility of winning. If nothing else, you cannot let down the thousands of volunteers who are pouring their hearts and souls into your candidacy. And furthermore, the strategic purpose of third-party "leverage" politics, the kind represented by New York's Conservative and Liberal Parties, is to demonstrate the size of the following your particular views can attract, in the hope that the demonstration will influence the selection of future candidates by the Republican and Democratic Parties.

Election day finally came around, Bill lost, and I returned to my normal life. It had been an interesting, exhausting exposure to the strange world of elective politics, and there were moments I would always remember. But I was certain my involvement in politics was ended.

But less than three years later, in 1968, the phone rang again. It was Bill. The Fathers of the Conservative Party had interceded with him to intercede with me to become, of all things, the party's candidate for the United States Senate. My opponent would be Senator Jacob Javits, one of New York's champion vote-getters.

I brushed Bill off with the observation that they must really be getting desperate. I hadn't lifted a finger in the political vineyards since the mayoralty campaign and they had no way of knowing whether I would be an effective spokesman for the conservative point of view. What the devil—I didn't even know how to give a speech! It was one thing to help out a brother who had allowed himself to be coaxed into being a political candidate; it was quite another to make the same mistake myself.

Two weeks later I received a call from Dan Mahoney, the Chairman and co-founder of the Conservative Party. He is a very persuasive man. First of all, Dan assured me that I had no prospect whatever of being elected. Therefore, for me to enter the race would involve only a short-term commitment of time. The campaign itself, he promised, would not be demanding (only two or three days a week), and I would find the activities interesting. He succeeded in arousing my curiosity. I had no idea how I would make out, and began thinking of the experience as a kind of intensified Dale Carnegie course as I went about the state trying to win friends and influence voters in a cause in which I believed. If I ended up making a fool of myself, well then, at least I would have learned something about my own limitations.

Once again I learned that there is no such thing as parttime campaigning, at least not for me. But I also learned that I could in fact give a speech, could hold my own in debate, could field reporters' questions. And more important, I found that my frankly stated views (the ability to state views frankly being one of the bonuses of running in a contest you know you can't win) struck a responsive chord in far more New Yorkers than the New York *Times* cared to admit. (The one issue, in the fall of 1968, which failed to draw much response was the need to do something about pollution. One supporter even dressed me down for wasting my efforts on a "nonissue." On this one I think I can modestly say that I was merely ahead of my time.)

The campaign was starved for funds. It was October before we could distribute basic campaign materials—leaflets, bumper stickers, posters, and pins. And by the time election day rolled around, we had received and spent $160,000, less than 10 percent of what each of my two opponents had expended, and none of it for statewide television or radio commercials. Nevertheless, because of the selfless work of an army of Conservative Party volunteers, and because my positions had so broad an acceptance, I managed to receive 1,142,000 votes, more than twice as many as any third-party candidate had previously polled in a New York election, for a total of more than 14 percent of the vote.

Once again it had been an interesting, exhausting experience, and I now knew what it was to be a candidate for elective office. This rounded out my collection of political experiences. The New York *Daily News* ran a story under the headline BUCKLEY'S LAST HURRAH, and as far as I was concerned, it was. And so I returned to the serious business of earning what it takes to feed, clothe, and educate a family of six children.

It was because of this offbeat exposure to politics that in March, 1970, I could find myself seriously considering the possibility of actually being elected to the United States Senate as a third-party candidate. I began to consider this possibility not because I had acquired a taste for campaigning (I had not; I had found my 1968 campaign as grueling an experience, physically and emotionally, as I had ever had), or because I had begun to have Walter Mitty fantasies about life in the public eye (it is the loss of personal privacy that I still find the most trying part of my present life).

I began to assess my chances of winning an election that March because I had become seriously worried about the future of the United States.

I had spent the prior four months on business trips abroad to places such as Canada, the Philippines, Indonesia, New Zealand, and Australia. In each country the newspapers were filled with new stories of outbreaks of violence and arson in American colleges and cities. The United States, for so long a symbol around the world of social stability, seemed to be falling apart.

We tend to forget the scope of the mindless rounds of destruction that seized the country during the late 1960's, reaching their peak in the riots that swept scores of campuses in the wake of the Cambodian incursion in April, 1970. Nothing better recaptures the mood of that period than a column written during the Cambodian spring by the distinguished American journalist James Jackson Kilpatrick. Kilpatrick had been on a speaking tour and had come back to his motel, dead tired, after an evening at the lectern. This is part of what he wrote:

> . . . I have been sitting for a while in the green-tweed chair watching Kansas burn on the TV screen. The color control is out of kilter; I am too tired to correct it, so the smoke comes out purple and the flames a putty yellow. This is the dawning, so they say, of the Age of Aquarius; I herald it from a motel, darkly, in the livid light of a University set afire.
>
> In the name of God, what has happened to our country? If this were Columbia or Cornell or Berkeley, the flickering image might not sear the heart. Scar tissue grows. But this is Lawrence, Kansas, heartland America; here, too, the arsonist's torch. And tonight it is not only Kansas.
>
> At Penn State, the President and his wife have fled their home to escape the stones of "dissenters." Demonstrators seize a campus building in upstate New York. The virus of nihilism, nothingism, spreads its destructive infection. . . .
>
> How have we fallen so weak, so sick, so spineless, nerveless, gutless? Is this the consequence of some lunatic obsession with equality—that all ideas are equally good, all modes of conduct equally permissible? Have we so corrupted our values as to accept the suicidal notion that in a society based upon order, disorder deserves equal time?
>
> So, it's the Age of Aquarius, is it? The fault, dear Brutus, lies not in our stars but in ourselves. We middle Americans have signally failed to look after first things first, to cultivate in our public institutions those rules of law, civility, and grace that might have kept the whole thing in balance.
>
> Somehow we forgot—and this is Burke again—that liberty exists only with order and virtue, and cannot exist at all without them. . . .

It was in a large sense the seeming disintegration of the social fabric in America described with such biting economy by Kilpatrick that played a central role in my own decision to enter public life.

I remember one night, in Darwin, Australia, talking with two Americans who just a few years earlier had pulled up stakes and emigrated. One had established a thriving business dealing in cement; the other had opened a large area to the cultivation of cotton, applying all the advanced techniques that had been developed in our own country. They had left the United States because they felt strangled by regulations, because taxes and inflation had been eating into their earnings faster than they could accumulate them, because the streets of American cities were no longer safe. They had decided that America was coming to the end of the line, and had concluded it was time to break loose from a society in which they saw no escape from an irresistible growth of governmental power at the expense of individual freedom and initiative. And so, they and hundreds like them sold what they had, moved themselves and their families 12,000 miles, and started afresh in what they felt to be a freer, more hopeful society.

I bridled as I listened. I was not about to write off the United States, with its magnificent history of freedom and hope and its beauty and strength and vigor and generosity. Yet, as I heard them talking, I found that for the first time in my adult life I feared for my country.

It was during this conversation in late January or early February that I began to think about the possibility of seeking the Senate seat occupied by Charles Goodell. Goodell, who seventeen months earlier had been appointed to fill the vacancy left by Robert Kennedy's assassination, by then had dramatically changed his political views. In so doing, he left an important—I believed a majority—segment of New York opinion unrepresented. I had no thought whatsoever of emigrating from the United States, but I did ask myself what I could do to help keep the predictions made by these new Australians from coming true.

I thought about this all the way back to the United States, considering the prospects of entering the Republican primary and trying for election to the United States Senate as the candidate of both the Republican and Conservative parties. One thing I was certain of, and that is that I would not consider running unless I had a reasonable chance of succeeding. A Senate race is not the sort that anyone will run a second time just for the exercise.

When I returned to New York in mid-March I set about checking the relevant political facts. Two things I learned in quick succession: I was not technically qualified to force a primary challenge against Goodell, and if I had any interest whatever in running, I would have to make a tentative public commitment within days. Under New York's election laws the Conservative Party's nomination could not be tendered later than March 25. That same law, however, did provide an escape hatch. I could withdraw at any time until April 7, when I would be required to file an affidavit legally committing me to the race. I considered the possibility of running without the Republican line, as Charles Goodell's change of political course had so angered a great majority of New York Republicans that it was conceivable I could win running solely as the candidate of the Conservative Party.

I had exactly ten days to decide whether or not to seek the Conservative Party nomination; and if nominated, just thirteen additional days during which I could open the escape hatch and avoid being committed to the race.

I had decided that I would make a final commitment only if I could satisfy myself that it was not romantic to believe victory possible; that my candidacy would be taken seriously enough, early enough, by the press to give it the credibility necessary for it to have any chance whatever; and that I could be assured, before I was finally committed, of initial financing of at least $100,000.

These were rather large ifs. To help me get the answers, I turned first to F. Clifton White, the political strategist who had been responsible for engineering Barry Goldwater's nomination for the Presidency six years earlier. Clif heard my story and then said that I couldn't have the answers to any of my questions without first conducting a poll to determine the views of New York voters on a series of questions. Only with these answers in hand could we determine whether or not I was a viable candidate, and it was only as a viable candidate that I could secure early commitment of money and hazard an educated guess as to how my candidacy would be viewed by the press.

We raised $15,000 to cover the cost of the poll and other incidental expenses. The poll itself, however, would not be ready until April 1 at the earliest. Screwing up my courage, I asked Dan Mahoney whether the Executive Committee of the Conservative Party would be willing to recommend my nomination to the Senate on the understanding that I might well withdraw before I was required to confirm my candidacy with an affidavit. He reported back that they would; and a few days later I appeared before the Conservative Party convention to accept the party's nomination.

The days went by with agonizing slowness while we waited for the results of the poll. In the meantime we were discovering the difficulty of securing significant financial commitments months before the campaign would actually get into full swing, months before the identity of the Democratic candidate would be determined in a primary election, and at any time before I was in a position to present evidence in support of the proposition that my candidacy actually had a chance for success.

The results were finally tabulated on April 4. They revealed that 23.8 percent of New Yorkers regarded themselves as conservative and 32.6 percent as moderate. Clearly there was a base to work on that could provide a victory, especially in a three-cornered race. Moreover, on all the issues then uppermost in the public mind, including Vietnam, my own positions coincided with those of a majority. If I were not preempted on the issues by whoever won the Democratic primary, I had a gambler's chance of winning, despite the institutional advantages that my opponents would enjoy because of their party affiliations.

It was now too late to try to satisfy my second and third conditions, but I nevertheless decided to file the affidavit confirming my candidacy. A friend had offered to put up securities as collateral for a $50,000 loan to be repaid out of future campaign contributions. This enabled us to set up a headquarters, begin hiring a campaign staff, and send out the first of a number of fund-raising letters. (Ultimately I was to raise more than $1,800,000 from over 40,000 individual contributors.)

Congressman Richard Ottinger, of Westchester, obliged me by winning the Democratic primary with the help of $2,100,000 borrowed from his mother. His views on the issues were virtually indistinguishable from those of Charles Goodell, which simplified my job in the three-way televised debates. I had no problem in distinguishing their collective positions from mine, whereas they never mastered the art of making plausible distinctions between their own views on any given issue.

As I crisscrossed New York State during the campaign I was struck by the change—or intensification—in attitudes since I had run the same course two years earlier. I saw a mounting concern over the outbreaks of social disorder. I watched hardhats by the thousands marching down Broadway to demonstrate their love of country, their deep belief in its values and institutions, and their concern for its future at a time when many of their countrymen were burning the American flag and marching under Viet Cong banners. I felt the frustration of individual citizens growing in proportion to the rising level of governmental intrusion into every corner of their lives. I talked to hundreds of industrious New Yorkers who found themselves increasingly trapped between taxation and inflation, unable any longer to plan for their own futures or the futures of their children.

For perhaps the first time in their lives they felt they could no longer be sure that the America they had inherited, with its values, its freedoms, its challenges and opportunities, would survive, reasonably intact, to be passed on to their children.

I was running for election in what is generally regarded as the heartland of American liberalism, and doing so as the candidate of a party that threw down the gauntlet at the feet of the New York political establishment by frankly designating itself "Conservative." As I moved around the state, it became manifestly clear, far more so than two years earlier, that conservatism had managed to shed its Wall Street, know-nothing, treading-on-the-poor image and had come to be understood as a position manifesting a true concern for the protection of higher values. Because of this I was able to campaign successfully in New York under the label "Conservative" and to speak to the public in terms of a conservative analysis of current problems.

It is true that many, perhaps most, of the people I met

during my campaign had probably never thought of themselves as conservative. But when an unapologetic and clear presentation of conservative alternatives was made to them, they responded by the hundreds of thousands. The voters of New York, including an estimated 900,000 members of labor unions, for the most part traditionally Democratic, did recognize the difference between the Goodell-Ottinger approach to current problems and mine, and when faced with a clear choice between them, they chose the one that I represented.*

While I never felt that my election was assured, after the first few weeks I was confident that I had a chance to win. And as I entered the final week of the campaign, the polls showed me ahead, but by a margin so slender that in its election eve issue, the New York *Daily News* declared the race too close to call. The campaign itself was a blur of rallies and journeys by plane, bus, and car, televised debates, with one event following another in such rapid succession that I had little time to worry about where I stood. All I knew was that I had a chance to present a viewpoint I believed in, and I took every opportunity to do just that. By election day I was satisfied that I had done everything I could.

---

*I suspect that eyebrows will be raised by this statement, as I won election in that three-way race by a plurality of 39 percent. I base my assertion that it was a clear victory for my point of view, for conservatism, on the authority of Charles Goodell. In a postelection interview the New York *Post* reported:

. . . in a wide-ranging election post-mortem, Goodell also defended his decision to remain in the race, asserting that his withdrawal would have "guaranteed" victory for Conservative Senator-elect James L. Buckley rather than for Democratic Rep. Richard L. Ottinger.

Goodell said he had concluded from a number of polls that his departure from the race "would probably have thrown more votes at that stage to Buckley than Ottinger.

"We analyzed where Buckley's strength was," he said. "Our analysis was that a good portion of it was Republican. A good portion was upstate and suburban.

"And if I had said, 'I'm withdrawing. Please don't vote for me. Vote for Ottinger,' that vote wasn't going to go to Ottinger. It was a Republican vote that would've gone to Buckley. My withdrawing at the stage would have guaranteed the election of Mr. Buckley."

My election-night headquarters at the Waldorf-Astoria was bedlam. The huge ballroom was filled with campaign workers and well-wishers. Upstairs in a suite I watched the returns on television with my wife and children, members of my family, close friends, and key members of my campaign staff. I began with an early lead, lost some ground between the first and second hours, and then steadily increased my margin over the second-place runner, Richard Ottinger. By 10:00, Clif White and Art Finkelstein (my volunteer analyst who called the final results within one-tenth of one percent based on a Sunday-night telephone survey) assured me that I had won. Within another hour I too concluded that I had won, but the CBS election-night computer (VPA) hung in there. It wasn't about to concede the election to an upstart conservative. But finally, after I went to the ballroom to tell the increasingly exuberant and restless crowd that I *appeared* to be the winner, and after my opponents had admitted that I appeared to be right, CBS reluctantly yielded to the inevitable, threw in the electronic towel, and (at 1:00 A.M.) declared me the victor.

2
A Minority of One

ON THE DAY after I was sworn in, when I consulted a large printed directory listing members of the Senate, I was startled to see my name looming out from the sheet in upper-case capital letters. Mine was the only name so printed. A quick check of the legend beneath the list of Senators, their states, office suites, and telephone numbers revealed that the names of Democrats were printed in ordinary type (*e.g.,* James Allen), Republicans in italics (*e.g., Jacob Javits*), Independents (HARRY F. BYRD JR.) in capital and small capital letters, and Conservative-Republicans (me) in the aforementioned style.

Clearly, along with Harry Byrd, I was a minority of one. Harry had won reelection the prior November, having run as an Independent rather than as a Democrat. For my part, I chose to be listed as Conservative-Republican to reflect the fact that I was elected to office as the candidate of New York State's Conservative Party while being enrolled in the state and working within the Senate as a Republican. An extraordinary fuss was raised over my insistence on this particular designation, which I believed to be the most accurate way of describing what I was and how I had arrived in the Senate. It provided the meat for at least one Evans and Novak column, and one of the arguments in Senator Javits' case for trying to have me excluded from the Senate Republican Caucus until I had had the opportunity to demonstrate my Republicanism.

For a fleeting moment, when we first met one another as roastees at a "little gridiron" banquet held at Hot Springs shortly after our elections, Harry Byrd and I discussed the desirability of forming our own caucus and occupying two

27

desks wedged into the aisle separating the Republican and Democratic members. I would nominate him to be Leader, and he would nominate me to be the Whip. In this manner each of us could lay claim to the emoluments of these positions, namely, a special suite of offices in the Capitol, a limousine and chauffeur, and an extra $5,000 per year in salary. We finally decided it was an idea whose time had not yet come.

I was soon to learn that in the unstructured life of the Senate, every member who is not vested with particular responsibilities as a committee or subcommittee chairman (and these positions, of course, are reserved to members of the majority party) operates essentially as a minority of one: as an individual with his own special constituent interests and responsibilities, his own understanding of what the role of a Senator should be, his own view of how the public welfare is best served and our constitutional system best preserved.

There are a variety of ways in which a Senator can present his point of view and seek to achieve his goals. In the course of each day he works on legislation in committee and on the floor. But he also works with his staff in becoming actively involved in a whole spectrum of constituent problems, and over a period of time develops innumerable contacts with members of the Executive Branch. Finally, access to the Senate floor and to the press offer him the opportunity to comment on pending legislation and on the larger issues of national and international policy.

In each of these areas I found that even a new Senator sitting on the minority side can exercise some degree of influence in the discharge of his three principal jobs, which I take to be (1) making such impact as he can on the shape and administration of federal laws and institutions; (2) serving the specific needs of his constituents in every way he legitimately can; and (3) preserving and protecting what Thomas Jefferson called "the bright constellation" of American freedoms.

One of my first on-the-job discoveries was that the New York Congressional Delegation rarely acts as a unit in support of specific legislation. The state is just too large and its population and interests far too diverse to permit the kind of unified front so often found in other delegations. New York has the nation's largest and most majestic city and its third-largest rural population. There are more New Yorkers engaged in manufacturing than in any other state, yet its single most important industry, dairying, is agricultural. New York ranks first in the production of cameras and computers and second in grapes and apples. New York contains the largest state-owned complex of forest and wilderness areas in the country—the 2,000,000-acre Adirondack Park.

There are probably as many New York importers interested in freedom of international trade as there are manufacturers seeking protection from foreign imports. New York has by far the nation's largest population of commuters using mass transit. But there are other millions in the state who must use their own cars to travel to and from their jobs, and who wonder why the cost of a New York subway ride should be any more sacred than the cost of the gasoline they use to drive to work.

Given such size and diversity, and given the all but infinite needs of its more than 18,000,000 citizens, a major problem faced by a New York Senator (and by any big-state Senator) is one of communication. The hazards of the mails notwithstanding, constituents are anything but shy about sending letters detailing their hopes, complaints, views, and needs. I have come to conclude that New Yorkers must be the free-style letter-sending champions of the world, if the volume of mail to the Buckley offices is in any way representative. I have averaged over 5,000 letters a week—more than 1,000,000 pieces of mail—during my first four years in office, each one of which was opened, read, sorted, and directed to me or otherwise handled by the members of my mailroom, legislative, and casework staffs.

It is obvious that I can personally attend to only a fraction of this enormous volume of correspondence. As the great bulk of the mail in any week will deal with a dozen or more issues of current public concern, most of them can only be answered through the use of standard replies. Unfortunately, a harassed typist or intern (usually students earning credits at high school or college for a few weeks' work in an office on Capitol Hill) will sometimes pick up the wrong form and a constituent anxious to have my views on, say, soybean price supports will receive instead a closely reasoned analysis of proposed changes in auto emission standards. The constituent is irate, I am embarrassed, and my staff and I try yet again to devise a truly fail-safe system.

Does this semiautomated handling of constituent mail mean that it is useless or foolish for a citizen to write his Senator? Not at all. Although I cannot see the great majority of letters written to me, I do read representative samplings, and I am kept current on what it is that most concerns those writing, where they stand on the issues, and whether the mail we are receiving on a particular matter is spontaneous or the result of an organized campaign. This creates an important link with home-state sentiment that as a practical matter cannot be gained in any other way, given the fact that the Congress is now in session most of the year. One of the interesting facets of this ongoing sampling of public concerns is its demonstration of how little connection there is between those matters that at any given time will agitate columnists, editorial writers, and television commentators and those that really concern the average American preoccupied with such mundane things as earning a living, inflation, the safety of neighborhood streets, and the quality of the education his children are getting.

The mail is also an important source of information about what is going wrong with federal programs and their administration. Each bag of mail contains letters describing in detail, and often with evident emotion, problems that are real: problems faced by parents of youngsters under long jail sentences in Turkey or Spain or elsewhere for the possession of drugs; school superintendents at their wit's end after trying to get a reasonable response from a functionary at HEW; mayors concerned over inequities in the distribution of revenue sharing funds or delays in the approval of plans for sewage treatment plants; elderly persons frustrated at having computers answer their letters complaining about lost Social Security checks; small-business men and women who see their livelihoods threatened by some new arbitrary requirement imposed by the federal government with which they simply cannot comply; dairy farmers faced with competition from Europeans who can export dairy products to the United States that would not meet domestic standards of production.

These letters not only educate me as to how government actually impinges on the lives of New Yorkers and New York businesses and communities; they also provide me with opportunities to try to cut through red tape and help harassed citizens get the service to which they are entitled.

This phase of a Senator's activities comes under the category of casework. Only with the growth of government in recent years has it achieved any significant role in a Senator's life; and strictly speaking, it has nothing to do with his constitutional responsibilities. Yet it performs a necessary function. Someone has to be the court of last resort in the attempt of a municipality, a hospital, a small business, or an individual to deal with the federal bureaucracy. It is inevitable that they ultimately turn to those whom they have elected to represent them in Washington. It is good that they do so, and not just because we can so often help. Constituent casework gives us a far better understanding of how the programs we create actually work. Clearly, however, there is a limit to how much of a caseload we are able to handle; and this highlights the fact that Senators from larger states are less equal than others.

A new Senator from a state like New York quickly learns that the Senate places great emphasis on the equal sovereign dignity of each individual state, which is a polite way of saying that when it comes to allocating rooms and funds, Senators from the larger states invariably feel shortchanged. It should be kept in mind that the volume of work that must be handled by a Senator's office depends to a substantial degree on the size of his constituency. Well over half my staff is engaged in handling mail and in trying to help constituents with specific problems involving one agency or another of the federal government.

Whereas the office workload of a Senator from New York (population, 18,190,740: 1970 census) may not be thirty-six times as heavy as that of a Senator from Delaware (population, 548,104), it certainly involves several times the volume of work. Yet, when I entered the Senate in 1971, the smallest number of rooms assigned to any Senator was five and the largest (California and New York), seven. Moreover, my staff payroll allowance was less than twice that for the smallest state. Thus, while a member of the House of Representatives receives a staff allowance equivalent to $.43 per constituent, and Senators from Rhode Island $.41, Senators from California and New York have to make do with a per capita allowance of $.03.

But even with more restrictive facilities, my staff and I have been able to help constituents in a surprising number of ways, both large and small. We estimate that during the first four years we have handled more than 30,000 cases, some with impressive results.

Casework tends to be invisible. Yet there are occasions when a Senator can best serve constituent interests by stimulating a few headlines to focus attention on a given problem. This I was able to do in connection with an ill-advised "scatter-housing" project for Forest Hills, in New York City. The proposal called for the erection of a series of federally financed high-rise apartment buildings that were totally inconsistent with the general character of the neighborhood and would place an unconscionable burden on existing school and transportation facilities. Because it involved the bureaucratic mentality at its most insensitive and was, in a way, representative of how constituent concerns are brought to a Senator's attention and acted upon, I offer the following brief summary of what came to be known in my office as the Forest Hills Case.

The roots of the controversy stretched back several years before my election. It had once been determined by the appropriate authorities in New York City (i.e., the Office of the Mayor, the City Planning Commission, and the Board of Estimate) that a new school was needed for the Forest Hills area of Queens, as the schools in Forest Hills were seriously overcrowded. In an unrelated decision, it had also been determined that a nearby section of Queens (Corona) would receive some scatter-site low income housing. ("Scatter-site" is a euphemism employed by City Hall for the integration of large numbers of welfare families into middle- and upper-class neighborhoods.) Such a policy, it was felt, would result in a cultural rub-off, in which middle-class values would be transferred to the welfare recipients, and thus a new sense of civic pride and neighborhood concern would be implanted in the newcomers. It was also believed that the extraordinary load that a slum area puts on municipal services (police, sanitation, etc.) would be lightened if a scatter-site approach were used to break up the slums.

Predictably enough (to anyone but ideologues), the announcement that Corona was slated for low income housing sparked protests by Corona residents, and City Hall quickly became aware of their displeasure. A plan was then worked out by City Hall to locate the new school on the Corona site designated for the housing. This left city officials with no housing site, and after some hasty calculations it was determined that the citizens of Forest Hills would be the lucky recipients of ideological goodwill. Thus began a dispute that ultimately involved several City Councilmen, all five Borough Presidents, several Assemblymen and state Senators, a Mayor, four or five Congressmen, one United States Senator, a Cabinet member, and the President of the United States, as well as thousands of bureaucrats, groups, and residents of Forest Hills.

Within three months after I had been sworn in, my office had been contacted several times by members of an ad hoc group called the Forest Hills Residents Association. The group opposed the scatter-site project, demanded the school be built in Forest Hills, and alleged a number of irregularities in the planning of the project up to that point. My staff began an extensive investigation of the project's history, the proposed site, the cost involved, the conditions in the community, etc. During the next few months there were a number of meetings and hundreds of phone conversations with members of the FHRA and their legal and technical experts. In due course I was able to advise the group that HUD had pledged not to proceed with the funding (it was to be 100 percent federally financed) until the community and I had had a chance to review the plan.

What followed was the ritual mating dance of the federal bureaucracy: a series of meetings between my office and HUD officials both in Washington and New York. About a week after these meetings, the Department of Housing and Urban Development announced it was going ahead with the funding. This activated the community the way nothing else had to that date. A number of increasingly bitter protest meetings were held in Forest Hills. Picketers were dispatched to block workers at the construction site (and were subsequently dispatched to picket City Hall). Articles began appearing daily in the papers about the protests.

An interesting phenomenon occurred during this period: the liberal establishment in New York City split down the middle on the issue. While the New York *Post* adhered to the orthodoxies of liberalism, the *Times* and the *Village Voice*, a Greenwich Village weekly generally known for its left liberal positions, took an antiproject position.

Unaccustomed, even at that early stage of my Senatorial career, to having the *Times* and the *Voice* agree with me on a controversial issue, I quickly inserted the articles into the *Congressional Record* if only to show that in the Forest Hills controversy, common sense knew no philosophical or political boundaries. On November 23, 1971, the *Times* paid obeisance to the "basic rationale of this bitterly controversial project," but also stated that the city administration had not shown "sympathetic understanding" to the Forest Hills residents. The *Village Voice*, as usual, was much more blunt. In an article entitled "The Middle Class Fights Back: Battle of Forest Hills" (November 26, 1971) the *Voice* writer began with a "primer" on how to go about blockbusting, according to the New York City Mayor's office:

> Don't just settle for chasing out the middle-class families. Break up the entire neighborhood. Turn Brownsville into World War III and the South Bronx into an open sore. Stick a string of welfare hotels into Greenwich Village and knock down a community of self-built homes in Corona. And if someone points out that these changes have made life worse,

not better, in the area, then stencil him with words like "racist" or "bigot" and open fire on another neighborhood. . . .

On November 16, I met with HUD Secretary George Romney and personally requested that the project be reconsidered. On November 22, Romney advised me that he could find no grounds on which to reverse the contractual commitments already made, and therefore was allowing construction to proceed. At that point I appealed directly to the President. Hints were dropped by Presidential spokesmen that the project would proceed, but there never was a formal response.

Later, in a series of sudden shifts the project was literally chopped in half: from three 24-story buildings containing 840 units to three 12-story buildings containing 430 units. In an interesting experiment, the buildings have been "cooped" and a screening committee is now looking over prospective tenants. As the federal government has retained financial responsibility for the project, the arrangement calls for the co-op organization to lease the buildings from the government. This will not prove to be one of HUD's better investments, however. One of our arguments to HUD from the beginning was that various conditions would make the cost of this project exorbitant. The last *per-unit* cost estimate was over $72,000. In other words, the federal government could have bought each of the 430 tenant families a $72,000 house for the price of the proposed project.

As in so many other areas of bureaucratic meddling, final victories were not forthcoming in the Forest Hills controversy. But half a victory in politics is not only better than no victory at all, but perhaps all that can be gained. The utopian urban nightmare of the bureaucrats of the City of New York and of the federal government did not become reality in its original disruptive form, but the citizens of Forest Hills could take small consolation from the fact as they watched the co-ops being built.

The Forest Hills case taught me something about the realities of urban problems and of bureaucratic life in Washington. But it wasn't until 1972, when I became involved in the intricate, complex, and seemingly endless problems involved in the grain shortage in New York State, that I really learned how important it is for citizens to be able to appeal to someone to help untangle bureaucratic knots. Looking back, what had seemed at the time to be the complicated problems of Forest Hills were in reality a kind of primer of bureaucratic mischief compared with the postgraduate course offered by the various aspects of the grain shortage of 1972.

As I have pointed out, New York is not only a state of big cities and large industries but also one of the chief agricultural and dairy states in the nation. In 1972 this was brought home to me in dramatic detail as I flew by helicopter over areas of New York ravaged by Hurricane Agnes. Reading about such destruction, or even seeing it on television, gives no true picture of the total nature of the disaster. Homes, farms, and factories—entire communities—lay in ruin.

Upon my return to Washington I sponsored or cosponsored several amendments to the Disaster Relief section of the Small Business Act. These amendments had the effect of helping the residents of the devastated areas rebuild their homes and their lives. But, as I was to discover, this was only the beginning of the story. The hurricane had destroyed much of the corn on which dairymen rely for winter silage. This, combined with the huge grain sales to Russia that year, caused a crisis of the first order for the New York dairy industry.

Late in December, 1972, mail and telephone calls to my office told of severe grain shortages in New York State. "Severe" in this case did not appear to be too strong a word—the supply of feed grain in the state, from what information we could gather, was limited to *three days*. On December 22 my office received an anguished call from an upstate farmer. "I'm finished," he said. "I don't have enough grain to feed my cows through the Christmas holidays." The dairy farmers of New York were facing nothing less than total ruin.

These calls and letters began for me one of the most exhausting but worthwhile bureaucratic battles I have faced as a Senator. Between January 3 and February 1 I did my utmost to convince the relevant bureaucrats that the best way to relieve a grain shortage is by sending grain to the affected area. With Mrs. Joan Carroll of my staff playing Virgil to my Dante, I descended the various rungs of the federal inferno, trying to find someone, somewhere, who would do something. I found myself becoming adept at deciphering the cryptic utterances, nods, winks, and shrugs of bureaucrats but unable to make anyone budge.

Finally, after fiery debates over boxcars, eligibility for government aid, and a complicated procedure involving the calling in of government loans (in the form of grain stored in the Midwest and pledged as collateral) in order to help New York's farmers, I was able to announce, on February 1, that my efforts had achieved success: a seventy-one-car unit train with 300,000 bushels of oats was on its way to Buffalo. An official of the Interstate Commerce Commission in Kansas City was assigned the sole responsibility of seeing to it that grain was expedited from there to New York.

But my Midwestern colleagues, from whose states this grain was coming, did not, understandably enough, see things quite the way I did. Their efforts to stop the grain shipment and the diversion of boxcars to the East resulted in the introduction of something called S.J. Res 59, the purpose of which was to stop everything quite literally on the tracks. The Midwest farmers, a powerful group, were claiming that these shipments to New York were resulting in (a) reductions in the price of grain and (b) a shortage of boxcars needed to ship their grain to storage. I testified before the Agriculture Committee, pleading the case of the New York dairy farmers, and opposed the resolution on the floor of the Senate. Eventually things were settled by one of those curious Washington "compromises": The resolution disapproving the shipment of grain was accepted, but the grain continued to be shipped.

Urban or rural, the needs of the citizens of New York reflect the diversity and size of the state. Many of the thousands of cases processed by my offices each year can be resolved through one or two telephone calls to the appropriate officials, while others may take months of work and lead to dead ends. And though the cases I have described to illustrate facets of a Senator's life have often involved arbitrary or evasive bureaucrats, in most instances we have found employees of federal agencies to be cooperative and anxious to help.

It is, in fact, to this kind of cooperation above the call of duty that I owe one of my happiest experiences with constituent work. This case had nothing to do with such major matters as the environment or housing or grain shortages. It concerned an eleven-year-old New Yorker, Maria Maniaci of Holbrook, Long Island. She is a normal and happy little girl in every way except one: She is almost totally deaf.

Several years ago the Town of Islip installed a sign on a heavily traveled road near the Maniaci home. It read: CAUTION—DEAF CHILD IN AREA.

The New York State Department of Transportation ordered the sign down, stating that it did not appear in the state's uniform sign manual, which in turn was required to conform with national standards set in Washington.

With that, Mrs. Maniaci wrote to me to protest the ruling. With Mrs. Maniaci's letter in hand, and with figures showing that almost 500,000 children in the nation are deaf, I was able to persuade the U.S. Department of Transportation to create a nationwide sign for alerting motorists. The new sign reads simply: DEAF CHILD AREA.

When told of the decision, Mrs. Maniaci, whose letter sparked the governmental process that authorized the new sign, wrote me: "Picture if you can, a 32-year old mother of three, jumping, laughing, crying, and hugging my deaf daughter and yelling, 'We won, we won!'"

As important as constituent work has come to be, a Senator's first responsibilities continue to be legislative, and the place an individual Senator can do his most effective legislative work is in committee. It is only here that he truly has the opportunity to present and argue a point and to persuade others under circumstances where it is actually possible to exchange ideas and reach areas of agreement. The Senator who does his homework and persists with the paragraph-by-paragraph discussion of new legislation for as many days as it takes to complete work on it can have a material impact on what ultimately becomes law—always assuming that points made in actual discussion are not overriden through the voting of proxies of absentee members. To be effective, however, a Senator must be reasonably selective. He hasn't the time to master all the legislation that will flow through his committees, let alone attend all the markup sessions in which individual bills take final shape.

Much of the work that I did during my first four years was concerned with environmental matters. Both as ranking minority member on the Environmental Pollution Subcommittee of the Senate Public Works Committee and as a member of various subcommittees of the Interior Committee, I was exposed to a broad range of laws that were either primarily or in important respects concerned with environmental matters. As this represented a confluence of committee responsibilities and a deep personal interest in conservation, I found myself devoting a significant part of my time to them.

It happens that since my earliest days I have been fascinated with nature, particularly birds. I grew up in the country with a host of pets, ranging from the conventional to such exotica as armadillos and flying squirrels, pythons and tortoises, and Cooper's hawks and South American honey creepers. I worked in a school zoo, banded birds, and at age sixteen spent a summer month working in New York's American Museum of Natural History helping classify a collection of Venezuelan birds. My leisure reading for more than thirty years has included books and articles on natural history, and in the course of this I have absorbed some knowledge of the intricacy of ecological relationships, and of man's ultimate dependence on the health of his physical environment.

In recent times I have developed a particular fascination with the Arctic, where vast areas can still be seen in their untouched state—but a state so fragile that unthinking human action can cause the most long-lasting damage. Arctic vegetation grows so slowly that it may take a century to erase the sledge marks left by explorers.

It was in the Arctic, on two expeditions to capture muskoxen, that I was introduced by John J. Teal, Jr., to a concept of human ecology in which man consciously adapts naturally occurring biological resources to meet his needs. For more than twenty years, Teal has been working to domesticate the musk-ox, a large mammal that ranges naturally as far north as land extends, in order to provide Eskimos and other peoples living north of the permafrost line with a form of agriculture that can take the place of their fast-disappearing hunting and fishing economy. It is a fascinating attempt to find new ways in which man can coexist with rather than exploit his surroundings, and represents a fresh viewpoint that needs to be encouraged.

The point of this digression (other than to exercise my hobbyhorse) is to indicate that over the years I have developed an appreciation of man's interrelationship with his biological and physical environment that ideally complemented some of my more important committee responsibilities. But before describing some of these aspects of my committee work, it might be useful to discuss a more general problem that I have had to face in this respect, and that is the failure of so many conservatives to grasp the essentials of environmental issues.

My conservative brethren often charge me with inconsistency because I favor federal legislation to bring air and water pollution under effective control. For my part, I frequently wince when reading articles in conservative journals—even that excellent one, *National Review,* edited by my brother Bill—that do nothing but illustrate their authors' ignorance of elementary questions of biological cause and effect.

This phenomenon saddens me because their every instinct ought to propel conservatives into the forefront of the environmental movement. Conservatives pride themselves on their understanding of the dangers that can accrue from the thoughtless destruction of systems or institutions that have successfully served man's needs; they perceive the existence of natural laws that man in his own highest interest is bound to observe; and they acknowledge a moral obligation to conserve the inheritance received from generations past for the benefit of those to come.

Too few conservatives seem to appreciate the extraordinary complexity and sensitivity of the interdependent ecological systems on which life literally depends. Too few acknowledge that unless man learns to modify some of his habits, this generation of "temporary possessors and life-renters" could well (in Edmund Burke's words) "leave to those who come after . . . a ruin instead of a habitation."

I suspect that in matters concerning the environment too many conservatives suffer from three sets of intellectual blinders. First, they are put off by the excesses and politics of the "eco-freaks," who seem to be demanding a return to the days of the horse and buggy. Second, they are unlettered in matters ecological. Finally, they rebel at the thought that the dangers cited by environmentalists could have developed, as it were, overnight.

Yet the incontrovertible fact is that they are real. While it is impossible to detail here all the factors that have combined to bring these dangers to a head, I will try to sketch certain of those that explain why the problems posed by pollution have suddenly loomed so large.

A body of water or an atmospheric basin has a certain capacity to absorb, to dissipate. Only when the limits of that self-cleansing capacity are reached do we notice that a problem exists at all, and by then it is almost out of hand. This is the result of what is known as the "exponential" effect of introducing ever larger volumes of pollutants into a system. By way of oversimplified illustration, let us take a 1,000-gallon tank with a 100-gallon-a-day outflow. One gallon of liquid is poured into the tank the first day and the amount is doubled every day thereafter: two gallons on the second, four on the third, eight on the fourth, and so on. The sixty-four gallons poured into the tank on the seventh day will drain out as fast as they are introduced. Only toward the end of the eighth day will we notice any accumulation. By noon of the eleventh, the tank will be overflowing. In other words, by the time a problem is first detected, it has achieved a momentum that may require herculean efforts to bring it under control.

So it has been with lakes and streams and the atmosphere across the country as we discharge increasing volumes of wastes into them. For many years the wastes disappeared from view and were thought to be harmless. But ultimately, as the systems became overburdened, the rate of degradation proceeded with alarming speed and often with sudden biological consequences. Many organisms are highly sensitive to even minor changes in their environment. Add a few degrees to the temperature of a body of water or increase the presence of a given chemical by a few parts per million, and overnight you will have eliminated whole populations of fish or plants.

Another factor has compounded the pollution problem. During most of man's history he has utilized naturally occurring materials and chemicals in his manufacturing processes. The wastes he generated, the goods he discarded, in due course rusted, dissolved, or rotted away, and their component elements were recycled into the earth's soil, air, and water.

In the past few decades, however, men have begun to produce a formidable variety and quantity of synthetic materials and chemicals that resist those natural recycling processes. Many synthetic compounds have been broadcast into the environment without any understanding of their ultimate biological effects. We have learned the hard way that when we deal with persistent substances there may be no such thing as "safe" concentrations when utilized on any scale. Certain chemicals such as DDT are subject to biological concentration as they move up the food chain, and once injected into the environment they cannot be reclaimed. Our production of these biologically indigestible substances has grown from virtually zero to hundreds of billions of pounds annually over the past thirty years.

In sum, our technology has propelled us into a new era where we have the power to disrupt the very rhythms of life. Clearly this is a situation that requires safeguards that only government can impose; and equally clearly, as the flow of water and air ignores political boundaries, only the federal government is in a position to impose them. The need for environmental legislation is self-evident. What is far less evident is how we are to achieve our essential environmental goals without incurring unnecessary cost or dislocation. The state of our technology is still such as to make it virtually impossible for even scientists, let alone legislators, to define necessary goals or the methods by which they are to be achieved with any degree of precision.

I was exposed almost immediately to the complexities of legislating in this area when, as a member of the Public Works Committee, I found myself deeply involved in work on the Federal Water Pollution Control Amendments that were ultimately enacted in 1972. One major consideration was the interaction between the Environmental Protection Agency, which was to be charged with drawing up the necessary regulations and monitoring compliance, and the states and their political subdivisions and agencies, which would be given the responsibility for developing their own water quality programs and implementing them, all in accordance with federal laws and regulations. I was among those urging a maximum state role, and in this I was able to enlist the enormously valuable help of the New York State Department of Environmental Conservation.

Time and again my staff and I would discuss specific problems with experts in the department and I would then be able to draw on their expertise and experience to develop modifications in the proposed legislation that I succeeded in having adopted. I was also able to contribute a number of other changes that I believe have served to make the goals somewhat more realistic, the procedures more flexible, and which give greater weight to economic consequences in determining what is feasible (in terms of the abatement of pollution) under any given set of circumstances.

One environmental cause that I have taken very much to heart has been that of protecting the integrity of the procedures mandated by the National Environmental Policy Act of 1969. Its most important (and controversial) requirement is that an environmental impact statement (nicknamed "NEPA statement") be prepared in connection with any federal activity or use of federal funds that will have a significant effect on the environment. Its purpose is simple and, I believe, important: namely, to make sure that environmental consequences are brought into the decision-making process in the same manner as are other considerations such as economic costs and benefits. This is necessary because many of the adverse effects that a dam, a nuclear power plant, a highway, or a pipeline are apt to have do not appear in conventional balance sheets even though their ultimate costs may be very great.

The new law tended to be ignored or to be complied with in only the most perfunctory way. Environmentalists were soon waging a series of successful lawsuits challenging everything from highways to the Alaska pipeline on the basis that the environmental impact statements had not been properly prepared. The law's requirements are now better understood and observed, and the whole NEPA process has become more effective and efficient. It has also become the target of collateral attack as advocates of special projects seek to exempt theirs from NEPA's requirements.

One example of this, which I was able to head off in committee, was the attempt to enact legislation that would have permitted the "interim" licensing of nuclear power plants at less than full capacity without filing environmental impact statements. I prevailed in part because I could demonstrate that completion of only one power station was being delayed by the NEPA requirements. More importantly, I was able to persuade the majority of the dangers of eroding this important procedural protection through special "hardship case" exceptions. It could well be that the law itself requires modification in the light of actual experience. If so, we should be addressing ourselves to its deficiencies and not to weakening it by attrition.

When it comes to NEPA, I am a sufficient purist to find myself at loggerheads with the Senate's premier environmentalist, Edmund Muskie. It is his position that the one federal agency that is and ought to be exempt from the sweeping mandate of the National Environmental Policy Act is the Environmental Protection Agency that is charged with implementing most of our national environmental laws. While I suspect he is right as to the legal fact of its exemption (the case is persuasive, but less than crystal clear) I believe the EPA ought to be made subject to its discipline. While the

EPA is professionally concerned with environmental matters, this in itself is no guarantee that it will not slip into habits of thought or practices that in time will fail to take into account the possible collateral adverse effects of its own directives. There is no reason why EPA officials should not be made to go through the same checklists that are required of the Corps of Engineers and others. We are, for example, now learning of possible adverse environmental consequences resulting from the use of the catalytic devices that the EPA had sanctioned as a means for meeting auto emission standards under the Clean Air Act.

But there is another aspect of our environmental laws that requires increasing attention from the Congress. We need to develop better techniques for measuring the cost/benefit ratios associated with the programs we are mandating. If we impose a disproportionate cost on the economy and on individual citizens, we will sacrifice that reservoir of support that is essential to progress.

This is why I was among those who proposed that the Public Works Committee commission the National Academy of Sciences to review all the newly developed scientific data to determine whether the EPA's air quality standards for automobile exhaust pollutants were soundly based on medical evidence, and also make a cost/benefit evaluation of the measures required to meet those standards. Billions of dollars in added automobile manufacturing costs depend on the answers. A far more thorough study is now proceeding under the National Commission on Water Quality (of which I am a member) that is designed to determine whether the long-term goals of the Federal Water Pollution Control Amendments of 1972 are in fact achievable, whether the cost of achieving them is worth the price, and whether there are alternative goals that represent a more acceptable balancing of environmental and social benefits with economic costs.

It is hoped that through these and other efforts we will develop some analytical techniques of broad application that will enable us to calculate with some degree of confidence the social and economic costs and benefits of the goals we set and the control measures we adopt in the field of environmental protection. This we must do if we are to succeed in displacing emotion with reason in the discussion of these objectives. Yet it will be very difficult ever to achieve a large degree of precision. How does one achieve consensus in any technique for measuring the relative "cost/benefits" of such disparate values as employment, health, public convenience, air-conditioned shopping malls, trout fishing, adequate and secure sources of energy, and the sound of wood thrushes singing at twilight? Value judgments are ultimately required, and it is the Congress that will have to make them.

Despite these and other considerable efforts on my part to develop prudent and effective approaches to our environmental needs, I find myself receiving less than the highest marks from several environmental groups who rate the performance of members of the Congress. Apparently one of my major sins is my insistence that the killing of unwanted children before they are born is no more appropriate a solution to the population problem than the killing of unwanted adults who have outlived their usefulness. I have also opposed the assumption by the federal government of responsibility over those forms of pollution that are clearly within the capacity of state and local governments to control. I find the sound of pneumatic drills tearing up the streets beneath my New York City apartment highly disturbing to my emotional stability, peace of mind, and health. But I do not see where it can be said to disturb the emotional stability, peace of mind, or health of the people living across the river in New Jersey. I am confident that between the resources of New York City and New York State there is all the knowledge and expertise and goodwill and sense of civic responsibility required to keep the level of noise within reasonable limits. The federal role, it seems to me (and seemed to me when I was called upon to work on a noise pollution bill), ought to be limited to those functions within federal jurisdiction such as the licensing of aircraft that routinely move from state to state. My one contribution to this legislation was to delete a requirement that any machinery *exported* from the United States be required to conform with domestic noise-suppression standards. It was my position that American enlightenment should not be extended to the point where we might price American goods out of markets in foreign countries that were less concerned than we over the impact of noise generated by bulldozers on the eardrums of their citizens.

I voted against the noise pollution bill because on very substantial balance it represented an unwarranted intrusion into matters that the states were competent to handle on their own terms. I have also opposed having the federal government preempt the field of solid waste disposal except where that waste is to be disposed at sea. Again, it seems to me that state and local governments have the competence to handle this problem without the added burden and cost of federal guidelines and directives.

There is one important bill with which I have been associated that demonstrated in another context the key role a single Senator can play. It required a kind of brinksmanship on which the outcome of joint conferences between representatives of the House and Senate sometimes depends.

This particular conference involved the long-delayed highway bill that was finally enacted in August, 1973. Perhaps its most significant provision was one that for the first time breached the "sanctity" of the Highway Trust Fund so that the monies collected in it could be used for the construction or improvement of mass transit facilities.

This proposal would allow local authorities the option to use certain highway trust funds allocated to metropolitan areas either for conventional highway-related purposes or for the purchase of rolling stock or the extension or improvement of mass transit facilities. As an original cosponsor of the measure, I argued that it was impossible to plan intelligently for the transportation needs of a great metropolitan area like New York City while wearing statutory blinders that would limit consideration to one form of transportation alone; that the majority of the monies in the Highway Trust Fund were made up from gasoline and other taxes collected from motorists in urban areas who had the most to gain from the reduced congestion that could result from improved alternative forms of transportation; and that Congress was totally within its power to modify the nature of the projects to be financed out of the Highway Trust Fund. We failed to carry the day within the Public Works Committee (the vote was 8 to 6 against us), but on the Senate floor we won by the narrow margin of 49 to 44. The House adopted its own highway bill without any comparable provision. After days of haggling in conference, we were able to resolve all the differences between the two bills save the one permitting the use of highway trust funds for mass transit purposes. Here the battle lines froze. Compromise after compromise was offered by the House conferees that would have made equivalent amounts out of the general treasury available for the purposes specified in the Senate bill, but the Senate conferees remained firm. The House was determined to protect what they believed to be the integrity of the Highway Trust Fund while the Senate conferees were equally determined to achieve a breach that in later years could open up the resources of the fund for a broader approach to transportation needs.

Each time a significant compromise was tendered, the Senate conferees would retire to consider its merits. Although the conferees were committed in principle to back the provisions contained in the Senate version as it was enacted on the floor, the process of negotiated compromise necessarily means that one side or the other must be prepared to back away if final agreement on a bill is to be achieved. Of the seven Senators who were members of the conference, four had supported the controversial amendment and the other three had strongly opposed it. These latter were naturally predisposed to accept some of the offers made by the House side.

The conference continued week after week. A total of fifteen meetings were held, without any resolution of the difference. In the meantime, the existing authorization was running out. The highway departments of state after state were beginning to curtail their programs; large-scale layoffs of highway construction workers were predicted. Mounting pressures were being brought to bear by Governors, Highway Commissioners, contractors, and unions on members of the conference to give ground. Any one of the four Senators who had supported the principle of tapping highway trust funds for mass transit purposes could have broken the deadlock by simply switching his vote and accepting one of the House compromises. Instead, we held the line with the House seemingly unanimous in its determination to scuttle the bill rather than to accede to the Senate position. But at the last moment, with just enough time before the August recess for the Congress to act on a conference report, the House conferees tossed in the towel. I believe this reflected, on their part, a realistic assessment of the support that had been gathering for a broader approach to the planning of our facilities for moving people and goods in and out of urban areas.

The conference process is a mechanism that frequently serves to weed out extraneous amendments that Senate procedures allow members to tack on to bills under consideration on the floor whether or not the amendments are remotely germane to the subject matter at hand. This weeding-out process saves the Senate from many of its election-year excesses. House procedures are much tidier and tighter and they do not allow members the same ability to bring a matter to the attention of the full membership.

The openness of the Senate procedures, however, allows them to be abused. We are often called upon to consider matters of tremendous substantive significance that we have had no chance to examine. We are required to vote yea or nay on them without quite knowing what we are up to, always hoping that the House will insist on the responsible course if what we have enacted should indeed prove to be irresponsible.

Yet, much can be done through the technique of floor amendments to improve existing legislation or to get action on a matter that has been stalled in committee or whose pros and cons are sufficiently well known to make its processing through committee essentially superfluous.

At one time or another I have been able to secure adoption of amendments ranging from requiring the development of a special cost of living index for older persons so that adjustments in Social Security payments would be more closely targeted to actual need (it was later lost in conference), to measures improving the quality of federally funded day-care centers. The most significant legislation I have been able to have enacted through the amendatory procedure was in regard to an education bill where I offered an amendment to protect the privacy of students.

My amendment had been developed over a period of months in close association with several groups which had become increasingly concerned over the misuse by schools of information about students that was collected over a period of years. Often, inaccurate and damaging information would be made available to police departments or prospective employers. Parents and students, however, would be denied access to the files and any opportunity to correct errors.

The amendment was circulated among the other Senate offices weeks before it was introduced. In due course it was adopted by the Senate, somewhat modified in conference, and became law as the Family Education Rights and Privacy Act of 1974.

There are other ways in which a member of Congress can make a contribution to legislative affairs and government policies. One is to stake out a public position and set forth your reasons for it in clear-cut terms so that the true range of views within the Congress can be understood and assessed both by the Executive and by the public at large.

The importance of this was brought home to me when I first met Henry Kissinger. He complained that conservatives had let President Nixon down through their failure to hammer home their own positions on matters affecting foreign policy and defense. Instead, conservatives seemed so anxious to protect the President that they were reluctant to speak their minds while he was formulating a position, thus leaving the field of public debate and influence to the opposition. The net effect was to restrict the political ground within which the President could maneuver.

I have since come to understand the validity of Kissinger's criticism and have determined that I can best be of service to a President whose positions I basically approve by presenting my own views as forcefully and effectively as I can and by urging like-minded colleagues to do the same.

In so doing, we can contribute to a general public understanding of the issues, something that, alas, the press cannot be relied upon to do on our behalf without a substantial assist. Spiro Agnew was not attempting to intimidate the national media when he commented on their pervasive bias. He was merely stating the obvious fact that some points of view are given a far wider and more sympathetic coverage than others. The Senate nevertheless offers even its newest members a whole range of opportunities to coax the press into reporting the other side of a story.

The way this is most often done is for one or more Senators to schedule time on the Senate floor, often in tandem, to deliver themselves of learned or impassioned speeches to an empty chamber. Their wisdom might be wasted on the Senate air, except that the exercise enables them to alert the press that Senator so-and-so will deliver remarks on such-and-such a topic at the appointed time. Copies of the speech are distributed, and the gist of the Senator's argument and the points he wishes to make become part of the nation's informational bloodstream. I have now participated in dozens of these "colloquies"; and though the point of view I represent apparently continues to be regarded as unfit to print in some of our most prestigious newspapers, it will usually leave a trace—in newspapers in various parts of New York State, in columns, in editorials.

A Senator has other ways of communicating his views on a subject: radio and television interviews, press conferences, speeches, articles, sometimes even in a book. By making use of these and other opportunities for public education, a Senator can help the electorate become more fully informed on basic issues. And this in turn bears on the legislative process because, in the last analysis, public opinion dictates the outside limits of the options available to the Congress. By joining in the public debate and articulating the arguments in support of his own positions, even the newest Senator, even one labeled Conservative-Republican, can contribute to the educational process which ultimately finds its reflection in national policy.

I have availed myself of one or more of these vehicles to try to contribute a better public understanding of any number of controversial issues, and in one case even launched a lawsuit to test the constitutionality of a campaign reform bill that Common Cause had lobbied though the Congress with trumpet blasts of self-righteousness in 1974. On the floor and at public meetings I had argued that the bill violated First Amendment rights and that it was outrageously slanted in favor of incumbents and the political status quo. An amendment I offered to allow challengers to spend 30 percent more in their campaigns than incumbents was handily shot down by a vote of 66 to 17. I was signally unsuccessful in calling any serious attention to the threats to freedom of expression and other constitutional rights contained in the bill until I found myself joining with former Senator Eugene McCarthy of Minnesota and the New York Civil Liberties Union in a press conference to announce that we would be instituting a suit to have the Campaign Reform Act of 1974 declared unconstitutional. This was an exotic combine that the press could not ignore, and it was not long before newspapers and magazines ranging from the *Village Voice* to *Newsweek* were echoing our arguments.

One of my most controversial attempts to focus public attention on an issue and to contribute to its understanding involved the question of abortion. Shortly after the Supreme Court issued two decisions that had the effect of striking down the laws of fifty states and the ethical tradition of more than 2,000 years of Western civilization, I introduced a resolution calling for a constitutional amendment that would restore protection to all human life at every stage, whether born or unborn. It is precisely because the issue is so controversial, because so many feel so deeply committed to and against the concept of permissive abortion, that I knew it was unlikely that final action would ever be taken on the issue in the Congress unless a sustained demand for action one way or the other could be mobilized. The strong instinct for survival that is sharply cultivated in political animals is such that a majority of Senators and Congressmen who did not feel a deep personal commitment on the matter could be counted upon to duck the issue rather than be forced to a vote on a matter that one way or another would be guaranteed to alienate a significant number of voters. It is a classic example of a no-win issue that no one welcomes having to face. It is for this reason that Senators Mark Hatfield of Oregon, Jesse Helms of North Carolina, Dewey Bartlett of Oklahoma, and I have devoted so much time trying to foster a fuller understanding by the public of the fact not only that abortion involves the taking of a biologically distinct and unique human life, but that the acceptance of abortion for reasons of convenience will lead inevitably to the acceptance of euthanasia for reasons of convenience. We have also worked to sustain the morale of the pro-life movement in the United States in its efforts to deploy effective political pressures for bringing the issue to a vote. This particular issue happens to be uncommonly controversial, but it and others must be faced if our system is truly to reflect the informed will of the people.

This is one aspect of life in the Senate for which I had not been fully prepared. In my innocence I had not anticipated the intensely political atmosphere that prevails on Capitol Hill or the impact that purely political considerations have on specific actions taken by individual members of the Congress. There is a tremendous tendency to cast votes with a view toward minimizing future political problems. When a Senator's vote is clearly not critical to the fate of a bill, it is often deployed for future political convenience on the grounds that it "wouldn't count anyway." Thus, the Senate will often cast a lopsided vote on questions on which public opinion and the real opinion within the Senate is much more evenly divided.

This protecting of political flanks seems harmless enough, but it vitiates the educational function that the Senate is in a position to perform. If citizens see that members of the Senate have voted overwhelmingly in favor of this or that piece of legislation, many not entirely certain of their own ground may decide that they have been wrong or backward or insensitive. Yet, if on such issues each member of the Senate had voted his true convictions, the breakdown might have been, say, 60 to 40 instead of 80 to 20. I can't help wondering to what extent this form of political expediency may affect the public's perception of the issues. Nor can I help wondering to what extent, in the months between this writing and November, 1976, I will yield to the temptation to act on the premise (motivated always by the higher patriotic considerations) that my own reelection would serve a superior public purpose than absolute honesty with my constituents.

The Senate may be a highly political place, but it operates with an extraordinary degree of fairness. I have rarely seen a committee chairman deny a member a full hearing, and although members of the majority party are clearly more equal than the others, they will usually go to great lengths to protect the rights of the minority. The Senate is a place where the rules of civility are still observed and the rights and independence of each individual still respected. It is a place where many of the major decisions affecting the shape of our times are made, and it is a place where even the least of its members may have a hand in making them. It provides an atmosphere that encourages each Senator to pursue his own goals and to develop his own style, and the institution is richer for its diversity.

It has been suggested that the particular role I have set for myself disqualifies me from being a mover within the Senate. Yes and no. There are those who have a particular talent for brokering a compromise between differing positions, and in the process they get things done. They play a vital role. But so do those who help define the positions to be reconciled, for they are the ones who define the limits of possible actions and the reasons for taking one course or another. Moreover, I have found in the Senate that those who earn a reputation for well-reasoned positions are respected, and that respect is in itself a source of influence, if not of mass conversions.

At any rate it is in this role, and in the various ways described in this chapter, that I have sought to serve both my constituents and my country.

3
The Anatomy of a Decision

On one occasion I shall never forget I found myself testing the limits of what it is to be a minority of one. It was the morning of March 19, 1974. The Watergate winter had been a traumatic one, and spring held little hope of relief.

I had just finished the last of a dozen telephone calls to advise Governor Wilson and a few colleagues and friends of what I was about to do. Dawne Cina, my secretary, buzzed to say that General Haig, President Nixon's Chief of Staff, was trying to reach me. At the same moment, Len Saffir, my press secretary, looked in to tell me that the press was waiting.

I told Dawne I'd call the General back later, knowing, of course, that by then there would be nothing left to discuss. I picked up a yellow pad and my prepared statement and Len and I walked the long hallway to the Senate Caucus Room, made famous by the Watergate hearings. It was the longest walk of my political life.

I stepped up to the bank of microphones and peered out through the television lights at more reporters than I had ever seen gathered in one room.

I began to read. The statement went quickly and soon I reached the critical passage:

> There is one way and one way only by which the crisis can be resolved, and the country pulled out of the Watergate swamp. I propose an extraordinary act of statesmanship and courage. . . . That act is Richard Nixon's own voluntary resignation as President of the United States.

That was it. I had passed the point of no return. It had taken weeks of agonizing thought and analysis to reach the decision to call for the President's resignation and days of writing and rewriting to arrive at a full but precise statement of my reasons for doing so.

And now, in a few brief moments, I had uttered words that could never be retrieved. There is a terrible finality about speaking into dozens of microphones connected to whirring television cameras and tape recorders—finality, but no relief, for the real ordeal was still to come.

Within minutes, my office switchboard was jammed with calls. I was Judas Iscariot, Benedict Arnold, Brutus. And this was not the predictable reaction of a narrow band of diehard loyalists. It was an outpouring of hurt and anger from thousands of men and women, many of whom had worked diligently for my election.

I had known in advance that my decision would be unpopular with the great majority of my particular constituency and I had been warned that the reaction to it would be vehement. But I was unprepared for the depth of the feeling that was ultimately reflected in more than 25,000 letters, telegrams, and telephone calls, running 3 to 1 against my position. (One Mailgram, sent by a gentleman in Winter Haven, Florida, particularly sticks in my mind. It consisted of the word "NUTS" repeated one hundred and three times.)

The reaction was, to put it mildly, depressing, and it did nothing for my state of mind when, as I walked to the Capitol later that morning, Senator Edward Kennedy—with whom I disagree on almost everything—crossed the street to congratulate me. And to top it off, I arrived on the Senate floor just in time to catch the last words of a denunciation of my stand by Senator Carl Curtis of Nebraska, a friend and ally from the moment I entered the Senate in 1971.

Chicken Little was clearly right. The sky was falling down. Yet I remained convinced that I had done the right thing. There was nothing impulsive about the decision that led to the most difficult two weeks of my life.

I had begun to think seriously about the desirability of a

Presidential resignation during that famous "firestorm" weekend beginning on Saturday, October 20, 1973.

First the President had apparently reached an agreement with Senators Ervin and Baker to deliver his taped recordings of White House conversations to Senator Stennis, a universally admired symbol of Senatorial integrity, who would in turn forward to the Watergate Committee those sections of the tapes relevant to the charges of misconduct made against the President and his aides. And, briefly, we all breathed easier. But just as we heaved the first sighs of relief, Nixon suddenly ordered Attorney General Richardson to fire the Special Watergate Prosecutor, Archibald Cox, and demanded that the Deputy Attorney General, William Ruckelshaus, be prepared to do so in case Richardson refused. The result: Both Richardson and Ruckelshaus resigned, and the country, seething silently for months, suddenly seemed to explode.

The reaction was extraordinary. Every office on Capitol Hill was flooded with calls and letters protesting the President's actions (my own office received well over 5,000). There was only one conclusion to be drawn: Watergate had reached the saturation point and the American people had finally had enough.

We witnessed, that weekend, a tidal shift in the public's attitude toward Watergate that would have to be taken into account henceforth as each new bizarre event unfolded.

Thus, on October 31, when Judge John Sirica announced the latest bizarre discovery—that two of the key tapes of Presidential conversations either did not exist or had ceased to exist—I issued the following statement:

> Judge Sirica's disclosure has dramatically shifted the burden of proof. As of this moment, President Nixon has the clear burden of satisfying the American people that he has been speaking the truth. If he fails in this, then we are faced with a political crisis of the most profoundly disturbing proportions.

After the Saturday Night Massacre, the presumptions of innocence, in point of fact if not in law, no longer held. From that moment on, any statement that Richard Nixon made would not be believed unless he could prove he was telling the truth.

As the Watergate winter dragged on, I became increasingly concerned with the viability of the Nixon Administration and the potential damage to the country that would follow Nixon's failure to reestablish the kind of credibility required for effective government. In December I considered the possibility of calling for Nixon's resignation, but concluded that his Administration could yet be salvaged—always on the assumption that the information on the tapes and in his private papers would support his denial of any direct complicity in the Watergate cover-up. It was becoming increasingly doubtful, however, that the President would release the material that alone could vindicate him.

A few weeks earlier I had visited the President's private quarters at the White House along with a dozen other Republican Senators who had been invited (in three groups alphabetically) for a "hair-down" talk about the crisis that was increasingly crippling the Administration's ability to operate.

The President received us warmly as we trickled in, chatting first with one and then another of us as drinks were served. After the last guest had arrived, we sat down, and Nixon began a lengthy discourse on current international and domestic problems, what he hoped to accomplish, and only then turned to Watergate. He ended with an affirmation that (a) he had been guilty of no wrongdoing; and (b) he had a duty to the Presidency—the need to protect the confidentiality of Presidential papers and conversations—that he could not and would not compromise. He then invited us to comment.

Even in the informal surroundings of the private quarters, it is impossible to forget who it is that occupies them. It is always difficult, especially as a guest in such a place, to tell a person things he would rather not hear. The temptation is not to lie, but to be less than candid; to soften what it is you really want to say.

I felt, however, that the stated purpose of this particular meeting required that each of us say frankly what was on his mind. Accordingly, when it came my turn to speak, I mustered up the courage to tell the President of the United States that the public simply no longer believed what he told them, that he now carried the burden of establishing his innocence, and that he could only do so by releasing to men such as Senator Stennis every tape and file cabinet and drawer and shoebox that contained any scrap of information remotely related to the break-in and alleged cover-up so that they could, in turn, give the Watergate Committee and the Special Prosecutor all information relevant to the charges that had been brought against the President.

He heard me out, occasionally nodding in a rather distant way. He thanked me for my comments, but I left the meeting doubting that he really understood what it was I was trying to say to him.

These meetings were the prelude to an exhaustive two-week offensive dubbed by the press "Operation Candor," during which the President raced around the country repeatedly protesting his innocence, assuring us that his protestations were corroborated by information on the tapes. Yet no tangible evidence in support of his assertions was ever released. The President was clearly digging in.

And as he dug in, his Administration began a marked retreat from the objectives endorsed so overwhelmingly by the American people in the election of 1972. To cite one example, the budget submitted in January, 1974, in striking contrast to the previous year's budget, abandoned every meaningful attempt to peel back the size of the federal bureaucracy, transfer responsibilities back to the state and local governments, and achieve some degree of balance between federal income and expenditures. It was, in short, a budget designed to mollify the Congress and blunt at least that source of antagonism.

By late February I was convinced that an effective Nixon Presidency could no longer be resurrected. Moreover, the infection was spreading far beyond the Presidency itself. The paralysis of decision-making in the Executive Branch became daily more apparent to those of us on Capitol Hill. Predictions of catastrophe for Republican candidates in the upcoming elections were becoming commonplace. And even in the area of foreign policy there were signs that Nixon was losing effectiveness as foreign leaders took note of the pace and direction of events in the United States.

It was at this point that I began to agonize over whether I should take a hand in precipitating a call for the President's resignation. I had earlier discussed the matter with Len Saffir, my executive assistant Dave Keene, and Clif White, who had managed my election campaign. They agreed that such a move would arouse the fury of many of my colleagues and constituents. But they also agreed that if I honestly felt I had to speak out and if I were willing to take the consequences, then I should do so.

After consulting by phone with two highly informed and candid friends in New York City, I scheduled a private dinner meeting with five people at the Lawyers' Club in Washington. Among the five was a representative of the Republican establishment, who would, I hoped, act as devil's advocate.

Over dinner we explored the questions I needed to answer: Was my analysis correct that the Nixon Administration was beyond salvation, and if so, was it important that someone attempt to focus national attention on the need for the President's resignation? And then, assuming the answers to these two questions to be yes, there were two others that needed answering: Why now, and why me?

To my surprise, even the designated devil's advocate answered the first two questions in the affirmative. Another of those present, who had held an important position in the Nixon Administration, eloquently argued not only the purely political considerations but also the nation's need for a cleansing act to sweep away the sense of moral rot and cynicism that increased with every new revelation flushed out by the Watergate investigations.

We agreed that if Nixon were to resign, he should do so quickly. It would be best for him and best for the country. He could still step down with some dignity, focusing on the welfare of the country and admitting that he had been stripped by events of the ability to provide the kind of leadership the country so desperately needed. If he waited too long, on the other hand, given the pace of events and the revelations that were daily coming to light, he might find himself backed into a corner and his resignation would then be interpreted as an admission of guilt or as running under fire from the threat of impeachment.

Granted. But why should I be the one to make the move? First of all, it was argued, the person urging resignation should be perceived as a supporter of Richard Nixon. In this way it would be apparent that the President was being asked to resign not because of any assumption of guilt, not because of important policy differences, but because of a profound conviction that he had lost irretrievably the ability to govern effectively. It was pointed out that Senator Edward Brooke of Massachusetts, who belonged to the liberal wing of the Republican Party, had caused only momentary comment when he proposed that the President resign.

Why me? Because I fitted the job description; because somebody had to do it and it would be impossible to recruit an alternate without risking the leaks that would rob the call of its shock effect; because I was known as a conservative and it was important to disassociate conservatism from the rank abuses of power and the moral leprosy conjured up by the word "Watergate."

By then it was 9:30 in the evening. I thanked my guests and told them I would sleep on it and make a decision the following day. I have had a better night's sleep.

The next morning I told Len that I had decided to go ahead, and asked him to schedule a news conference the following Tuesday. I then telephoned Jim Burnham, who had attended the dinner the night before and who is one of the nation's most thoughtful writers, and asked him if he would prepare a working draft of the statement I would be delivering. On Friday morning in New York I sat down with him and went through the draft, paragraph by paragraph. We revised some of the thoughts and included others. And then, after he had gone, I spent the balance of the day working on the statement.

I continued over the weekend to rework the language, trying to anticipate and answer every question, every charge, as carefully and accurately as possible. My particular concern was the reaction of my friends. I cared deeply that they understand my reasoning and motivation, while realizing that only one in five thousand would ever see or read the full text.

On Monday morning I called in one other member of my staff, Bill Gavin, who had previously been a speechwriter for both Nixon and Agnew. I told him what I was going to do and asked him to review the statement. He sat on the couch in my office, reading silently. He finally looked up and told me that while arguments could and perhaps should be made for Nixon to resign, this action would destroy me politically. He argued that some of the points in the draft he was reading would not hold up under the grilling I would get from the press. More importantly, he said, my arguments, no matter how nicely phrased, no matter how detailed and precise, would be lost in the torrent of emotion that would inevitably follow. It would destroy my political base in New York State. It would crush the spirits of thousands of men and women who had worked to elect me to the Senate.

It was a blunt, candid analysis, strong medicine from a man whose feel for popular sentiment I greatly respect—not the best way to start the week. Nevertheless I was by then sure in my own mind that my decision was right and I was prepared to take the political consequences. I told Bill that I was standing by my decision. Finally, he said, "OK, if you've really made up your mind to go ahead, the only thing to do now is for us to make the best of it." He recommended some final changes in the statement and we invoked tight office security while it was typed in final form. By late afternoon a copy with a covering letter to the President was hand delivered to the White House. I had not sought an interview with the President, as had been my inclination, on the advice of a friend who had had firsthand knowledge of how the "palace guard" operated. He told me I would be subjected to pressures that would make my life a positive hell and that I would be inviting a massive campaign to discredit me in advance.

That evening I telephoned a friend who is an important political figure, a man whose opinion I deeply value. It was one of the most difficult conversations of my life, for when he heard what I was about to do, he was neither angry nor bitter. Instead, he begged me not to go through with it. I would be making a terrible, irretrievable mistake, he told me, for myself and for the cause of conservatism. As I tried to catch some sleep that night, I began to understand for the first time what Scott Fitzgerald meant when he wrote that in the dark night of the soul it is always three o'clock in the morning.

The next day, Tuesday, March 19, after my press conference and after word began to spread that I had called for Richard Nixon's resignation, I went to lunch at the Monocle Restaurant near the Senate Office Building with Len and Bill. As we ate, a passing waiter accidentally spilled coffee on me. It broke the tension. "See," said Len, "what did I tell you? You're already getting it from all sides."

We laughed and proceeded to eat. Gradually we began to talk of other things, of legislative proposals, and of other, less traumatic ways in which a minority of one can make himself a more effective Senator.

er sentence might be imposed if he cooperated. Yet he adamantly refused to cooperate with his torturers and fully expected a sentence of death. Finally, he was sentenced to ten years in a strict-regime labor camp.

It was only the accident of his mother's birth that enabled him to secure his release. She was born in Brooklyn shortly before her family returned to Lithuania. She was able to claim American citizenship, and in so doing enabled her imprisoned son to do the same. Thanks to pressures mobilized by the devotion and persistence of a number of Lithuanian-Americans, and sustained by several congressional offices (mine included), the State Department was finally able to persuade the Soviets to release Simas Kudirka, and to allow him and his mother, wife, and two children to leave for the United States in November, 1974.

At his press conference, a reporter asked Mr. Kudirka why, having been denied asylum, he had refused to denounce the United States. His answers to this and to another question tell us much about the world struggle in which we are engaged, and about what is ultimately at stake: "I have never had any ill feelings toward the Americans at all, even when it actually happened aboard the *Vigilant* and not even when I was in prison. . . . The incident probably happened because on one side there was a gentle man—the American—and on the other side a man without conscience . . . a man who, as a Soviet citizen, represents up until this day a very barbarous society." Why had he refused, under torture, to denounce the United States? "Because I loved freedom and because the United States represents greatly this freedom."

Extraordinary as it is, the Kudirka story is anything but unique. He is just one of millions who in recent years have demonstrated that fierce passion for freedom that is bred into the fabric of human nature, a passion that even a totalitarian state cannot destroy. This drive to freedom was summed up in the lead paragraph of a news item I came across in the fall of 1968, and which I have kept ever since. It is datelined Giessen, West Germany, October 25, and reads as follows: "The young East German, his tan scarcely hiding the strain of a wild ten-day escape through four communist countries, anticipated the question. 'I know it sounds trite,' he snapped, 'but I did it for freedom.' After a pause, he added, 'I would have tried anything to be a free man.'"

Not Simas Kudirka, or this young East German, or the millions of others like them have ever had a moment's doubt as to where liberty stands in the order of human priorities. They view it as being quite literally more precious than life itself; and it is to this same belief that our nation has been consecrated. Yet there are times when I wonder how many Americans still understand the priceless nature of the liberty they take so much for granted; how many still have the desire for freedom that history teaches us is so essential to its ultimate survival.

It is said that when he left Independence Hall after the conclusion of the Constitutional Convention, Benjamin Franklin was asked what form of government the nation now had. His reply, "A Republic, if you can keep it," remains today the definitive challenge that must be met by those concerned about the nature and the guarantees of freedom in the United States. Our Republic was carefully structured to resist the accretions of power and authority that had ultimately destroyed every prior experiment in human freedom. But Franklin understood, as did the other delegates to the great Constitutional Convention of 1787, that only a people's continued vigilance could guarantee the preservation of their liberties.

Almost 200 years have elapsed since the birth of the American Republic, and we still have it. Yet there are too many signs of an erosion of the safeguards written into our constitutional system to allow anyone to be sanguine over our continuing ability to "keep it." These concerns form the unstated arguments that lie at the heart of most of the debates in the Congress on issues that are perceived to divide along "liberal" and "conservative" lines. These points of difference are anything but academic. They go to the heart of our attitudes and institutions, and directly affect the lives and ultimately the liberties of our people.

It has now become fashionable to view with suspicion anyone who approaches government from a systematic or, if you will, a philosophical frame of reference. Anyone who raises essentially constitutional objections to a new proposal for expanding federal authority, or who approaches new problems from an intellectually consistent point of view, is apt to be dismissed as an ideologue, as if there were some virtue in a seat-of-the-pants, spit-in-the-wind approach to decisions that may profoundly affect the form and substance of governmental institutions to which past generations of Americans have looked for the preservation of their liberties.

If I am charged with approaching my job with a constitutional bias, I plead guilty. The Constitution is anything but haphazard. It represents far more than the detailing of offices and responsibilities and rights. It reflects its authors' understanding of the nature of man and their extraordinary grasp of the reasons why prior attempts to protect and enhance human liberty had ultimately failed.

It is no accident that the nation they created has proven to be mankind's most enduring experiment in freedom. What concerns me deeply now, however, is whether we have grown so accustomed to our freedoms that we are in danger of forgetting the conditions on which their long-term survival depends.

If I had serious concerns before my election over the concentration of power in the federal government, those fears have only deepened since I arrived in Washington and have had to live on a day-by-day basis with its consequences. Every aspect of my work has reinforced my belief that my constitutional concerns are anything but academic.

As I hope to demonstrate in later chapters, there is nothing academic about a proliferation of grant-in-aid programs that have served to transform state and local governments from independent governments with distinct responsibilities into agencies for the implementation of centralized policies; there is nothing academic about the proliferation of paperwork and regulations that threatens the ability of small businesses to survive; nothing academic about the excesses of a consumerism that is increasing costs while reducing the variety of goods available to the consumer; nothing academic about placing more and more of our citizens at the mercy of bureaucrats armed with arbitary discretion over a thousand and one areas of their private lives. What I fear has happened in the past forty years is that there has been a gradual but unmistakable erosion of the safeguards written into our Constitution. If we are to understand what is happening to us and seek to find the remedy for much of our social and political ills, we must refer to that basic document of our freedom.

Therefore, anyone who chooses to discuss the actual or potential threats to American freedom owes it to his readers—and to himself—to first set down his understanding of the broad principles incorporated in the Constitution. If what follows seems to some readers to be obvious and to smack of the civics primer, I can only say that it is precisely because these principles are not always obvious in current American political discourse that this book was written in the first place.

I believe it is first of all essential to understand that the Constitution is far more than a document establishing a frame of government for an entire nation; it is also a charter of individual liberty. It is not just a blueprint of government; it is a document of human freedom. It is this aspect of the Constitution which commands so fierce a passion; which makes each of us feel entitled to assert that this or that decision or law is or is not in accordance with what we understand to be true constitutional doctrine. But—and this is the important point—we also recognize that each of us cannot be right at the same time. Even though we may fervently believe that this or that judgment is rightly or wrongly taken, we are bound in the end, as responsible men and women in a self-governing society, to abide by that decision—even when, perhaps especially when, it does not go our way. This acquiescence in the decisions of the Supreme Court, or in the decisions of a majority of the voters or of the Congress, derives not only from a calculation of long-term self-interest, but also from a deep and abiding faith in our system of government, a faith that the courts and the laws they are asked to enforce will, in the end, prove correct, not only for us but for everyone.

This reflects the long-run optimism that has distinguished our nation from the beginning. It is captured in a passage from Benjamin Franklin's *Report on the Constitutional Convention*. Referring to an emblem—a sunburst—carved on the President's chair, he wrote: "I have often and often in the course of the Session . . . looked at that behind the President, without being able to tell whether it was rising or setting. But now at length I have the happiness to know it is a rising, not a setting sun."

For most of our history we have seen the American sun as always on the rise, our horizons unlimited. In recent years, however, we have witnessed changes that have caused many thoughtful men and women to question whether that optimism is still justified. For despite the strength of our constitutional system, there are signs that it is being strained to its limits.

A written Constitution may be indispensable in preserving freedom once achieved, but it will not impose it on a people that has lost the will or taste for it. This is something which that quite remarkable group of men who founded this nation understood to the marrow of their bones. They understood that freedom as we have been privileged to know it is not the natural state of human society, as a glance through the pages of history or about the globe today will so readily confirm. Nor is it the accidental state of society. Rather, freedom represents the highest and most fragile achievement of the political arts. This fundamental fact, coupled with this country's extraordinary stability, gives us the measure of the unique accomplishment of the architects of the American Republic. The institutions which they designed have survived for nearly 200 years because they were grounded on the lessons learned from more than 2,000 years of the Western world's experiments with free institutions, and because they were founded on an understanding of the realities of human nature illuminated by the insights of the Old and New Testaments.

While the Founders of this Republic were profoundly optimistic about what men could accomplish in a free society, they were not utopians, and they harbored few illusions about the perfectibility of human beings. On the contrary, they understood that while each man has within him a thirst for freedom, he also has within him the seeds of its destruction. They therefore recognized that if the new nation were to survive as a free society, if it were to avoid those dangers rooted in human nature on which all previous experiments in freedom had always foundered, it would be necessary to insulate it against man's ambition, against his innate drive to dominate other men. In explaining the need for the checks and balances which had been introduced into the Constitution, James Madison wrote in *Federalist Paper No. 51* as follows:

> It may be a reflection on human nature that such devices should be necessary to control the abuses of government. But what is government itself but the greatest of all reflections on human nature? If men were angels, no government would be necessary. If angels were to govern men, neither external nor internal controls on government would be necessary. In forming a government which is to be administered by men over men, the great difficulty lies in this: You must first enable the government to control the governed; and in the next place, oblige it to control itself. A dependence on the people is, no doubt, the primary control on the government; but experience has taught mankind the necessity of auxiliary precautions.

We are all familiar with the auxiliary precautions through which James Madison and the other architects of the Constitution sought to prevent the few from acquiring power at the expense of the many; and although volumes can be written as to what has happened in the intervening years to the safeguards summed up in the phrases "separation of powers" and "rights reserved to the states," the basic structure of the federal system has survived and it continues to function. The Founders also sought to protect the individual from the predations of government through the adoption of the Bill of Rights, and they instilled in us a reverence for the rule of law as our best protection against the capricious or arbitrary acts of those in authority.

But the Founders of this nation understood that these

safeguards could constitute only part of the equation of freedom; that it requires more than a diffusion of power among different branches and levels of government, more than the protection of the individual from the aggressive and arbitrary acts of the state. They understood that freedom also depends to a critical degree on the citizen's capacity for self-discipline and self-reliance, on the extent of his reverence for the law, and on his continued insistence on personal freedom as his first political goal.

It is against this background that, at our Bicentennial, we should pause and assess the present situation in America, and determine how secure we are in our freedoms. We need to examine whether or not our institutional safeguards and public attitudes are such as to give us the confidence we would like to feel as we enter our third century as a nation. These are not the questions we have been in the habit of asking ourselves. But neither have we, in years past, witnessed such fundamental and rapid changes as those that have been brought about during the past generation.

Something revolutionary has happened in the life of this country when governors and mayors, most recently the Mayor of New York City, and increasing numbers of ordinary citizens, whether they be rich or poor, farmers or pharmacists, taxpayers or the aged, must stand in line, hat in hand, to plead their cases before federal functionaries possessed of vast discretionary power over matters of vital importance to them.

Over the past forty years we have seen an extension of federal authority that is converting the states from autonomous sovereignties with clearly defined areas of exclusive competence into the role of administrators of federal programs seeking to implement federally defined goals. This has served to concentrate a degree of authority in Washington over the whole fabric of the nation that the framers of the Constitution had hoped to prevent. It threatens to subvert the division of power and responsibility that for so long has been considered the special genius of the American Republic, and that moved the great British historian Lord Acton to write of our Constitution as follows: "By the development of the principles of federalism, it has produced a community more powerful, more prosperous, more intelligent and more free than any other the world has seen."

As I slump back in my seat in the Senate chamber and hear the arguments advanced for imposing a federal authority on still further areas of state activity, be it automobile insurance, or public libraries, or municipal parks, or primary education, or the maintenance of child-care centers, I can't help wondering how many in America today really understand what it was about the American system that caused Lord Acton, a man not given to rhetorical extravagance, to make so generous a compliment to our distinctly American principles of Federalism. While I am encouraged by my own experience and by recent studies of American attitudes to believe the average citizen *does* understand the virtues of the federal system, I am less certain about his representatives in the Congress, who continue unabated in their work of concentrating power in Washington.

But the dangers run deeper than the threat to Federalism. They go to the heart of Franklin's challenge: Will we, the people, be able to keep the Republic? I find myself deeply concerned over the long-term effects of Congressional actions and rhetoric on both the ability and the willingness of the American people to maintain that personal independence which is the ultimate guarantee of our liberties. We are in danger of forgetting that freedom can flourish only where a people have the character and self-discipline required to keep the calls on public authority or public assistance to an absolute minimum. For more than a generation, however, we have been encouraging the American people to turn to government instead of to themselves or to the Deity for the satisfaction of every need, real or imagined; and in so doing we have been undermining their self-reliance. Similarly, our justified and continuing concern for the protection of the individual rights of each American has at times become so obsessive as to cause us to lose sight of the fact that neither these nor any other rights can exist in a social vacuum, nor can they be divorced from their concomitant responsibilities, nor pursued to the exclusion of all others. We are in danger, in short, of losing that balance wheel of common sense, of proportion, that was so striking a characteristic of the Founders of this Republic.

These current tendencies are nowhere better illustrated than in the wringing of hands that in the late 1960's accompanied just about any attempt by our public authorities to prevent rampaging mobs from giving vent to their discontent by burning down a college building or immobilizing a section of a city. Because these mobs had managed to co-opt the language of the legal process by describing themselves simply as demonstrators exercising their lawful right of protest, they were able to bring the undiscriminating wrath of our intelligentsia down upon the heads of those luckless officials who sought to enforce the laws against arson and to maintain that minimum degree of civil order required to permit a university or a city to function.

Now, I do not mean to suggest that our public authorities never resorted to excessive force. Certainly they did, but not nearly so often as their critics would suggest, and almost never without the severest provocations. What we witnessed time and again, however, was a bias against the forces of law and order and in favor of the militants whose worst excesses were somehow excused because of the well-advertised purity of their goals. But what has concerned me most is that in echoing the militants' charges of political repression, so many of the most influential voices in this country—voices that ought to have known better—encouraged the view that these resorts to violence and intimidation were somehow legitimate, or, at least, under the circumstances, excusable extensions of the constitutional "right of the people peaceably to assemble and to petition for the redress of grievances." In so doing, they exhibited what can only be described as a dangerous blindness to the historical fact that freedom cannot coexist with anarchy.

Happily, at this writing it is possible to speak of this epidemic of mass resorts to violence in the past tense. The psychic shocks they delivered to the body politic seem to have had a cathartic effect both on and off the campuses; and without any doubt, they have added a significant impetus to the trend toward conservatism. It may well be that we have learned some lessons, and that we will not soon again tolerate, let alone passively encourage, a return to the streets and to arson and intimidation as instruments of political action. It will take another major test, however, before we know whether those in authority have really learned from this experience.

I wish that I could be as confident of the instincts of the American people in another area where the ultimate threat to their freedom is less obvious. I wish that I could be satisfied that a majority of Americans fully understand the implications of the increasing dependence on the federal government that the Congress has been so assiduously encouraging on an ever broader scale. We cannot surrender responsibilities to the State without at the same time to that extent subjecting ourselves to the authority of the State; and thus, imperceptibly, step by step, we have allowed government to expand at a real cost to our ability to order our own lives. This acquiescence in the expansion of the federal role suggests that Americans, who for so many generations now have come to take their liberties for granted, may be losing that passion for individual freedom that is the best guarantee of its survival.

I do not mean to suggest that there exists today an immediate threat to our freedom. By and large, our institutions and our people remain strong. My brief exposure to public life has served to confirm my high confidence in the fundamental good sense and toughness and sound instincts of the great majority of Americans. And although it has been some time since we have witnessed the tar-and-feathering of a tax collector, most Americans still maintain a healthy suspicion of those in authority.

As time goes on, however, it will be increasingly difficult to mobilize that good sense and toughness and suspicion behind a move to peel back the scope of federal authority. Too many Americans are becoming the beneficiaries of special federal favors to make likely a broad-gauged attack on the wisdom of allowing the federal government the power to grant such favors in the first place. Too many businessmen, for example, will preach the virtues of unrestricted trade while defending to the last the sanctity of the quotas that protect their particular markets from the hazards of a too-energetic foreign competition. Big labor will champion the rights of the little man to fight the monopolists—unless, of course, the monopoly in question happens to be big labor itself. We all rightfully grumble over the complexity and inequities of federal tax regulations, but how many of us are ready to surrender those particular loopholes (such as the deductibility of interest paid on mortgages) which happen to serve our own convenience? No, I fear we may have grown too accustomed to the federal face, too docile for our own good, too willing to be expedient.

So I believe it is timely to hoist a few storm warnings and to keep them flying until we see signs of a sustained move to reverse the flow of power to Washington, and until we see Americans in sufficient numbers once again proclaiming against the dangers of becoming too dependent on government. We need to keep them flying until we see a new commitment to the insights and institutions that today, as in 1787, are best designed to "secure the blessings of liberty to ourselves and our posterity."

5
The Winter of Our Discontent

LAST YEAR an article in the *National Observer* analyzed a number of nationwide surveys undertaken to discover the views of Americans concerning their own lives and aspirations. The polls covered many areas of national life and, in summary, the *Observer* reported this as their conclusion: "America is still a great place to live and work, most Americans believe, but not as good as it was 5 or 10 years ago. And along with the sense that things are getting worse, public opinion polls show, a substantial percentage of Americans have a growing feeling that they are losing control over important aspects of their lives. . . ."

This is still a good country. I am losing control over my own destiny.

Americans continue to love their country and to believe in its greatness. They know that in most respects it is the society that comes closest to the ideals of freedom.

And yet . . .

And yet, there exists in America an undeniable, growing discontent. It takes many forms and can be attributed to many causes. But its symptom is the sense of powerlessness. Too many Americans have a feeling they are being forgotten or ignored, used and manipulated, and that there is nothing they can do about it. They see wrongs they want to right, actions they want taken, but they are unable to move the movers.

Alienation. Doubt. Discontent. Frustration. Whatever name is given to this phenomenon, one thing is certain:

77

Americans have grown not only less confident of their own abilities to lead their own lives, but less confident of their ability to shape their government and institutions.

The growing dissatisfaction has been recorded in the polls and at the polls. Public opinion surveys in recent years have traced a steady decline in public confidence in governmental institutions; and in the 1974 elections, only 38 percent of registered voters bothered to participate. A postmortem analysis revealed that more than half of those who failed to vote did so because they no longer believed it made any difference whether they voted or not.

I need look no further than my own mail to see the extent of this pervasive sense of powerlessness. My office receives an average of more than 1,000 letters and telegrams a day on almost every conceivable topic. But there is reflected in each day's mail an underlying theme that, I am convinced, is the most important political fact in present American life: the extent to which the average American feels he is helpless to control events.

It is far too easy to blame a disenchantment with "the system" and with politics and politicians on the eruption of social disorders and violence in 1968–1972, or on the Watergate scandals of 1973–1974, or on the inflation and recession that were gathering momentum in 1974. But the light turnout in the 1974 elections represents a phenomenon that runs much deeper. The American people sense today that government has become what John Courtney Murray in *We Hold These Truths* refers to as "being everywhere intrusive and also impotent, possessed of immense power and powerless to achieve rational ends. . . ." Yes, the federal government *does* possess immense power: power to debase the currency, power to dictate social policy, power to tax away the earnings of the American worker. "Powerless to achieve rational ends"—yes, but still powerful enough to whittle away at the ability of its citizens to manage their own affairs.

It is not only government that is increasingly gaining control over the lives of American citizens. There are other forces at work as well that set the tone of American life and define its objectives without condescending to consult those who will be most affected. Together they have affected virtually every aspect of the life of the individual, to the point where it is not much of an exaggeration to describe a day in the life of an average American as follows:

In the morning he sends his children off to the school bus which by federal court order will transport them halfway across town. He himself goes to work and learns the federal "affirmative action" program has kept him from getting a deserved promotion because his employer felt he had to give the job to a less qualified member of a minority group in order to meet employment goals set by the Department of Labor. He receives a call from his wife, who tells him that his brother is in trouble with the federal government because the repair shop he runs is in violation of obscure and unreasonably exacting Occupational, Safety and Health Administration (OSHA) regulations of which he had no prior knowledge. His wife also reminds him that there is a PTA meeting that night which will further discuss the plan of a private foundation to use the school district for experimental programs the parents neither asked for nor want. On his lunch hour he walks to a restaurant, past shops filled with pornographic books and past movie houses showing X-rated films that sprang up like mushrooms after a court struck down the antiobscenity ordinances that had been adopted by the City Council with overwhelming popular support. That evening, as he listens to the commentators on different television news shows, he hears himself condemned as a racist because he is opposed to forced busing; as being insensitive to the needs of others when he complains about a welfare system that allows some welfare families to live better than his neighbor is able to on earnings of $9,500 a year; and as being callous because he is against amnesty for draft dodgers. None of these commentators has a thing to say in support of his values or the positions he believes in. That night he has a nightmare about the mortage payments coming due on his house. Between higher taxes and the inflation caused by government deficits, he doesn't see how he can continue to make ends meet.

The government bureaucrats, the elitists in every area—education, the foundations, the media—each claims to know what is best for him and the country. They ignore what he wants or thinks. As they go about directing other people's lives and planning for brighter tomorrows, they never condescend to consult the one who has to pay for it all: the ordinary American whose total tax burden represents the fastest-growing item in his family budget.

There is no single answer to what is bothering the American people. There is no single solution that can be offered to solve the problems and to erase the feeling shared by millions of middle Americans that they are being overwhelmed by events they are unable to influence. But a look at some areas of our national life might serve to show how we got into this situation—and how, possibly, we can get out of it. Three of these go to the heart of the widespread feeling among Americans that they are no longer able to shape their destinies through the political process. The fourth has to do with a perception that society itself is losing its ability to maintain the public safety.

I
The Threat to Federalism

Let's call him Governor X. One evening I found myself seated beside him at a dinner. We exchanged pleasantries for a few minutes and then he began to unburden himself of all the frustrations he had felt since taking office.

I had heard similar stories from almost every other Governor I had met. They had different regional accents, different political philosophies, different views of the world, but they had one thing in common: each felt he couldn't get the job done in his state because he was being forced to conform to federal procedures and regulations and priorities, or suffer the forfeiture of federal funds.

My evening with Governor X stands out in my memory because he was not only frustrated, he was angry. He had campaigned on a specific program, and had been elected by a substantial majority of the voters of his state. Yet at every turn he found himself hedged in and blocked by the regulations, delays, and arbitrary requirements that accompany just about every dollar that flows from Washington back to the states. And since almost every state program nowadays receives some measure of federal funding, he found that the federal tail was wagging the dog. He finally said in exasperated tones: "Jim, I *know* what the people of my state want. I *know* how I can deliver better services at a lower cost. I *know* what our priorities have to be, and I am tired of being preached at and dictated to by bureaucrats in Washington who don't know how to run their own agencies, let alone a state. If we don't do things the federal way, why they just cut off the funds. And that's something that neither I nor any other Governor can stand politically. You refuse to go along with some stupid federal boondoggle and the next thing you know you see headlines blaring out that GOVERNOR X LOSES STATE $30 MILLION IN FEDERAL FUNDS. Jim, let's stop fooling ourselves. We don't have sovereign states anymore. All we have are a bunch of provinces. A governor can't develop an original program. All he is is a damn administrator of federal programs. I can't do a thing my people want. I can't make policy. Washington makes it for me, and never mind the fact that the policy doesn't make sense in our state. We are becoming conveyor belts for policies signed, sealed, and delivered in Washington.

"Am I frustrated?" he asked. "You're damned right! I'm frustrated, my department heads are frustrated, the Mayors of all my towns and cities are frustrated, and so are our citizens. They ask us questions, ask us to do things, and we simply can't give them straight answers. We don't make the decisions anymore. No wonder the voters are turned off."

We talked for a few more minutes and then turned our attention to the introduction of guests and the speaker. As I sat there, I pondered what he had been saying.

What, indeed, had happened? Why was the federal principle, which the Founders had made the cornerstone of our governmental structure, now being eroded and chipped away?

It would take a book the size of *War and Peace* to document the intellectual, social, historical, and political events that have led to the abandoning of the federal principle. But essentially the basic facts of the story can be summed up as follows:

The heresy that has resulted in the concentration of authority and responsibility in Washington has its source in the arrogance that assumes that a majority in Congress and the central planners in the bureacracy are better able to establish governmental priorities, design and build roads, meet social responsibilities, educate children, etc., than are the elected representatives of the several states. Democracy operates slowly, and some states are inevitably more alert than others to old and new problems. Yet if the concept of Federalism is important in the equation of American freedom—and I profoundly believe it is—then it necessarily requires a willingness to put up with inefficiencies, with delays, and with the fact that the electorates of some states may have different views as to what constitutes social responsibility and the rights and interests of their citizens than transient majorities in the Congress of the United States.

One of the unspoken premises behind the compulsion to centralize authority in Washington is that the states cannot be trusted to meet the minimum social needs of their own citizens—as Washington measures those needs. This, of course, is a repudiation of the proposition that individual Americans are capable of responsible self-government. But while it would be political suicide to say this, the repudiation remains implicit, and the apostles of centralized power praise the "common man" while at the same time espousing a philosophy that is contemptuous of his ability to exercise his franchise in a responsible manner.

I would suggest there is nothing in the record of the past forty years to support the smug belief that Washington has a monopoly on compassion or that it has a special competence in meeting human needs. Indeed the evidence is all the other way. George Romney, after four years as Secretary of the Department of Housing and Urban Development, said: "We have been throwing billions of dollars into these problem areas without making a dent upon them. It is now foolish to say that if we will only spend a little more money we will resolve these difficult issues. . . .

"The truth is—none of us are now sure what are the right things to do."

In the area of welfare the record of the federal government has been one of outrageous failure. More than that, the rigid regulations imposed by Washington on the states have made it exceedingly difficult (though not totally impossible) for the states to do anything sensible in the way of welfare reform. I say "not totally impossible," because Governor Ronald Reagan of California was able to push through reforms in his last term in office that (a) increased benefits to the truly needy by 42 percent, (b) reduced the California welfare rolls by 400,000 (they had been the fastest growing in the nation), and (c) cut total welfare costs by more than $4 billion. He had, however, to fight the bureaucrats both in the Department of Health, Education and Welfare, and in his own state down the line before he could institute his own program. When Governor Nelson Rockefeller tried to institute similar reforms in New York, he too had to fight the welfare bureaucracy, and some key elements in his plan were blocked in court on the basis of federal preemption of the welfare field.

It is argued, of course, that many states do not have the financial resources to do what is required to be done (as viewed from Washington). This is to a degree true, but there are other ways of addressing this problem than that of conjuring up massive federal programs that distribute funds to all the states irrespective of need, while imposing the most rigid requirements on how the funds are to be used.

But this concern for the less affluent states tends to obscure the heavy cost that federal grant-in-aid programs impose on every state whether rich or poor. The political shell game that suggests that money from Washington is somehow free makes the offer of matching federal funds almost irresistible. This in turn causes state and local governments to come up with their share of the funding for programs of marginal utility at the expense of others that would serve far more important local needs. This effect of federal grantsmanship was illustrated in a *Wall Street Journal* article (March 3, 1971) which discussed the special revenue-sharing proposals then being advanced by President Nixon. The article quoted an official as saying: "If the federal government were giving away gold-plated octagons, and the cities had to pay half the cost, every damn city in the nation would have one."

Not only does the intervention of the federal government serve to distort local priorities and divert funds from areas of greater need, it has also created administrative delays and costs that at times exceed the amount of the federal contribution. Nowhere is this aspect of federal aid more strikingly demonstrated than in testimony given by Governor Marvin Mandel of Maryland before the Senate Finance Committee in 1972 on how federal "help" works in real life:

> I might say to you without trying to appear too critical, it used to take us about a week to prepare an application to get a sewage treatment plant built, to prepare an application for the Federal Government. It now takes us 11 months to prepare that application to just apply for the funds because of the rules and regulations that we are tied up with. . . .
>
> It used to take us about one year to prepare a plan for a highway and to get it out for bid. Now it takes us six and a half years by the time we can get approval from the Federal Government to build that highway. That construction cost has gone up 18 percent a year. . . . We are starting to refuse Federal money because it is costing us more money than if we build with our own money. . . .

In other words, the State of Maryland found that it would be considerably cheaper to build its own highways with its own money in accordance with its own specifications than to accept federal funding and be required to build the highway the federal way. The Maryland experience is by no means unique. Few political officeholders, however, have the courage to risk the charge that they had failed to collect and use millions of federal dollars just because they found it would be net cheaper to meet their own needs with their own funds.

In January of 1973, the *National Journal* asked Allen E. Pritchard, Jr., Executive Vice-President of the National League of Cities, to give his views on the categorical grant system which between 1962 and 1974 has grown from 300 programs costing about $3 billion to more than 1,000 programs having an annual cost of $43.9 billion. Said Mr. Pritchard of these grant-in-aid programs:

> Over a period of time we have reached a point where the management of the programs, the maintenance of an awareness of their status and financial potential and the coordination of them—the whole business—has become a major function of any governmental unit. It really has so distorted the ability of local units to do any intelligent planning, let alone any implementation, that in my estimation, local planning is practically nonexistent. We say it is there, but really an awful lot of it has been planning a response to what is available and how it's available, rather than planning to meet needs and then looking for resources to meet those needs.
>
> The same thing has been true in terms of the structure of government. The categorical system builds bureaucracies not only in the federal government but within the state and local governments, and outside the scope of these governments. . . . They are always up against the wall, because independent agencies learn to play the ballgame on these categorical grants, and they are always coming in at five minutes to 12 and saying, "We've got to sign off on this application or we aren't going to get the money," or, "We don't have any options because if we do it the way we want to do it, we can't get the money." So even the most vocal people in the community or the strongest political leadership has a hard time shaping things, because the categorical system has set the trend within which they can work. In many cases, the programs are not broad enough to really allow any significant flexibility. The system has really made it almost impossible to essentially relate activities and policies at the local level. . . .

Thus, even though participation in federal programs is theoretically optional with the states and localities, the political effect is to force them to substitute Congressional and bureaucratic priorities for their own.

This brings us to still another aspect of the centralization of power and planning that has occurred in this country during the past forty years. We are destroying one of the great creative aspects of the federal system: the extraordinary degree of innovation that it encourages. Historically, individual states have acted as laboratories in which to experiment with new approaches to problems that are common to all the states. When one of them develops an effective way of meeting a particular need, the others are free to follow. On the other hand, when one adopts what proves to be a wrong approach, its patent failure will spare the sister states the cost of making the same mistake.

What I have just written used to be commonplace in schoolbooks describing the advantages of the federal system. Yet such is the current obsession in the Congress for a federal answer to any and every problem that captures public attention, that we rush pell-mell to cast in concrete a federal solution that is apt to be worse than the problem it attempts to address, and we destroy the ability to find a better one through the process of trial and error by the individual states.

Two examples of the tendency of Congress to run roughshod over the prerogatives of the states come immediately to mind. At the present time, neither is law although one of the proposals was adopted by the Senate in the fall of 1974. Both, however, are likely to be enacted before the Ninety-fourth Congress moves into history.

The first of these examples involves legislation to impose national no-fault automobile insurance. This concept is an interesting one, of which I approve in principle. It represents an attempt to eliminate or reduce the incredible costs and delays that result from lawsuits trying to fix the blame for automobile accidents. The no-fault concept would require that injured persons be compensated directly by their insurance companies irrespective of which driver was responsible for the accident.

This approach was adopted by the State of Massachusetts in January, 1971, and there has been every indication that the plan has worked well while Massachusetts drivers are realizing substantial savings in the cost of their insurance premiums. Other states soon followed suit, and as of the end of 1974, the legislatures of twenty-three others (including

New York) had adopted various forms of no-fault insurance laws. This created seemingly irresistible pressure in the Senate Commerce Committee to adopt a federal no-fault insurance policy that would, in effect, require every state to conform to a narrowly defined federal pattern. In due course a bill was reported out for debate on the floor.

Now it happens that till now, the regulation of insurance companies and the terms of insurance policies have been determined by state laws and by the insurance commissions established in the individual states. The first question I asked myself, therefore, on learning that I would be called on to consider federal legislation in the field, was whether, as a matter of practical necessity, uniform federal standards were required in order for the no-fault concept to work. Although historically each state set the standards for insurance policies sold within its own jurisdictions, it was possible that the extent of travel across state lines would make federal preemption necessary. I soon found, however, that this was not the case. Insurance policies issued to New York drivers gave them full protection whether or not they were involved in an accident in a "no-fault" state. There was, in short, no overriding *national* imperative for moving the federal government into this entirely new field.

But what were the objections to having the federal government preempt the field? In the first place, it would do further violence to the concept of federalism that has reserved admittedly diminishing areas of responsibility to the states; and it was largely on this basis that I determined to oppose the new law. But there were other, practical objections as well. There is a great deal still to be learned about how the no-fault concept will work in practice. What are the circumstances under which litigation ought to be permitted and special damages assessed? What kind of coverage should be required of motorcyclists and others using the highways? Which of the several plans in existence would prove to be the fairest and cheapest? The answers to these and a number of other questions would be provided over a period of time by actual experience at the state level. Yet, in its hurry, the Senate was determined to rush through its own version and impose it on all the states including those whose legislatures had specifically rejected this new approach to automobile liability insurance. Moreover, the Senate was determined to do so even though in certain instances it would require states to violate provisions of their own Constitutions guaranteeing their citizens access to the courts to litigate claims of the kinds that would be outlawed under the no-fault approach to automobile insurance.

It will be argued, of course, that in this state or that one, an unholy alliance between trial lawyers and insurance companies will thwart a move to a no-fault system that has already been demonstrated to be in the motorists' interest. The silent premise is that members of the Congress are immune to special-interest pleading. Those who really believe this would have had their illusions shattered in the fall of 1974 when the Senate passed legislation that would require every radio sold in the United States at a price of $15 or more to be able to receive both AM and FM broadcasts, and never mind the costs to or the preferences of the consumer of whose interests the Congress is so notoriously solicitous. Every reason but the real one was argued in support of this extraordinary measure; the real reason being the pressures that had been brought to bear on individual Senators by the FM broadcasting industry.

The other example I have in mind involves a contemplated intrusion into the area of labor relations between state and local governments and their own employees. The Ninety-fourth Congress now has under serious consideration several measures that would require mandatory unionization of employees working for state and local governments and the requirement that they be granted the right to strike.

If the states and localities are to be conceded any vestigial rights, if the Tenth Amendment to the Constitution is to have any meaning, then we must at the very least accord to the states the right to establish the conditions under which their own public employees will work. Yet, because of the assumption that no constitutional barriers any longer stand between the Congress and what it unilaterally deems desirable, there are those who are intent on demanding that the states snap to and adopt employment standards and practices that thoughtful citizens across the country consider a prescription for disaster in the cost and delivery of public services.

There is no doubt about it. One of the sharpest departures from the grand plan designed by the architects of the Constitution is the current compulsion to concentrate power in Washington, to impose a Washington-approved uniform mold on a vast, sprawling, and diverse population. Even though lip service is now being paid to the notion that the federal government has grown too large and too rigid, whenever a new problem, real or imagined, arises, the only solution one is apt to hear proposed inevitably involves the creation of still another federal program. Is there a shortage of energy? Establish some bureaucracies to spread the misery around, and perhaps form a federal corporation to go into the energy business rather than consider the removal of the restrictions and regulations that have contributed so substantially to creating the problem in the first instance. Are medical services becoming too expensive? Let us adopt a massive $60 billion federal health insurance program that will cover all Americans irrespective of need, and never mind the fact that, according to the Health Insurance Institute, 183,000,000 Americans (88 percent of our population) are already covered by one or more varieties of private health insurance. Are federal agencies designed to look after specific consumer interests falling down on the job? Let us set up still another superagency to ride herd on all those other agencies that are not functioning as well as they should.

The net result of all this is to atrophy local and state initiatives, and to destroy governmental accountability at those levels that are most directly accessible to the people. This in turn encourages citizens who ought to be looking to their state and local governments to look instead to Washington.

The more dependent he is made on a growing variety of services dispensed by the national government, the more difficult it becomes for the average unorganized citizen to influence the policies that increasingly shape his life. This more distant level of government, however, is sensitive to pressures from well-financed, well-organized groups, and to opinions generated by the media. The feeling of helplessness experienced by so many Americans, in other words, is not imagined. It is a fact—and a fact dangerous to the morale and therefore the future of a self-governing society.

At the risk of sounding flippant, I would suggest that the alternative to Federalism is best illustrated by a photograph that I came across in the weekly journal *Human Events.* It showed a man leaning out of a second-floor window of a building in Vienna, Virginia, a suburb of Washington. In his hand he held a long government form. When I say long, I mean *l-o-n-g.* The paper spilled from the second floor down to ground level, where it was held by a woman, and then extended ten or twelve feet beyond her, finally ending in the hands of another man. The accompanying story read:

> City officials of the Washington, D.C., suburb of Vienna, Va., a town of 18,000, are disturbed by the 40-foot long form EEO-4 sent out annually by the Equal Employment Opportunity Commission. The above photo shows Vienna Mayor Joseph R. Spriggs (second floor window), Secretary Lois Savia and Town Manager C. Clay Harrell holding the form. Compounding the waste, Harrell pointed out in a letter protesting the form, is the fact that it is in quadruplicate and thus requires some 160 feet of paper and additional lengths of carbon. "Multiply this by all of the other little municipalities, all other big municipalities, all of the counties, all of the independent or semi-independent boards, commissions and authorities, all the states and state agencies that have to complete this form and you begin to appreciate the volume of paper generated by one agency for one law. . . . How long can our short paper supply support programs of this nature?" Town Manager Harrell did not comment on the amount of time required of local governments to fill out the mandated form.

II
The Fourth Branch of Government

The development of the federal bureaucracy as a *de facto* fourth branch of government is a major source of the current discontent. For the first time in our history Americans feel hemmed in, manipulated, driven by nonelected bureaucrats who are protected by the civil service and endowed with broad discretionary powers over other people's lives. These bureaucrats belong to agencies and departments that as a practical matter cannot be disciplined by other than a most determined President or Congress. They are cloaked with the full authority of the federal government and have access to its resources. As a result, too many citizens involved in a dispute with the bureaucracy find themselves engaged in an unequal struggle in which they have little choice but to capitulate even when they know they are in the right. The average citizen simply cannot afford the fight, especially as the administrative laws governing the relationships of the regulator and the regulated have a way of reversing the normal presumptions. It is assumed that the federal regulator is in the right unless the aggrieved citizen is able to demonstrate that that regulator is acting in an arbitrary and capricious manner. This is a burden that is difficult and expensive to meet. The laws normally endow the regulators with wide discretionary powers; and the issue too often is not whether or not they are right, but whether they can be said to have abused their discretion.

Simply trying to get the name of the right person to write to in the federal bureaucracy can take weeks. Legal fees for those who choose to fight the federal government are invariably large. But perhaps the most aggravating and, in the final analysis, the most effective tool the bureaucrat has to keep citizens at arm's length (and at wit's end) is the bureaucratic answer. This is usually couched in bureaucratese, a form of English invented for the sole purpose of not saying what appears to be being said.

I once wrote to the Commissioner of the Social Security Administration to discover why the Social Security Administration demands that applicants for a Social Security card identify themselves racially. It seemed to me to be an uncomplicated question. I was informed by the Social Security Administration that the matter is one of "continuing concern" to them, that "very serious consideration had been given" to the correctness of including a question on race, and that "in light of present concern" they were "currently reviewing" the question.

I still did not know why the question was on the Social Security form, so I decided to try again. This time I received a two-page, single-spaced answer. It began with the hardly surprising claim that the Social Security Administration "attempts to work for the best interests of individuals affected by its decisions." Following this bit of news, I found that "constructive use" of racial data was needed in order to discover if "programs and resources" were reaching those intended. "Presentation and awareness of information are necessary for staff personnel . . . eligibility data are useful in analyzing the effectiveness of program outreach. . . ."

Then came this gem of bureaucratic prose: "Sorting people or sorting records in a decision-making process may affect the individuals, beneficially, harmfully or both, but sorting data for statistics does not directly affect the individuals counted in the statistics." I *still* do not know one clear, understandable reason why the Social Security Administration continues to ask Americans to list their race when applying for a Social Security card. Small wonder that the average citizen, unused to the Byzantine complexity of the Washington bureaucracy and unlettered in the mysteries of bureaucratic prose, feels lost when attempting to find a simple answer to a simple question.

This expansion of government regulation exercised by men and women with discretionary authority means, in practical terms, that we have moved away from the concept of government by law to a system of government by men.

"Bureaucracy" was once a scare word used by anti-New Deal propagandists, but it meant little to the rest of the nation. Then, within a relatively few years, more and more citizens' lives were being directed, shaped, and twisted into pretzel knots by that Faceless Bureaucrat who hitherto had been considered a myth. Several thousand New Yorkers each year are driven to write or telephone my office for specific help with regulations or decisions they feel to be unreasonable or unfair. Their complaints cover a wide range of problems. Sometimes they can be resolved with a telephone call or two to people in federal agencies who do their best to help. In other cases I find myself drawn into a prolonged battle with an entrenched and stubborn bureaucracy that will mobilize every weapon in its considerable arsenal. One such case involved the Mount Vernon school system.

Mount Vernon is a city in Westchester County, New York, with a population of 80,000 who live within a four-square-mile area. Its homes are largely single-family dwellings built in the thirties and before. The city's population is currently two-thirds white. The school system contains 11,000 students, about 55 percent of whom are black. The city is divided, in a way familiar to many Americans, by railroad tracks. The south side of the city is almost completely black, whereas the north side is predominantly white, although recent trends disclose a movement of blacks into the more affluent north side.

The Mount Vernon controversy climaxed in 1972 when an educational consultant reported that the Mount Vernon schools were in poor condition and that basic reforms were necessary. This report gave rise to several questions which became of interest to the Federal Department of Health, Education and Welfare (HEW). A federal administrative law judge eventually held that the school system was operating in violation of the Civil Rights Act of 1964 because of what he found to be intentional denials of equal educational opportunities. His ruling gave HEW's Office for Civil Rights (OCR) the chance to enter the picture.

Limitations of space and the feeling that the attention of even the most sympathetic reader might wander when confronted with the mind-benumbing chronicle of bureaucratic tactics in the Mount Vernon Board of Education's protracted battle with HEW zealots, persuade me not to attempt more than a sparse summary of the case. Suffice it to say, HEW/ OCR, with a display of footwork that would be the envy of Muhammad Ali, managed to keep the Mount Vernon school administrators off balance by coming at them from every direction. When the administrators attempted to make the inferior school facilities acceptable, to a degree that moved even an HEW official to acknowledge that "substantial progress" had been made, HEW decided that a school that had been renovated and reactivated in order to meet HEW complaints about congestion was inferior to others in the school system because its beautiful old hard-oakwood floors were a fire hazard. This "inferiority" was held a violation of the 1964 Civil Rights Act.

The school authorities were also guilty of having acceded to the request of minority parents that more minority teachers be hired in predominantly black schools because the children felt more comfortable with them. HEW found this accommodation to black parents unacceptable and forced the Mount Vernon Board of Education to transfer a black principal from one school to another solely on the basis of his race. This racist demand was begrudgingly consented to by the school system, which feared it would otherwise lose vocational education funds which were being withheld by HEW as it sought to enforce its orders.

Grimes School, the school with the hard-oakwood floors, became, for me, a symbol of the paradoxical nature of HEW's demands. It is an old, attractive brick building which outwardly does not appear rundown. The inside has been renovated, including new lighting, at a cost of more than $50,000. I found myself wondering if our plastic age finds wooden flooring "unconstitutional" per se.

When the Mount Vernon School Superintendent first proposed that the Grimes School be reopened in order to ease the congestion that HEW had earlier complained of, the HEW consultant was delighted. It was only after the school had been reopened with a highly predictable predominantly black neighborhood enrollment that HEW/OCR discovered the oak flooring. When it finally backed away from this particular ground for objection, HEW/OCR advanced the more serious charge that since the Grimes School was "racially identifiable," the decision to reopen it was a *de jure* act of discrimination even in the absence of any discriminatory intent on the part of the school authorities. At this point, HEW/OCR was asserting a novel constitutional doctrine that a financially strapped school board could not possibly be expected to litigate all the way to the Supreme Court.

Happily, the Department of Health, Education and Welfare was finally persuaded to abandon its more extreme position and release the vocational training funds whose principal beneficiaries would be the minority children for whose welfare HEW/OCR had been so extravagantly solicitous. But what bothered me more than the attempt to claim *de jure* discrimination without any showing of intent was the disturbing tendency on the part of OCR and HEW to ignore the views of the people most directly involved. While in Mount Vernon I was able to determine through conversations with parents, teachers, and administrators that the reopening of Grimes School was generally supported. A confidential poll of the parents was taken by the principal of the school, Mr. G. Allison Wells. One-third of the 340 parents responded to the unsigned questionnaire. The result showed major support for the decision to open the school as a neighborhood facility. It allowed their children to attend a school closer to home. School discipline improved markedly. Absenteeism was down. It simply could not reasonably be contended that any child's educational situation had deteriorated with the reopening of the school. To the best of my knowledge the only destabilizing influence in the school picture had been the Office for Civil Rights.

It is small wonder, then, that the school administrators and the citizens of Mount Vernon came to look upon HEW/OCR not as civil servants but as persecutors. Many felt that it was not entirely a coincidence that each new demand by the federal zealots was accompanied by the suggestion that all of Mount Vernon's problems, oak floors included, could be solved if the school authorities would only adopt forced busing to achieve racial balance throughout the district.

In any event, HEW/OCR never seemed to run out of new reasons for withholding federal funds. "No matter what we do, they ask for more," one administrator told me. "We think we've done everything we have to do, but then there's another letter or a visit from one of them and we're back where we started. This is costing us a lot of money, money that could be better used in other ways, in educating our children. But they keep coming back with new demands, something different each time. It's too much."

It was—and is—too much.

Other examples of bureaucratic interference in the lives of citizens abound, but perhaps no agency can match the Occupational Safety and Health Administration for the sheer rage and frustration its agents generate as they go about their appointed rounds. In its five brief years of existence, OSHA has become the symbol of the substitution of bureaucratic red tape for due process.

The stated purposes of OSHA are laudable enough. To quote the language of the Occupational Safety and Health Act of 1970, they are "to assure so far as possible every working man and woman in the nation safe and healthful working conditions and to preserve our human resources." It is the way OSHA has gone about preserving our human resources that has raised hackles throughout the American business community. As the Department of Labor's pamphlet, *All About OSHA*, is careful to point out, "The Act covers every employer in a business affecting commerce who has one or more employees." This means that virtually every business enterprise in the country, from the smallest corner grocery to General Motors, is subject to OSHA. To be subject to OSHA in turn means that you can be visited by one of its investigators at any time without notice, and fined on the spot for violations of regulations you not only have never heard about, but in some instances couldn't find the text of even if you had.

In 1972, in the course of Senate debate over OSHA, Senator Carl Curtis pointed to four stacks of books, each over three feet high, that he had placed on his desk. They contained a portion of the safety and health regulations that American businesses were being expected to abide by. His collection, he explained, was incomplete, as a number of the volumes were unavailable even in Washington. "Had I been able to get all the books telling the regulations," he said, "it would have been a stack seventeen feet high. There is scarcely a state in the Union that has a library that a small-business man can go to and find out what the regulations mean."

The seventeen-foot-high stack referred to by Carl Curtis is something more than a good debating point—it is a reality businessmen have had to live with, and it is symbolic of the problem inherent in so much well-intentioned legislation. In September, 1972, the Boulder, Colorado, *Daily Camera* carried an editorial which told of the plight of a local small-business man with six employees. A federal inspection led to a notification of a violation of a section of OSHA. The businessman did not have a copy of the regulations he had allegedly violated.

> . . . he was told no copies were available. He was fined $16.
>
> Two weeks later he received a 248-page list of OSHA regulations. There was nothing in the document about the violation he was charged with, so again he asked for a copy of the pertinent regulation.
>
> After a month he received a 48-page supplement to the 248-page rule book. The new document covered his situation but did not indicate he was violating any rule. So the small-business man appealed the case.
>
> After four hours of hearings with seven federal officials, the charge was dismissed—in a 19-page decision. . . .

As a practical matter, the average businessman will not go to court to protest a $16 or even a $1,600 fine. He has no recourse but to pay the amount and mutter about high-handed bureaucracy and the denial of due process, especially when OSHA regulations are patently absurd. One upstate New York businessman complained to me of being held in violation because he had constructed a guard rail out of iron piping even though it was stronger (and therefore safer) than the wooden guard rail stipulated in OSHA regulations. Another told me that it would cost over $200,000 to install new bathrooms to comply with OSHA regulations (some workers had to walk a few steps farther to reach a toilet than OSHA thought appropriate) in a factory building in which men and women had been happily, healthfully, and safely working for more than fifty years.

To give the reader some idea of how OSHA has affected American business practices, reference should be made to an ad that appeared in the New York *Times* on Sunday, March

23, 1975. The ad told of a new book that "could save you thousands of dollars on OSHA violation penalties." All "228 pages, 71 illustrations," and the "outsized 8½ inches x 11 inches format, ringbound" were designed to provide the buyer of the book with "a complete preparation plan" in order to get ready for an OSHA investigation. All this could be had for $29.95.

I do not know how successful the publishers of the book have been, but the fact that a book like this can be advertised as a necessity for every businessman shows the extent to which OSHA has transformed many American businessmen from productive members of society into puzzled and harassed victims of bureaucratic rules, regulations, and guidelines.

I am, unfortunately, all too familiar with the excesses of OSHA, because New York State has innumerable businesses, ranging from very small to very large, most of which, it would seem from my mail, have at one time or another come into contact with OSHA. Needless to add, it is the small- and medium-sized businesses that suffer most.

One case concerned alleged safety violations by a company that used tremolite (a mineral mined in New York State) in the production of industrial talc. Through a process of hopelessly complex reasoning, OSHA officials decided that the tremolite was a carcinogenic substance. The company which used the tremolite and the members of the New York State Local of the United Steel Workers of America, who mined it, disagreed on the perfectly reasonable grounds that the OSHA conclusion about tremolite was scientifically incorrect. But OSHA knew better—or its officials thought it did—and the company began to lose business as it couldn't manufacture under the new ruling of OSHA.

It took sixteen months, one United States Representative and his staff, one United States Senator and his staff, numerous meetings, countless letters, debates, quibbles, presentations of expert opinions and other forms of bureaucratic fun and games before progress was made. In the midst of the controversy, the head of the company wrote to me that his company was being held "hostage without documentation"—as ringing a phrase as I have heard in recent years, and a perfect rallying cry for every victim of the whims and moods of some Washington bureaucrat. Through the able assistance of caseworkers in my office and—to give OSHA its due—some late but welcome signs of reasonableness on the part of an OSHA official, the company was given, in effect, permission to certify to its customers that they were not risking cancer by using the company's product. This permission, I might add, was temporary, pending the results of an investigation. But it was only after sixteen months, the investment of a substantial sum of money and time by the company, and a more than substantial effort on the part of the Congressional caseworkers, that common sense prevailed.

Other small businesses are not so fortunate. The head of a tool and dye plant in upstate New York wrote to me that "we travel like a ping-pong ball between decisions by OSHA" and those of New York State officials. Another New York businessman, whose factory was investigated by the state Labor Department "one to two times a year," suddenly found himself in violation of safety standards after a quick visit from OSHA. "This procedure is un-American," he wrote. That a small-business man who has operated a safe shop for many years feels driven by Washington rulings to call a safety inspection un-American says something very important about how OSHA and other agencies are inexorably driving many citizens to the breaking point.

In February, 1975, I came across a case that exemplified the bureaucratic tyranny that can and does lead to excessive costs and additional burdens on businessmen (and, of course, ultimately, on the consumer as well).

Columnist John Lofton addressed himself to the woes of the Caterpillar Tractor Company of Peoria, Illinois. It seemed that this company did not mount fire extinguishers at the height required by OSHA regulations. After much discussion, debate, letter writing, telephone calls, and paper shuffling, OSHA finally agreed that Caterpillar's method of mounting fire extinguishers was, after all, not bad. Indeed,

OSHA indicated it would probably abandon its fire-extinguisher-mounting standards and adopt Caterpillar's. Lofton had this last word:

> Now what's so incredible about this whole ridiculous, time-consuming idiocy, is that in the good old days, before there was an OSHA, the Caterpillar Company hung its fire extinguishers just as OSHA now recommends they be hung.
> But, as the company's assistant safety manager Bob Keller explained to me, Caterpillar spent $60,000 in their Decatur, Ill. plant to rip this system out and install their own.
> Why? Because fork-lift drivers kept smashing into the extinguishers and damaging them. They were simply too low to the ground.
> So, here we see government in action. Big Brother in Washington makes a law, already found to be unworkable years ago by private industry, then after a year of consideration, ends up scrapping it and adopting the heretofore illegal standard as its own, in a ruling which should never have been any of the government's business in the first place.
> It's this sort of stupidity which makes the arguments for anarchy not entirely unappealing.

And it is having to put up with this sort of arbitrary stupidity that is causing increasing numbers of Americans to wonder whatever happened to the idea that ours was to be a government of laws and not of men.

III
Judicial Activism: What the Court Decides

Such is my respect for the Supreme Court that it has taken me a long time to admit to myself the extent to which this guardian of constitutional stability and the rule of law has contributed to the current sense of instability. The evidence, however, is clear.

For a generation now, the Supreme Court has too often

been a significant source of dissension as time-honored constitutional doctrines have been upset in case after case. Judicial activism during the years when Earl Warren was Chief Justice reached such heights that in August, 1958, the Tenth Annual Meeting of the Conference of Chief Justices was moved to adopt a resolution that can only be described as a stinging rebuke. Addressing themselves to the problem of federal-state relations, the attending Chief Justices of the states' highest courts, by a vote of 36 to 8, respectfully urged

> that the Supreme Court of the United States, in exercising the great powers confided to it for the determination of questions as to the allocation and extent of national and state powers . . . exercise one of the greatest of all judicial powers—the power of judicial self-restraint—by recognizing and giving effect to the difference between that which, on the one hand, the Constitution may prescribe or permit, and that which, on the other, a majority of the Supreme Court, as from time to time constituted, may deem desirable or undesirable. . . .

Given the deference that the Supreme Court commands, this is strong language. Certainly it illustrates the extent to which that body's recent ventures into judicial activism has alarmed thoughtful observers.

The Supreme Court is, of course, the institution farthest removed from popular control. Hence it is of special importance that it be seen as *judicial*; that is to say, as being above politics and ideologies. But in recent years, in far too many cases, it has appeared to be acting arbitrarily or precipitously, to be pursuing the thread of constitutional theory far beyond the limits of either precedent or common sense. In so doing, it has not only forfeited a substantial degree of popular support and respect, but it has weakened the perception of ours as a government by consensus: of institutional consensus represented by a Constitution that can only be modified through the amendatory process, and of the consensus represented by the decisions of elected officials. Instead of serving as mediator, the Court has too often been a major innovator acting without any mandate from, let alone the willing consent of, the governed.

The revolutionary character of the Court's activity in this period is scarcely denied even by its defenders. In area after area of law, the Court laid down novel rules of breathtaking scope and detail on everything from whether children should be allowed to pray in the public schools, to whether a police officer acted with perfect propriety prior to making an arrest, to whether the percentage of black and white children in a schoolroom was sociologically or psychologically desirable, and more recently to whether any form of meaningful protection could be extended to the unborn.

As a result of such decisions the Supreme Court emerged as a principal instrument in making major rearrangements in the way citizens have gone about their daily lives. As a result of totally novel constructions made by nonelected officials holding lifetime tenures, any form of funding or tax relief is denied parents wishing to exercise their right to send their children to religious schools. State legislatures have been required to upset systems of representation that antedate the Constitution and to adopt a "one man, one vote" concept not even required by the Constitution of the federal government.

Americans are told by the Court that pornographers are protected by the same First Amendment that forbids their children to join in classroom prayer in the public schools—schools which, to add insult to injury, their children may not be attending next month or next year because a federal judge finds their racial mix less than ideal. State and municipal courts find it increasingly difficult to bring those accused of crime to a speedy trial because of roadblocks made possible by a series of 5-to-4 decisions that have reversed longstanding rules affecting the admissibility of evidence and the rights of the accused. The litany could go on. What is more, the Supreme Court's lapse from judicial restraint has encouraged lower courts to mind-boggling extremes.

My own favorite example is the case of Mark Twain Junior High School, in Coney Island, New York City. In January,

1974, Federal District Court Judge Jack B. Weinstein determined that this predominantly black school represented a case of *de jure* segregation because federal-city financed housing for low income families had changed the racial mix of the neighborhood. In his preliminary order, he proposed to remedy the situation by mandating a change in the entire social and housing pattern of the area. In one way or another, federal, state, and city housing authorities were to haul middle and upper income whites into the school district and disperse the low income blacks whose children provided most of the student population at Mark Twain. We were not to learn precisely how Judge Weinstein proposed to bring this all about, because a subsequent order adopted the more modest goal of requiring school authorities to convert the school into a special school for gifted children that would attract students from across the city—presumably in ratios more representative of the racial and ethnic mix of the city's population. It should be noted in passing that Judge Weinstein did not believe it at all relevant that the low income housing that provided decent homes for black families was not constructed for the purpose of converting Mark Twain into a predominantly black school. Nor would he be deflected from his single-minded pursuit of his private ideological vision by the fact that Mark Twain was a superior school offering a variety of special educational help to the children of parents most of whom felt fortunate to have so excellent a neighborhood school.

I believe that most Americans are perfectly able to live with the fact that what they want may not always be compatible with the Constitution. But there are also limits on what they will accept in the name of constitutionally mandated decrees issued by federal judges.

Certain members of the Supreme Court are highly sensitive to this danger and are attempting to pull back on the reins. Other members of the Court, as well as many lower federal judges, seem bent on continuing as if there were no valid constraints upon their power. This latter group is, to say the least, shortsighted. Their problem is not one of intention, for I believe they are men of goodwill. Their problem, rather, is that they are isolated from the complex experiences which surround and mold the life of the man in the street. Elegant theories of constitutional law have a very different impact in the everyday world that most of us inhabit than may be apparent in the rarefied atmosphere of the Supreme Court's chambers. Constitutional rule-making in a nation as complex as ours should always be tempered by a healthy dose of common sense. Indeed, if there is a single fault—and there are many—common to the great gush of precedent-shattering decisions of the past twenty years, it is the persistent indulgence of ideological abstraction at the expense of common sense.

One measurable result of the judicial excesses of the past twenty years is that the High Court's docket is now perpetually clogged, which means that the members of the Court have quite literally only minutes to dispose of matters that have great impact on the everyday lives of common citizens. Another result, more important but less measurable, is that federal judges and would-be litigants have been encouraged to believe that virtually every imperfection or injustice in American life can somehow be converted into a constitutional claim of right. Even now, as I write in early 1975, the Supreme Court is at it again, decreeing by the narrowest of margins (5 to 4) that every schoolchild charged with a disciplinary infraction is entitled, as a matter of constitutional right, to a due process hearing before he can be dismissed. Now, I have no doubt but that a certain number of schoolchildren are unjustly or arbitrarily suspended from school every year. But for the life of me I cannot see that any great good will be advanced by making the federal judiciary the ultimate arbiter of disciplinary rules for public schools.

How did the transformation from a tradition of judicial restraint to one of judicial activism come about? I am not sure I know, but my own theory is that it has its genesis in the publication of Oliver Wendell Holmes' classic work of legal scholarship, *The Common Law.* In it Holmes marshaled evidence to demonstrate that despite the claim of common-law jurists that they did nothing more than apply immutable principles of law on a case by case basis to new fact situations, the common law tradition of Great Britain and the United States actually represented an evolutionary process in which legal principles were gradually modified to meet new situations in response to what he called "the felt necessities of the times." At the time he published his work, this flew in the face of the accepted understanding of the judicial process. Judges did not make law. They interpreted it and applied it to the facts before them.

The process he described was an unconscious one. While the judges deciding a case thought they were applying immutable principles, they were nevertheless unconsciously moved by what they perceived to be the demands of justice as they addressed themselves to situations for which they could find no direct precedent. I suspect, however, that the effect of Holmes' scholarship has been to translate an unconscious process into a conscious one; and this has created temptations to transform judicial decisions into what can only be described as legislative ones.

But whatever the reason for their current activism, it is clear that our courts have wandered a fair distance from the role Alexander Hamilton had in mind when he described the judiciary as being "the least dangerous branch." It is time our courts rediscovered the virtues of judicial restraint. It is time they rediscovered their constitutional role as interpreters of the law, and left social policy and the writing of the law to the states and to the Congress.

Centralized power, bureaucratic arrogance, judicial activism—these are causes enough for the pervasive feeling among too many Americans that they have lost effective control over the society in which they live. But they are more than that. They are symptoms of an underlying view of the world which, in recent years, has dominated the institutions that now shape the thought and tone of American life. It is the prevailing view of the mass media, including such pacesetting newspapers as the New York *Times* and the Washington *Post,* of the academic world, of the major foundations, and of government itself.

This complex is characterized by an elitism that is removed

from the mainstream of American experience; an elitism that explains our curious flight from the enlightened common sense that once enabled us to strike the appropriate balance between private rights and public order and to understand the limits of governmental power in a free society. It is an elitism that disdains the values, needs, and aspirations of those inhabitants of the middle ranks of American life who man our factories and farms and who provide the bulk of the revenues required to support a vast array of programs whose merits they seriously question. And this in itself is a source of profound frustration among a vast number of Americans who feel themselves ignored and taken advantage of.

There is a never-ending movement among the various worlds of the new elite that can be easily discerned. Those who share the same views go naturally from one field to another, carrying along the same ideological baggage. The "educrat" who becomes the head of a foundation after having served as an administrator at a prestigious college, and who is then tapped to be Assistant Secretary of a federal government department—this is an archetypical figure of our time. In each of his manifestations he reflects the same unstated assumption: that he is one of a relatively small number of benevolent human beings who know what is best for the majority of Americans. And so he goes about the task of restructuring society according to his vision with sublime self-assurance and without any reference to the desires or goals of the majority. In fact, all too often he regards the views of the majority with an indifference bordering on contempt.

It is when this attitude is found in government that Americans usually begin to feel its effects at first hand. The educator who uses his classroom as a forum to propagandize his social and political views may be resented. But when the same person becomes a top-level bureaucrat with the power to put his theories into practice, he is perceived as a threat.

Those of us in government have a responsibility to do something about limiting the opportunities of the ideologues to use the coercive power of the State. It is a battle worth fighting and, in the view of history, may well be seen as one of the most important battles to be fought in this country.

IV
Crime and Social Order

As I have indicated earlier, there is another, qualitatively distinct source of the current perception that the times are out of joint, and this one goes to the heart of the social contract: the ability of society to maintain public order and safety. No discussion of the reasons why so many Americans are beginning to feel a sense of helplessness would be complete without touching on the problems summed up in the phrase "law and order." Nor can any book concerned with the state of our liberties ignore the fact that too many Americans have come to see government as impotent in the face of mass disorders or massive crime.

While government, in most areas, has grown in power and arrogance at the expense of the individual, when it comes to protecting the individual against the lawless, government appears to be increasingly helpless—even to control the juveniles now terrorizing too many of our urban schools.

This was a matter of central concern to the people of New York when I was seeking office in 1970. The campaign was played out against a backdrop of arson, mob violence, and rampant crime that had reached epidemic proportions. Flags were being burned. Self-styled revolutionaries had proclaimed guerrilla warfare in our cities. Citizens everywhere were beginning to be afraid to walk their streets at night.

These immediate worries, coupled with a profound concern over the explosion of drug addiction throughout New York and the nation, made central issues of the need to restore social stability, to revive respect for the law and law-enforcement officers, and to make the administration of criminal law and the prosecution of criminals more effective.

What disturbed New Yorkers even more than the actual acts of violence and destruction that were becoming so commonplace was the fact that they could occur at all on so wide a scale. They saw the twin phenomena of rising crime (especially violent crime) and riots as symptomatic of a major social and institutional breakdown.

For years Americans had read reports of student riots

abroad with the smug assurance that they couldn't happen here. The American character would not allow it. We had too great a respect for the law, too much confidence in the fairness of our institutions, too great a respect for the right of any dissident voice to make itself heard for a systematic resort to violence for political ends ever to be launched, let alone excused.

Yet it had happened here. We proved ourselves not only capable of mob action in every part of the nation, but we tolerated it. We tolerated it because too many in authority failed to make the necessary distinction between a lawful exercise of the right of assembly and petition and an unlawful assault on the rights, persons, and property of others. Criminal acts were excused because they were committed in some higher cause. They were excused by too many in positions of responsibility who had forgotten the elementary fact that civil order is indispensable to civil liberty.

Any reading of history will demonstrate that when people are required to choose between anarchy and civil order, they will inevitably opt for the latter even if they must sacrifice some of their freedoms in order to achieve it. It was a search for "domestic tranquility" that caused the German people to turn to Hitler in 1933.

The elementary distinction between authoritarian and free societies is that in the former, order is imposed from above, while in the latter, it is largely self-imposed. It is only when citizens are willing to submit voluntarily to the principles of ordered freedom, to observe the law, that freedom can flourish. The breakdown of law and order, therefore, is not only a problem that today is putting our system of justice to the test—it goes to the root of our liberties.

Happily, the violence that crippled so many American campuses in the late 1960's and early 1970's has all but disappeared. But criminality in America continues to increase at an alarming rate, and we seem less and less able to cope with it.

According to the Index of Crime published in the *Uniform Crime Reports* of the United States, between the years 1960 and 1973 total crime increased by 158 percent, violent crimes by 204 percent, murder by 115 percent, forcible rape by 199 percent, and robbery by 256 percent. During that same period, violent crime was spreading faster among youths than among adults. The number of those under eighteen arrested for murder increased by 201 percent, for rape by 132 percent, for assault by 206 percent, and for robbery by a staggering 299 percent. And the incidence of serious crime continues to soar—in 1974 by a startling 17 percent, the largest annual rate of increase in more than forty years.

Once we have agreed on the seriousness of the problem of crime, we are confronted with the much more difficult question: What if anything can be done about it?

Because most of the specific functions of the criminal process—deterring crimes, enforcing the law, the conduct of criminal trials, etc.—occur and ought to continue to occur at the state and local levels of government, those of us operating at the national level are of necessity limited in what we can do to help stem the current incidence of crime. There are, however, certain areas in which the federal government can make significant contributions. These include cooperation with state and local police officials in the exchange of information, the testing of reforms and innovations in every area of law enforcement lying within the jurisdiction of the federal government, the launching of truly effective measures to curtail the illegal importation and distribution of drugs,* and a reassessment of various recent rulings of the Supreme Court that have had the net effect of greatly prolonging the trial process in both state and federal courts. I believe, however, that most of the long-term answers are going to be found not in Washington, but in the cities and counties and states across the country, and also in the homes and schools and churches—which brings us back to the original question: What can be done?

Certainly one aspect of the problem that has for too long

---

*There is no area where effective federal action can do more to relieve human misery and reduce the incidence of crime. In 1971, it was estimated that 98 percent of New York City's 100,000 narcotics addicts turned to crime in order to support their habits.

been disregarded is that of attitude. I was reminded of this by public service advertisements that appeared all over Washington, D.C., in 1974, and by television messages that were shown over major channels. The message in both cases was the same: *Shoplifting Is Dumb.* Dumb? Well, yes, but more important than that, shoplifting is wrong. Why didn't the signs and commercials use "wrong" or "criminal" instead of "dumb"? Even granting the fact that "dumb" had taken on the status of a new "in" word used by teen-agers to describe anything from World War II to an unattractive dress, the deliberate avoidance of the ethical term is informative. Not only do we seem to have succeeded in effectively diluting the legal sanctions that discourage crime, we are rapidly destroying the social and moral sanctions as well.

The idea of objective standards of right and wrong is in a sharp decline, as is that of personal accountability. It is argued these days that the criminal ought not to be held responsible for his acts because he is the victim of social conditions, such as poor housing and poverty, that are said to be the underlying causes of crime.

But is the argument sound? Using figures taken from the census of 1960 and 1970 (including statistics on "dilapidated housing") the Library of Congress estimates that over 32.5 million Americans may be said to have been "ill-housed" in 1960. In 1970, the figure had dropped to 20.4 million. During the same ten years the number of Americans living below the poverty level had also decreased—from 39,851,000 (22.2 percent of the population) to 25,851,000 (12.6 percent of the population). Thus, during a period when it is estimated that the number of poor, ill-housed Americans decreased by roughly 37 percent, the rate of crime was *increasing* by well over 100 percent. If bad housing and poverty are major causes of crime, it would certainly follow that during a decade when living conditions improved significantly, the incidence of crime should have decreased. But precisely the opposite was the case.

We should, indeed must, work toward the lessening of poverty, disease, ignorance, and urban decay. But we should seek these ends in the name of social justice, and not because by achieving them we will somehow find a solution to the problem of crime.

There is a far more rational reason for the extraordinary rise in robberies and thefts and white collar crimes in America today. The fact is that contrary to the old adage, crime nowadays does indeed pay—and, for those who are prepared to undergo certain manageable risks, it can pay rather handsomely. As the *Wall Street Journal* pointed out in an editorial in 1973, "it pays because the average criminal no longer fears being punished, even if he is caught. Overworked police forces, crowded court calendars, misplaced social concern and a penological reaction against imprisonment on the ground that it fails to rehabilitate, have given criminals the edge—and given society the short end of the stick."

This fact undermines one of the most treasured assumptions of latter-day criminology. The tendency in recent years has been to regard the criminal as a patient and crime as a disease, from which it follows that a "soft" rather than a "hard" approach to crime is the order of the day.

I cannot help recalling in this regard the story of Willie Sutton, the dapper and ingenious bank robber whose exploits during the 1940's and 1950's kept him on the front pages of the nation's press. Following what proved to be his final arrest and conviction, the sociologists, criminologists, psychologists, and psychiatrists descended on him in hordes. They pinched and poked and prodded him, exploring each and every aspect of his life, from toilet training on, applying each and every available hypothesis they could contrive to explain his life of crime. Almost without exception, these hypotheses began with the assumption that Willie was somehow abnormal, that his genetic endowment or environmental experience, or some combination of both, virtually compelled him to pursue a criminal career. After months of exasperating study and conflicting conclusions, it suddenly occurred to an enterprising young interviewer to ask a really intelligent question. "Willie," he asked, "why do you rob banks?" Without a moment's hesitation, Willie shot back: "Because that's where the money is."

That simple and honest explanation is worth a world of

learned treatises on the causes of crime. Most of those who commit crime do so because they *choose* to do so; and today they choose to do so because the potential rewards, weighed against the risk of being captured and punished, are highly attractive. The *U.S. News & World Report* (December 16, 1974) put it this way:

> For too many criminals, crime *does* pay. The risk they run is too small, compared with the profits, to be an effective deterrent. "They feel the odds are largely in their favor," says FBI Director Clarence M. Kelley. And they have reason, as Mr. Kelley explains: "Our crime statistics plainly tell us that a high percentage of the criminals beat the risk. They are able, for a variety of reasons, to make a profit out of their crimes."
>
> The statistics are that only 21 per cent of all serious crimes are "cleared" by arrests. Only about 5 per cent are "solved" by convictions as charged. And a steadily diminishing percentage of those convicted are sent to prison. . . .

If the law is in any way tolerant or indulgent, criminals will be the first to discover the fact. And should they nevertheless run afoul of the law, they cannot help but form a cynical opinion about a legal system in which punishment, precisely because it is employed halfheartedly or irregularly, is thought of as being employed inequitably.

It is clear that the first quality we need is level-headed common sense in dealing with criminal activity, a new determination to restore speed and the certainty of punishment to the criminal process. This calls for a policy of firmness that is fully compatible with the protection of constitutional liberty—that of society as well as that of the accused. It also calls for a reexamination of some of the more rarefied rulings issued by the Supreme Court under Chief Justice Earl Warren.

Many of these decisions, through the expansion and extension of the exclusionary rule (in which wrongfully obtained evidence is excluded irrespective of its value in establishing the guilt of the accused) and other newly discovered constitutional principles, have created infinite difficulties for prosecutors while only marginally adding to the protection of the accused. As a result, trials too often take on the character of tests of the evidence or of police behavior, rather than of the defendant. Many patently guilty criminals walk away scot-free because the evidence against them has been ruled inadmissible. Criminal proceedings are drawn out to unconscionable lengths through technical challenges unrelated to the question of the guilt or innocence of the accused. Court calendars have become clogged, and plea bargaining ensues. And even after conviction, the case is open to endless appeals on highly technical grounds leading the late New York District Attorney Frank Hogan to complain that nowadays "there is virtually no such thing as finality in a judgment of conviction."

This is clearly an area that can only be resolved through federal action, although that action is made more difficult because we are dealing with newly defined constitutional rights. The Congress has moved to limit the adverse effects of the Warren Court decisions in several areas, and other proposals are pending. Moreover, the Burger Court has rendered decisions that restrict the application of some of its predecessor's rulings, and it may well go further.

In determining where and why our criminal process is breaking down, we might do well to examine the English example. I proposed in 1972 (and will continue to propose) that we undertake a systematic comparative study of British and American criminal jurisprudence. The United States and Great Britain share a common legal heritage. We hold in common fundamental concepts as to what is required to guarantee a fair trial and to safeguard the rights of the accused. For years after American independence, our criminal procedures remained virtually indistinguishable. But in time they began to diverge, and, in recent years, in most significant ways.

Today the British are able to find a defendant innocent or guilty within a few months after his arrest, and a certain finality normally attaches upon conviction. In our country, years can elapse between arrest and the conclusion of the trial, and a conviction merely marks the beginning of a procedural ballet that can continue indefinitely. In Britain today, the incidence of crime is small in comparison with ours, and respect for the law and for the legal apparatus remains undiminished.

A comprehensive study of the kind I recommend may suggest any number of improvements we can make in our own procedures without sacrificing the substantive rights of the accused, and it may also be instructive in telling us what purely local developments in American life may have contributed to our current criminality. If such a study does nothing more than help us restore speed to the trial process, it will have proven well worth the while. Justice delayed continues to be justice denied.

There is a final point I would like to make, and it is directed at those who still equate calls for firm law enforcement with racism or an insensitivity to the plight of the poor, especially those in our inner cities. The fact is that a "get tough" approach to crime might well be the greatest single contribution that enlightened public policy could make to the lot of men and women of all races in urban America today.

This point was underscored in an exchange that took place at a meeting of the National League of Cities in Houston, Texas, in March, 1975. Many of the delegates criticized the use of Law Enforcement Assistance Administration funds for the purchase of weapons as a means of reducing crime. According to a New York *Times* report, the question constantly asked was, "Why aren't the funds used for social programs that might reduce the root causes of crime?" The answer was provided by a black city official: "If I can spend the money in my city to cut crime in a poor neighborhood where some poor black women are afraid to walk home after they finish their day's work, that will be a social program well worth the spending."

The black official knew that the poor in our inner cities are disproportionately the victims of crime. Professor Herbert Packer has estimated that a resident of a black ghetto is at least one hundred times more likely to be victimized by crime than a relatively affluent, white resident of the suburbs. It is no wonder, then, that the New York City chapter of the NAACP in 1968 called for "the use of whatever force is necessary to stop crime and apprehend a criminal," and a minimum of five years in prison without parole for armed robbery, and ten years for the sale of narcotics.

The fact is that unless we are able to come to terms with the problem of crime, we may find ourselves incapable of dealing with our other problems as well.

We need to reform our criminal procedures. We need to restore a reasonable certainty that criminal acts will be punished. But if we are to avoid the measures with which authoritarian states maintain their social order, we will need to do more. We will need to rediscover self-discipline and a true commitment to the rule of law.

In this day when disrespect for authority of all kinds—religious, parental, legal—is so pervasive; when allegiance to anything other than one's own passions is condemned as illegitimate; when "civil disobedience" is used as a defensive cloak for criminal behavior, let us never forget that it is only the rule of law that holds our society together and protects our freedom.

Our nation and its rule of law are still strong. But for all its strengths, the rule of law can only abide so many attacks, and the delicate webbing of our liberties can, like the veil of the temple, be rent. Liberty and a people's willing submission to the law: one cannot long exist without the other. No one has spoken to this truth with greater passion or eloquence than Abraham Lincoln, when he said:

> Let every man remember that to violate the law is to trample on the blood of his father, and to tear the charter of his own and his children's liberty; let reverence for the law be breathed by every American mother to the lisping babe that prattles on her lap—let it be taught in the schools, in seminaries, and in colleges;—let it be written in primers, spelling books, and in almanacs;—let it be preached from the pulpit, proclaimed in the legislative halls, and enforced in courts of justice. And, in short, let it become the *political religion* of the nation; and let the old and the young, the grave and the gay, of all sexes and tongues, and colors and conditions, sacrifice unceasingly upon its altars.

6

The Congress: How Strong a Reed?

ALONG WITH OTHER hitherto revered institutions, Congress has in recent years been weighed and found wanting by the American public. One poll might differ from another in detail, but basically it is accurate to say that the performance of the Congress is viewed by the American people as less than inspiring. This is a sobering datum when we are asked to look to the Congress for a new assertion of leadership. It is not that the men and women who today constitute the Senate and the House of Representatives are less able, or highly motivated, or experienced than their predecessors have been in years past. Rather, the Congress has permitted an accelerating growth of business that now exceeds its institutional capacity to handle.

I can best illustrate the institutional reasons why it is now virtually impossible for the Congress as a whole to discharge its current responsibilities with any degree of intelligent thought by describing in some detail how this member of what was once accurately and proudly described as the world's greatest deliberative body must go about his work.

Perhaps I can convey the flavor of what a Senator's life is like by detailing my activities during the five days of December 9 through 13, 1974.

Monday, December 9, 1974

The first day of the next to last week of the Ninety-third Congress began at 8:00 A.M. with one of the breakfasts that

117

the Republican members of the Interior Committee periodically schedule with officials whose responsibilities fall within the committee's jurisdiction. In this case, we wanted the chance to meet and question Robert Seamens, whom President Ford had nominated for the highly important job of administering and coordinating federal energy research programs.

These breakfast sessions prove enormously valuable in enabling us to keep abreast of the Administration's thinking on a number of issues while giving us the opportunity to provide the Administration with an understanding of our own views on a wide variety of areas involving policy and personnel.

Ever since the Arabs imposed their oil embargo, we were concerned by the preoccupation of the Interior Committee's Chairman, Senator Henry Jackson, with elaborate petroleum allocation machinery and price controls that would do little more than spread around the misery caused by energy shortages while doing nothing to alleviate them. Worse than that, we were convinced that Senator Jackson's policies would prolong our reliance on foreign sources by removing the economic incentives required to increase domestic production of oil and gas. This particular series of breakfast meetings helped us hammer out common policies and strategies for holding the line against some of the more ill-conceived proposals.

I moved on to my office at around 9:00 and glanced at the New York *Times* and the New York *Daily News* (I had already read the Washington *Post* at home). Because we were in the final days of a session with most of our committee work behind us, I wasn't faced with my usual morning's dilemma of trying to decide which of two or more concurrent committee meetings it was most important for me to attend. As a result, for the first time in weeks I could enjoy the luxury of several uninterrupted hours within which to tackle a variety of tasks within normal working hours.

On this particular day I was able to make substantial headway on two legislative fronts. The first involved a series of telephone conversations to discuss strategy with Senators who were supporting my efforts to force a vote on a proposal to deregulate natural gas. This can be a time-consuming and frustrating procedure as you try to track down a Senator who has either just left or not quite reached his office, or a committee room, or the floor. I also had the time to discuss with one of my legislative assistants, John Kwapisz, the language of proposed amendments that I was working on with Senator Claiborne Pell of Rhode Island. These were designed to eliminate some ambiguities (real and imagined) in the Family Educational Rights and Privacy Bill that I had introduced earlier in the year, and that had been signed into law in August as part of the Education Amendments of 1974.

I also found time to work on a floor statement I was to make in support of the Jackson Amendment to the trade bill (about which more later), redraft a speech I was to deliver two days later, and make a small dent in the mound of accumulated correspondence and required reading that is always to be found on my desk. There was only one roll-call vote that day, on a noncontroversial supplemental appropriation bill.

At 4:00 P.M. I met, at my request, with Mr. William Highland, Director of the State Department's Bureau of Intelligence and Research, who briefed me on the President's trip to Vladivostok. I had been very much concerned over press reports of what President Ford and Chairman Brezhnev had agreed upon as the basis for the negotiation of a second round of strategic arms limitations agreements (SALT II). It appeared that we were prepared to make concessions that would enable the Soviets to achieve significant advantages in certain critical categories of strategic weapons. Mr. Highland failed to reassure me on these points. Afterward, I met with Judges Lee Gagliardi, Charles Briant, and Charles Stewart, all of whom serve on the United States District Court for the Southern District of New York. They were attending a conference in Washington, and stopped by the office to make a courtesy call and to express a few thoughts on matters judicial.

After my visitors left, I signed some mail, reviewed the next day's work, and left my office at around 6:30, in time to arrive home, change, and drive my wife to a small dinner.

Tuesday, December 10, 1974

After dropping my two resident sons off at school, I arrived at my office (per usual) at around 8:20, hurriedly skimmed the newspapers, and then, at 9:00, invited in the Washington correspondents of New York newspapers and radio stations with whom I meet each Tuesday morning for a "coffee and doughnuts" news conference lasting about half an hour. I answer questions on matters currently in the news, and often receive in exchange advance warning of issues that will be of special interest to various communities of New York State. I have found these weekly meetings to be invaluable sources of information about the facts, data, gossip, problems, proposals, opinions, and political esoterica that make New York the marvelously complex and fascinating state it is. The New York State Washington correspondents are unusually well informed, and by the time the half-hour session is over, there is not much of either national or state interest that has been overlooked.

Immediately after this meeting I placed a call to Dr. Andrei Sakharov, the Russian physicist and champion of human rights, in Moscow. I told him of the status of matters that we had discussed when we had met in his Moscow apartment two and a half weeks earlier. He had recommended telephoning because letters might never reach him. (A few weeks later I was to read that Dr. Sakharov was no longer allowed to receive foreign calls.)

After finishing my call, I was required to pick and choose between conflicting committee work—either a 9:30 meeting of the Public Works Committee or a 10:00 meeting of the Interior Committee. I chose the former since there were several pending items that required final action.

Just before noon I returned to my office to meet with Mr. Wilson Talley, the newly appointed Director of Research and Development for the Environmental Protection Agency.

This was in the nature of a get-acquainted visit. I was especially interested in seeing him because a firm on Long Island had developed a new approach to one phase of municipal waste treatment that if successful could save hundreds of millions of dollars. I wanted to make sure that the EPA's research and development people would give it a fair assessment.

After this, I met with Lieutenant General Edward L. Rowny, who was a member of the SALT negotiating team. This appointment had been made at the request of Secretary of State Kissinger, who was unhappy about the reservations I had expressed over the announced framework for a second SALT agreement. The meeting, while highly informative, was like so many in Washington: not long enough for me to learn all I wanted to know, but long enough to make me late for the Republican Policy Committee luncheon which, together with a meeting of the Republican Conference, lasted until around 2:30, when the buzzer (by which Senatorial lives are ruled) summoned us to the floor for the vote confirming Nelson Rockefeller's nomination to the Vice Presidency.

After voting, I retraced my steps: through the door of the Senate Chamber; an elevator ride to the subway; a subway ride to the Old Senate Office Building; another elevator ride to the third floor; a walk down the long corridor to Room 304-C. (On clement days I usually forgo the elevators and subways and walk instead for the exercise. It rarely takes more than five minutes to get from place to place, but over the course of a day I will have walked an average of more than 2½ miles.)

I arrived in my office just in time for a meeting with Joe Sobran of *National Review,* who was there to interview me on my visit to the Soviet Union the month before. After the interview I met with Mr. Frank T. Cary, the head of IBM, who was concerned over reports that I might offer an amendment to the long-awaited trade bill that might trigger a filibuster. I assured him that I believed the trade bill was vitally needed while expressing great misgivings as to whether IBM's and Control Data Corporation's more sophisticated computers should ever be the subject of trade with the Soviet Union. I recalled other meetings with businessmen in which I suggested that in dealings with the Soviets, what is good for IBM (or other firms selling highly sophisticated technology) might not always be good for the United States. Needless to say, my views on the subject are not always persuasive with businessmen, who are apt to take the not unreasonable position that it is up to the government to determine what ought not be sold to our potential adversaries.

Again, I found myself in the usual Senate dilemma. At the same time I was discussing trade with this gentleman, I was supposed to be attending a meeting of the Senate Steering Committee (an informal association of conservative Senators who meet weekly to examine issues and coordinate their work so as to increase their effectiveness). I said good-bye to Mr. Cary at 5:20, joined the Steering Committee for the last half of their deliberations, and at 6:00 returned to my office to sign mail and tidy up a few details, and then left for home at 6:45.

Wednesday, December 11, 1974

This day was a dandy. After an 8:30 breakfast meeting with Clif White (political adviser in my campaign of 1970) and two members of my staff to discuss certain internal organizational matters, I rushed off to the office to prepare for a joint press conference with former Senator Eugene McCarthy and Ira Glasser of the New York Civil Liberties Union. We were announcing our intention to test the constitutionality of the new campaign reform law placing strict limitations on what individuals could spend on behalf of political candidates. The press conference lasted until well after 10:30, leaving me with time only to duck in and out of a conference of Republican Senators before reporting to a leadership meeting in Senator Robert Byrd's office that was concerned with expediting the passage of the Trade Bill. As I had long ago introduced an amendment to the bill calling for deregulation of natural gas, and as several Senators had publicly announced that they would engage in a filibuster if I called it up, there was more than passing interest in what I planned to do.

A scheduled 2:00 meeting with Secretary of HEW Weinberger (to discuss various aspects of HEW regulations) was interrupted by a call from a reporter. It seems that in the course of a press conference in Washington, the New York State Republican Chairman had suggested that I might be inviting retribution if I failed to support Senator Javits in his bid for election as Chairman of the Senate Republican Conference. I had hoped that the whole issue would be kept private; but now that public pressures were apparently being applied to influence my vote, I had to prepare and "go public" with a statement that I would be voting for Senator Curtis. The day was further complicated by five roll-call votes involving three separate bills and rather complicated amendments thereto, and by a Senate-House conference on deepwater ports legislation that was so frequently interrupted that it eventually had to be abandoned.

That evening I was scheduled to receive the Freedom Award from the Conference on Soviet Jewry in Westchester County. This meant a 6:30 departure for National Airport, a 7:15 flight to White Plains, New York, and a car ride to the rally. I was able to put the hour between my arrival in White Plains and my arrival at that gathering to good use by meeting with a member of my New York City staff to discuss a number of pending matters. The program consisted primarily of a series of presentations—singing, dancing, recitals—interspersed by brief and often moving talks. I was "front and center" not at 9:45, as scheduled, but closer to 10:45, and I finally arrived at the home of George and Susie Lawrence, who had kindly offered to put me up for the night, well after midnight.

Thursday, December 12, 1974

I was up at 6:30, had breakfast with two young Lawrences (and two older ones), and then caught an 8:15 flight at White Plains that landed me at National Airport at 9:20. At 10:00 I was in an Interior Committee mark-up session which was in-

terrupted by a roll-call vote on final passage of the Special
Employment Assistance Act of 1974—a highly expensive
proposal for the creation of 535,000 public service jobs. It
had been rushed through as an antirecession measure at
such a speed that we were being required to vote on a measure involving the spending of many billions of dollars (no
one seemed to know whether we were talking about three or
four or six billions—so it goes in the Senate) even before a
committee report describing what was in the bill was generally available. I reiterated my complaint that this was a rather
irresponsible way to handle the nation's business; suggested
that no adequate attention had been paid to alternative ways
of meeting the problem of unemployment on the basis of an
accurate analysis of who was losing jobs and why; asked why
it was imperative to act now instead of the following week;
and announced that I would vote against the bill "because
this program is being rushed through in such a way that
makes rational inquiry and thought impossible."

The 3 x 5 schedule card that my secretary had handed me
the day before indicated that I was to spend much of the afternoon with Simas Kudirka (whose trials and courage I described in Chapter 4) and his family. Specifically, I was to
lunch with him at 12:30, and then act as co-host of a reception in the Capitol being given for the Kudirkas by members
of the Congress who had helped secure their release from
the Soviet Union. As is so often the case, my written schedule
was but a pale (and inaccurate) shadow of reality. I wish I
could have spent the afternoon with the Kudirkas; but instead I had to abandon the luncheon in their honor at 1:00
for a vote, rejoining them only long enough to help organize
a receiving line at the reception crowded not only by members of the Congress, but by more Lithuanian-Americans
than I understood existed in the United States.

Most of that afternoon was devoted to a crash session with
Senator Pell to perfect amendments to the Family Educational Rights and Privacy Bill. Despite frequent interruptions for
telephone calls that could not be put off, we completed our
work by late afternoon.

I was back in my office by 5:30, signed mail, glanced at memos on pending legislation, discussed some matters coming up the following day with members of my staff, and was home by 7:00.

Friday, December 13, 1974

My day began with a 9:00 appointment with my dentist to have a cap replaced. As things turned out, the thirty-five minutes I spent reclining in the dental chair were to be the only moments of relaxation (of a sort) that I was to have until thirteen hours later when I finally joined my wife and some friends for the second act of a play at the Kennedy Center.

On arriving at the office after my dental appointment, I found I had to attend an emergency meeting of minority members of the Interior Committee to determine how best we could derail an emergency energy bill that "Scoop" Jackson was trying to rush through before we adjourned—a bill that we were convinced would make the nation's serious energy situation even worse. I was assigned the task of maintaining liaison with members of the Administration, which triggered a series of telephone calls to people who had *just* left the office, or were in conference, and who in turn returned my calls while I was on the floor or otherwise unreachable, which return calls I eventually returned. In time I spoke to the individuals I had to reach, but the whole process was enormously disruptive.

Meanwhile, back at the Senate, we were called to the floor eight times, once to form a quorum and the other seven times for record votes. Except when votes are made "back to back," each one involves an interruption of anywhere from ten to twenty minutes in whatever it is one is doing. On this particular day, the seven votes and the quorum call took place at the following times: 11:32 A.M., 11:49 A.M., 12:06 P.M., 12:16 P.M., 12:30 P.M., 3:48 P.M., 5:21 P.M., and 6:41 P.M.

But that was not all. I also found myself more than normally engaged in the chamber. Prior to the first vote, I had routine business to attend to on the floor. Later, I had to interrupt my lunch with a representative of the West German

Parliament (the Bundestag) because debate on the Jackson Amendment to the Trade Bill (conditioning the extension of "most favored nation" tariff treatment and government-financed trade credits to Communist countries on the latter's liberalization of emigration policies) was about to begin. On my visit to the Soviet Union three weeks earlier, I had discussed aspects of the Jackson Amendment with a number of Soviet dissidents, and wanted to make sure that the legislative history as reflected in the *Congressional Record* fairly defined the Senate's intentions. I also wanted to secure agreement to certain safeguards and procedures for monitoring Soviet performance on a continuing basis independently of the State Department. This I was able to accomplish, but it required about an hour and a half while I awaited my turn for recognition.

I was able to interrupt my floor vigil (after protecting my position by asking the Senator then holding the floor to keep talking until my return) to keep an appointment with Messrs. Blostein and Hazlitt, the incumbent and former County Executives of Chemung County, New York, in the crowded reception room off the Senate floor, less than ideal conditions for the discussion of constituent concerns. (As with so much else in the Senate, meetings with constituents are almost impossible to schedule with any degree of certainty. Each week brings its flow of visitors with special problems or proposals they want to discuss with me or with members of my staff. Too often, the unpredictable nature of Senate business forces last-minute cancellations.)

Toward the end of the day, Senator Pell and I took to the floor to introduce the clarifying amendments to the Family Educational Rights and Privacy Act, and secured their adoption by voice vote.

The business of the day having come to an end, I hopped into my car and drove off to the Kennedy Center to catch up with my wife and Secretary and Mrs. Dent in time for the second act of *In Praise of Love*. It was then after 8:00.

So ended a not untypical five-day period that constitutes the normal week of scheduled work in the life of the Senate.

(That week the Senate also met on Saturday to take care of certain year-end matters, but such sessions are not the norm.) During those five days I attended perhaps a dozen meetings on almost as many subjects, worked on half a dozen statements to be delivered on or off the floor, trundled to and from New York, worked on the minutiae of four bills, voted on a dozen others, and tried to catch up with accumulated mail. Although between 8:00 A.M. Monday and 8:00 P.M. Friday I had been on the job more than fifty-six hours, I could salvage no more than five or six for concentrated thought or study on matters of great importance, or even for catching up with correspondence. This meant that I had to carry home a full briefcase for review over the weekend. The fact is that much of a Senator's productive work must be done at home on Saturdays and Sundays, away from the interruptions of the Senate.

In session and out, a Senator is constantly on the run, trying to keep abreast of the most immediately pressing matters through meetings, briefings, and staff memorandums, his attention drawn in a thousand different directions.

As for trying to do all the "necessary reading"—the bills, reports, studies, background material; all that is required to develop in-depth personal understanding and knowledge—there is only one thing to say about it and that is that it can never be done. The amount of reading necessary to keep a Senator minimally informed on matters of maximum importance is always double that which he can possibly accomplish in the time allotted. My reading takes place in my office, at home, in airports, on airplanes, in taxicabs, in waiting rooms, and just about anywhere I can find sufficient light and (as always) time—and there is never enough.

But what about maintaining contact with one's home state? Here we have the Senatorial paradox. One is elected to the Senate as the representative of his state. But in order to give the state the kind of representation it deserves, one must (a) be in attendance in the Senate and (b) be in constant personal touch with the people and problems back home. Given the fact the Congress nowadays is in session on a virtually year-round basis, the more one attends to (a) the less time he has for (b). And vice versa. Yet one attempts to do both.

I try to keep in touch with New York and New Yorkers in a number of ways, some of them suggested in my description of the week of December 9–13, 1974. There are, first of all, visits from constituents. This can mean anything from a five-minute "drop-by" in my office to a longer session with a New York local or state official with a serious problem. There are, of course, visits from representatives of groups eager to present their views on pending legislation. These range from small farmers to major corporations, from patriotic and religious organizations to "one-issue" lobbying groups. Finally, there are before-hours breakfasts and after-hours receptions and dinners where it is possible to meet individuals from home who represent the widest variety of interests and views.

All this is helpful, but a broader view is required than that derived from the usual visitor who has made the trip to Washington in order to grind a specific ax. Over a period of four years I have tried to maintain contact with my constituency by visiting virtually all of the sixty-two counties, all the major cities, and many of the smaller communities of New York State, often several times a year. These visits have proved enormously informative, but they exact a heavy cost in terms of strictly legislative work.

The present-day demands on a Senator are such as to make it virtually impossible for him to find the time for any consecutive thought or any detailed study of the mass of legislation that reaches the floor, or even much of the legislation that flows through the committees of which he is a member.

Inevitably, Senators have come to place major reliance on members of their individual or committee staffs for an analysis of the issues, an examination of relevant facts, and a definition of policy alternatives. And just as inevitably, as the press of business crowds out their ability to focus on the matters before them, members of the Senate find themselves reduced on an ever-larger scale to making essentially snap judgments on the basis of information and a description of policy options made by usually highly informed and intelligent individuals whose views are nevertheless freighted with their own goals and prejudices.

When it comes to voting, an individual Senator will rely heavily not only on the judgment of staff, his own and his committees', but also on a select number of fellow Senators whose knowledge he has come to respect and whose general perspective he shares. The fact is that in the majority of cases a Senator will arrive on the floor in response to the bell announcing the beginning of the fifteen-minute roll call without any clear idea of what it is he is being called upon to cast his vote. Individual staffs are simply too small to follow most of the legislation—let alone the unprinted amendments and motions—on matters that lie outside their Senator's special areas of interest. When there is sufficient advance notice of what is coming to a vote, a staff member can consult the committee report (if available) and/or discuss the legislation with committee staff or other sources in order to prepare a summary of what the bill or amendment is all about; but when the legislation is at all complex, and the time short, the summary is necessarily superficial. It very often happens, moreover, that a bill is reported out and called up for debate and a vote without adequate notice, or an unprinted amendment is called up and discussed with only a dozen ears on hand to hear it. Even where amendments have been printed, so many are apt to be placed in the legislative hoppers that it is virtually impossible to assess even a handful of the more significant, let alone know of their existence.

At any rate, more often than not, after the bell rings to announce a vote, a Senator will find himself rushing from a committee meeting or another engagement to a rendezvous with a member of his legislative staff outside the Senate chamber; and if his staff is unable to provide him with the necessary guidance, he will rush onto the floor and search out a friend on the appropriate committee for a hurried explanation and recommendation. In extreme cases, when time is about to run out, the inquiry will be limited to a simple "How do I vote?" and the answer may be a simple "yes" or "no," or even only a gesture of thumb up or thumb down.

It is small wonder that each one of us has found himself intensely embarrassed by a vote after he has found out what he was really voting on.

The great debates we have read about in our history

books—the great debates in which eloquent orators were able to present their cases and carry the day through the sheer force of their arguments—no longer take place. Most Senators are too preoccupied with their own individual concerns, their appointments, committee meetings, correspondence, telephone calls and constituent work, to spend any time on the floor to listen to other people talk.

Floor debate today has become a sort of theater without an audience, a presentation of arguments largely for the benefit of the *Congressional Record* and those few reporters who happen to be in the gallery. Usually there are no more than half a dozen Senators on hand to follow the presentation of a bill, and more often than not these are members of the sponsoring committee who are joined together to explain the virtues of the bill and none of its shortcomings. Even where there is sharp disagreement, those present are apt to be knowledgeable partisans rather than uncommitted Senators seeking to understand the pros and cons so that they may arrive at their own informed judgments.

Thus the Senate no longer performs one of the most important of its original functions, that of providing a forum for the presentation and testing of opposing views in meaningful debate. It no longer provides a mechanism for the education of its membership as a whole. This is a grave loss, as I am persuaded that many votes would be changed (my own included), and we would enact far better laws, if most members could hear controversial measures fully aired, with the arguments presented by the Senate's best-informed members.

Both the desirability and impossibility of such debate is now reflected in a formality at the beginning of each legislative day. After the majority leader asks unanimous consent that the reading of the prior day's proceedings be dispensed with (which consent is essential because, after the reading of the *Record,* no time would remain in which to conduct any other Senate business), he asks unanimous consent "that all committees may be authorized to meet" while the Senate is in session. Whereas it was once possible to organize the business of the Senate so that no one was required to be absent from the floor while legislation was being debated, the proliferation of both committee work and legislation now makes it impossible for members to absent themselves from the former in order to attend to a discussion of the latter. I am advised by Dr. Floyd Riddick, the Parliamentarian Emeritus of the Senate, that it is only since 1947 that committees have been permitted to meet as a matter of course while the Senate is in session.

It is common knowledge that today the important work of the Senate is done not on the floor, but in committee. This, of course, raises the necessary question as to how effectively the committee system operates as a substitute for the full discussion by the Senate as a whole that was originally contemplated.

The committee system is itself of ancient vintage (dating back to 1803), and reflects a necessary delegation of responsibility for legislative spadework and recommendations in designated areas. The responsibility for final action remained (and remains) with the body as a whole; and for that body to act responsibly the ability of its members to make informed judgments on legislation reported out by a given committee must be presupposed.

Now that full debate has been virtually eliminated as a technique for testing the merits of legislation that a committee has reported to the floor, it becomes all the more important that the committees themselves operate effectively. Unfortunately the same forces that have served to splinter a Senator's attention, and to transform the institution of debate from the active crucible in which legislation is finally formed into a formalistic exercise, are also at work eroding the ability of committees to do their job.

The first thing to be understood is that most committees are anything but representative of the Senate as a whole. Senators naturally gravitate to those committees that interest them or whose work is most important to their particular constituencies. Given the broad range of viewpoints represented on each side of the aisle, the requirement that each committee have a majority and minority membership roughly proportionate to that of the Senate as a whole is no guarantee that it will reflect the political spectrum in any other sense. Thus particular committees become zealous advocates for governmental action in their own areas of jurisdiction, and their reports are too often selling documents that do not provide the Senate as a whole with the kind of balanced information essential to a reasonably educated opinion on a particular bill's merits.

Further, bills reported out by committees cannot even claim to represent the informed judgment of their own members. Just as the work of the Senate has been divided up and delegated to committees, so has the work of almost every committee been divided up and delegated to subcommittees, each of whose work tends to increase as the Congress expands the scope of federal responsibilities. Thus, while it was once expected that each Senator would understand and master every aspect of his committee's work, and carry the responsibility for explaining it to his colleagues, this has now become impossible.

Under current Senate rules, each member is assigned to two standing committees and to one minor or joint committee. At this writing, I am a member of the Public Works and Commerce Committees and of the Joint Atomic Energy Committee. I am also a member of the newly formed Budget Committee which will become fully operational as a major committee in 1977. In the meantime, members of the Budget Committee are expected to serve on two other major ones. On the Public Works Committee I have been assigned to the Subcommittees for Environmental Protection, Transportation, and Buildings and Grounds; on Commerce, to the Subcommittees for Surface Transportation, Consumer, Foreign Commerce and Tourism, Environment, Oceans and Atmospheres, and the Special Subcommittee to Study Transportation on the Great Lakes and the St. Lawrence Seaway. It is hardly surprising that day after day I find that two or more of these committees or subcommittees are holding meetings at identical times. I am therefore required either to bounce from one to the other in order to put in symbolic appearances, or I must choose to attend that one where I feel I can make the most effective contribution. In any event, on every such occasion I of necessity must neglect a significant proportion of my primary institutional responsibilities.

It is hardly surprising that the professional staffs assigned to each committee and subcommittee should assume so important, even dominant, a role in the legislative process. These staffs are usually heavily loaded in favor of the majority party in terms of both outlook and availability to committee members. They provide continuity and detailed expertise, they select the witnesses to be heard, the issues to be followed. Thus they exert an enormous influence over the shape and scope of the legislation that passes through their hands. Time and again after new points are raised in committee on complex and controversial legislation, the staff will disappear to return the next day with what is often a significantly new or considerably refocused piece of legislation.

Even those changes that the staff is asked to incorporate into the legislation under consideration will not necessarily represent a consensus of the committee. In the first instance, it is a rare day that a committee or subcommittee can muster the majority required to form a quorum for the conduct of business; and as time goes on, some of those who formed a quorum will melt away and others will appear and disappear in the middle of discussions of important points. Even when a quorum can be held in place long enough to argue through a particular point to a conclusion, there is no guarantee that the action taken at the meeting will reflect the consensus of those present. It is the use (and abuse) of proxy voting that makes this so. Time and again, during mark-up sessions on such legislation as the land use and strip mining bills, I would offer an amendment, explain my reasons in support of it, and persuade a majority of those present to back it, only to have the chairman reach into his pocket, pull out a handful of proxies, and vote the absentee members against my amendment.

As consideration of complicated legislation is extended day after day, it becomes extraordinarily difficult for committee members, even those particularly concerned with the legislation in question, to keep up with what is happening to it. There simply isn't time for a member to rethink and reconsider every interlocking provision of a complex bill each time a substantive change is made. Furthermore, committees often work under enormous pressure to report out particular bills by deadlines that at times are set not so much by the natural rhythm of the legislative process as by political considerations. Thus major legislation is often rushed through committee, reported out, and put to a vote even before all the members of the relevant committee fully understand what is in it.

It must be understood that it is virtually impossible for a Senator to keep up with most—let alone all—of the significant legislation being considered by committees other than his own. I do not refer to legislation that commands the headlines and occasions national debate. A Senator has to examine such legislation in some detail if only to answer his mail and reply to reporters' questions. It is, after all, by his positions on conspicuous legislation that he establishes his political identity. But most of the bills considered by the Senate are relatively inconspicuous—though by no means unimportant. They may involve new programs that will have an enormous impact on American society, on the states, or on the economy; programs that in time may grow into multibillion-dollar commitments. Yet many of these bills will be enacted with little real examination by most of the members who will have to vote yea or nay on them, and with less than adequate comprehension of what the bill involves.

Technically speaking, any Senator can ensure that adequate time is allowed for debate of any bill. He can simply register his refusal to agree to a unanimous-consent agreement limiting the time allotted to debate. This presupposes, however, that he has had enough advance warning of the particular mischief at hand to record a timely objection to any agreement to which he is not a party; that he feels strongly enough about the matter to be willing to devote the time required to launch a minifilibuster to call attention to what is afoot; and that he will be able to educate and energize a sufficient number of his all-too-preoccupied colleagues to assure himself of sufficient floor support to make the effort worthwhile.

For these and other reasons, the committee system today operates as something less than an effective agent of the whole in selecting and presenting bills that can then be examined with care and acted upon. Rather, the system operates in such a way that legislation reported out by a subcommittee, often without the active participation of all its members, is normally adopted by the full committee; and most legislation reported out by a full committee will be adopted by the Senate as a whole. With the exception of headline-catching legislation about which most Senators are required to form positive opinions, there is an institutional tendency to assume that the relevant committee has done its job, and that the resulting bill represents the informed judgment of members expert in the area of concern. This assumption continues to prevail in practice, I think, because the only other alternative is for a Senator to try to arrive at an independent analysis and judgment that time and available facilities simply will not allow.

Thus, what emerges from a committee and becomes law too often reflects the work and views of a few rather than the considered judgment of a majority of the hundred Senators who have been elected to shape the nation's laws. Let me cite one example that served to illuminate my own understanding of the limitations under which the Congress operates.

In early 1971, when sharp cutbacks in government aerospace programs, combined with a business recession, caused major layoffs at Boeing and other businesses in the Seattle area, Governor Daniel Evans of Washington suggested the need for legislation to cope with economic disasters similar to existing legislation designed to cope with natural disasters. The law he proposed would be narrow in its focus, providing relief on a short-term, emergency basis to help communities ride out sudden economic catastrophes.

Two bills incorporating this approach were introduced, and hearings on them were held by the Public Works Committee's Subcommittee on Economic Development, of which I was then a member. Several months later the subcommittee met in executive session to consider the legislation as revised by staff after the hearings. To the astonishment of at least some, the draft bill differed in fundamental respects from both of the measures that had been introduced. The basic concept had shifted from that of bringing maximum effort to bear on specific, localized economic emergencies to an amorphous bill that would also cover areas of chronic unemployment or chronically low economic activity for which there already existed thirty or forty other federal programs. The definition of areas which could be made subject to the legislation was such that even a neighborhood could qualify for the most exotic kinds of federal grants and aid.

Nevertheless, this basically new legislation was approved in a single day by the full committee and reported out. The legislation was then rushed to the floor of the Senate, debated before a largely empty chamber, and put to a vote—all within a day or two of the time printed copies of the bill and of the accompanying committee report had become available to Senators. The bill opened up a whole new area of federal intervention; it carried no price tag; and it was approved by Senators only a few of whom had any grasp of its scope.

The Congress, of course, is involved in far more than the enactment of new laws. One of its major responsibilities is, or ought to be, that of overseeing how laws already enacted and agencies already established are operating. Another is to establish broad national policy. These are areas of responsibility that are most directly relevant to the question of whether the Congress has the institutional capacity to assume a position of effective equality vis-à-vis the Executive Branch.

With respect to the exercise of oversight responsibilities, we need look no further than the sheer size of the job to be done, the inflexible limitation imposed by the clock and the calendar on available time, and the press of competing business to know that Congress can no longer do the job required.

There is no doubt whatever that Congressional committees and special committees can do superb work in seizing upon a particular problem, in shaking facts loose, and in identifying abuses that have occurred. The Congress can do excellent work in correcting the abuses uncovered in a particular situation and in establishing safeguards. But these individual successes, and the routine requirement that major agencies periodically appear before authorizing committees to report on the discharge of their responsibilities, should not obscure the fact that the Congress doesn't have the time or the facilities to intelligently review and assess the performance of the vast majority of the agencies or the effectiveness of the vast majority of the programs that are now in operation. Even if the Congress were to create a dozen watchdog agencies, such as the General Accounting Office, to help it do the job, it would still face an impossible task even in overseeing the watchdogs over so vast a bureaucracy.

What needs to be understood is that the Congress by its nature operates under an unavoidable limitation. Whereas the Executive Branch can build new buildings to house and hire specialists to man the new agencies created by the Congress under the supervision of a new department of the Cabinet, each member of the Congress is expected to cast an independent judgment on every matter that comes before the body as a whole. The Congress can only try to cope with the ever-expanding number and variety of federal activities by dividing ever thinner the amount of time its members can devote to any one. Once, when the Congress was in session only six or seven months each year, and its members, even during those months, enjoyed sufficient leisure to be able to spend full days participating in debate, it was possible to expand the length of a session to accommodate the expanded areas of responsibility without reducing the quality of the attention that could be focused on the work. We have long since run out of days and months, however, and we are now cutting the days into ever finer fragments.

Moreover, as government has expanded into more and more areas affecting the everyday lives of individuals and businesses and communities, the members of the Congress have found themselves assuming new areas of nonlegislative responsibilities that are overwhelming them and their staffs. Increasingly, they are asked to intervene on behalf of constituents who have reached the limits of their resources in the too-often-unequal battle with the bureaucracy. Whether members of the Senate and the House of Representatives ought to be acting as ombudsmen for their constituents is subject to intellectual debate; but as a practical, political matter, the role is unavoidable. All of this has resulted in a startling expansion of the workload on the Congress, a workload that a 1970 study of the Association of the Bar of the City of New York estimated to have doubled every five years since 1933.

Another way to illustrate the extraordinary increase in the demands that have been made on the time and attention of the finite members of the Congress is to observe that in 1940, a New York Senator could operate comfortably with a staff of nine. Today I am shorthanded with a Washington staff of forty. In 1940, the Commerce Committee staff consisted of six members. Today it numbers eighty-nine.

All this has a direct effect on the Congress' institutional attention span; and this, in turn, on its capacity to develop comprehensive policy in areas that are complex and controversial. Nowhere has this been more clearly illustrated than in the area of energy.

For years it has been apparent that the United States has been moving from a position of substantial sufficiency of cheap energy to one in which we would become increasingly, and dangerously, dependent on external sources for the fuels required to sustain our standard of living and maintain our industrial and agricultural bases. Our principal fuels, oil and natural gas, were becoming more difficult and expensive to find and produce; and while our consumption of energy was growing at an annual rate of between 4 and 5 percent, it was evident by 1970 that under existing conditions our production of oil and gas would soon be on the decline. These trends pointed to an early, unhealthy degree of dependence on foreign oil largely under the control of a handful of Arab states. The time was overdue for a carefully considered, comprehensive energy policy that would assure us of a better long-term balance between domestic consumption and production.

The Senate responded, in May, 1971, by commissioning a National Fuels and Energy Study under the direction of the

Interior Committee and with representation from the Public Works, Commerce, and Joint Atomic Energy Committees. Three and a half years and one oil embargo later, it had yet to reach a tentative conclusion or issue a report. By the end of 1974, the National Fuels and Energy Study had spent almost $1,500,000 and published more than 60,000 pages of hearing records. Yet it had proven itself incapable of formulating a policy on natural gas (which it attempted to do, without success, in the fall of 1974), let alone one encompassing the whole field of energy.

True, the Congress did enact a number of energy bills, some of them important, in 1973 and 1974, but most of these were adopted as individual, uncoordinated responses to the prodding of the Executive or the clear necessities imposed by the Arab embargo. Virtually nothing was done to encourage energy conservation on the one hand or to stimulate the near-term development and production of energy resources on the other. For well over a year every prominent member of the Congress had been declaiming about the need for an energy policy and had identified our long-term need for secure sources of energy as being at the top of any list of national priorities. Yet when the crisis was upon us, the Congress was unable to come forward with anything that remotely approached a conscious, comprehensive framework for addressing every aspect of the energy problem.

Why this institutional paralysis in the light of so clear a need for the development of national policy? There are a number of contributing factors. One of the more important is that the existing committee structure, with its jurisdictional jealousies, is such that it becomes extraordinarily difficult for the Congress to address in a concerted, sustained way a major policy objective that extends beyond the jurisdictional boundaries of any one standing committee. The establishment of the special-purpose National Fuels and Energy Study with representation from four committees reflected an attempt to bridge jurisdictional barriers. But as experience has demonstrated, while the study was able to amass a vast amount of information, it was not able to bring together the combined will or expertise of the member committees to develop policy. In point of fact it was not even able to eliminate duplication in the accumulation of information.

I have in mind the efforts in the Senate to do something rational to reverse the downward trend in the discovery and development of natural gas for commitment to interstate pipelines. Whatever one's particular solution, there is a broad consensus that our present and growing shortages of interstate gas are attributable to the requirement that the Federal Power Commission establish wellhead prices for natural gas committed to interstate markets. As the Federal Power Commission falls within the jurisdiction of the Commerce Committee, and as that committee began to express interest in addressing the problem, Senator Jackson decided that neither the Interior Committee nor the National Fuels and Energy Study, both of which he chaired, would propose specific legislation. Even though the Commerce Committee had representation on the latter, it proceeded with its own series of hearings that virtually duplicated the work already done the prior year. The result has been vast delays in addressing one of the most easily understood and most readily resolved problems affecting energy supply. Although the Senate, as a body, was in possession of the information in 1973 that would have permitted the making of a decision one way or the other on the future role of the FPC in the area of natural-gas pricing, none had yet been made more than a year later when President Ford included gas deregulation as an integral part of a comprehensive energy policy.

I believe few Americans understand (this one certainly didn't until he entered the Temple and was admitted to its mysteries) the extraordinary obstacles to the legislative process that can be created by the jealously guarded prerogatives of individual committees. Every legislative proposal must be referred to the "appropriate" Senate and House committees for consideration. If it fails to pass muster with the Congressional specialists in the field, it generally fails to become law—on the face of it, a reasonable procedure.

Unfortunately, it is not always easy to determine which committee is appropriate. Too many of today's problems escape the old categories. Inevitably, committee chairmen compete for control of important legislation, and where a new area having political sex appeal is discovered, such as energy or the environment, a form of imperialism can be observed as various committees try to stake their claims to portions of it. Too often the results have been unnecessarily awkward legislation (as an attempt is made to accommodate conflicting jurisdictional claims) or legislation unnecessarily delayed.

Let me cite an example involving the area of comprehensive land use planning.

The Coastal Zone Management Act, which is really a land use control bill for coastal zones, was written in the Ninety-second Congress by the Oceans and Atmosphere Subcommittee of the Senate Commerce Committee. The Nixon Administration threatened to veto the bill, stating its preference for the more comprehensive Land Use Policy and Planning Assistance Act then being written by the Interior Committee that would cover all lands, coastal and otherwise. President Nixon finally signed the Coastal Zone Management Act in October, 1972, which assigned administrative responsibilities over coastal areas to the Secretary of Commerce. Responsibility for administering the Interior Committee's land use bill would, of course, be vested in the Secretary of the Interior.

While logic and efficiency suggested that land use responsibilities ought to be exercised within a single department whether the lands in question lay along the sea or a few miles inland, rather than invite an in-house quarrel, the Senate Interior Committee deliberately excluded from its "comprehensive" bill those areas to which the Commerce Committee had staked a prior claim. Thus, in the interest of Senatorial comity, the Senate adopted two bills that would impose on coastal states two distinct programs subject to two sets of regulations under the supervision of separate departments.

But that was not the only accommodation made to other committees in the land use bill that the Senate ultimately adopted in 1974.* Section 306 of the Senate bill smoothed

---

*As the House failed to act on a land use measure, the bill died with the Ninety-third Congress.

other jurisdictional feathers by granting the Secretary of Housing and Urban Development and the Administrator of the Environmental Protection Agency a form of veto over certain of the Secretary of the Interior's actions in the administration of the act. This was done to assure the cooperation of the Banking and Public Works Committees, which also had interests in certain phases of land use planning (urban development and regional approaches to air and water pollution controls).

The Congress faces additional problems in trying to focus its work. Individual members are under such pressure to work on a vast array of measures of special interest to special constituencies that it is easy for priorities to be lost sight of. And this, too, must rank among the reasons why it seems so difficult for the Congress to assume a position of leadership in the definition of broad national policy. In the last analysis, the Senate and the House operate as loose federations of individual satrapies, each under the direction of the chairman of a committee or subcommittee who follows his own understanding of what needs to be done without any necessary relationship to or integration with the whole. Whether there is anything within the scope of our existing institutions that can correct this essentially aimless drift without the risk of greater disadvantages, I do not know.

The Democrats in the House of Representatives are currently reviving the party caucus as an instrument of institutional reform and policy direction. If it chooses to, a majority party caucus can maintain tight discipline because it has the power to reward and punish its members through distribution of committee assignments, chairmanships, and other emoluments of Congressional office. A well-organized group within the caucus has unseated several of the most powerful committee chairmen, and a few others appear to be serving on probation. This is all pretty heady stuff, until one recalls the abuses that some years ago led "King Caucus" to be replaced by the seniority system in the name of reform.

The problem with strong caucus rule is that it is apt to be neither representative nor responsible. A majority of the majority may have the naked power to force its will on the caucus, and therefore on the whole; but the policies and laws it can impose on a legislative body may be anything but representative of the views of that body's membership. Furthermore, because under our system a government will not fall because of the excesses of a majority of a caucus, we do not have the restraints that in parliamentary systems will force the majority to assume full responsibility for its actions.

Yet failing such a mechanism as the caucus, I do not see how, under existing circumstances, the Congress can adapt itself to deal on a truly comprehensive basis with such major problems as energy, or the protection of the environment (taking economic and other consequences into full account), or a redefinition of what ought to be the respective responsibilities of the federal government and the states (assuming any sustained interest can be revived in a revitalized Federalism).

Having said this, I hasten to point out one area where the Congress may well establish the capacity to develop policy of the most important kind. The Congress is currently putting into effect machinery designed to enable it to assume intelligent responsibility in the area of fiscal policy. The machinery was developed over a two-year period and was formalized in the Congressional Budget and Impoundment Control Act of 1974.

The legislation calls for the establishment of an independent Congressional Budget Office and for the establishment of budget committees in each house of the Congress that will, among other things, take into sober account estimated federal receipts and expenditures and measure the impact of federal fiscal policy on the economic health of the nation. Based on the recommendations of the budget committees, the Congress is to adopt, by each May 15, for the guidance of the authorizing and appropriations committees, a joint resolution estimating revenues during the ensuing fiscal year, establishing the overall level of expenditures to be made by the federal government, and allocating the spending among a number of broad categories. After the appropriations bills have been adopted, the budget committees will review them and recommend to the Congress whatever adjustments are required to reconcile them with the spending levels earlier adopted.

On paper, the new budget process makes a great deal of

sense, and it provides the Congress with its first opportunity to exercise conscious control over fiscal policy. It suffers, however, from the perhaps fatal flaw that the limitations to be adopted by the Congress may be upset by simple majority vote. It will provide an interesting test of Congressional self-discipline, especially in election years.

This attempt by the Congress to develop the means for asserting its prerogatives in the area of fiscal policy may well prove successful, and may provide a pattern for similar assertions in one or two other areas of permanent Congressional concern. It took two years to develop the machinery in the first instance and it will take another two to put it fully into effect. If it is successful, it will without any doubt become the prime interest and responsibility of the members of the budget committees. To the extent that it does, they will necessarily have to reduce the time they are able to devote to other responsibilities. The Congress itself will be no better able to respond effectively to new crises and needs.

When I am asked whether I see ways in which the Senate can overcome some of its problems, my answer is yes, but only to a degree. There are large opportunities for procedural reform, none of which have been even hinted at by such professional reformers as Common Cause.

What we need to concentrate on is not such essentially peripheral matters as how committee chairmen are selected or whether or not reporters are invited to sit in on every meeting of two or more Senators, but on a restructuring of the work and the flow of business in the Senate so that its members may be able to use their scarce time more effectively and bring a greater degree of thought to bear on legislation.

We need to sort out the various components of legislative work and address each in appropriate sequence so that we avoid the extraordinary inefficiencies and distractions that result from frenetic attempts to keep track of a dozen different activities at the same time—committee hearings, floor debates, markup sessions, and joint conference meetings all piled on top of one another in a manner that makes concentration or consecutive work impossible. Hours are wasted daily waiting for Senators to arrive from other commitments in order to form a quorum so that a committee may begin its work. Witnesses summoned from across the country find the flow of their testimony interrupted time and again as a buzzer rings to summon the Senators to the floor for still another roll-call vote. Members trying to hammer out the provisions of a particular bill in committee markup sessions find themselves having to relearn its essential provisions time and again because of the near impossibility of assembling the same group of Senators for the consecutive hours and days of work that are required to do the job in the most efficient way. Meetings of joint conference committees trying to iron out the differences between the Senate and House versions of a given bill will often find their work extended over a period of weeks, even months, as one set of conferees or the other, or both, are called away by other business.

We need to divide the legislative year into parts in which only certain kinds of activity will be undertaken. This would make it substantially easier to arrange for periods of uninterrupted committee work, and also make it possible for the Senate to return to the days when floor debate could be scheduled without competition from the committees.

We might even consider placing as much of the legislative business of the Congress as possible on a two-year cycle. One year might be devoted to debate and action on bills reported out of committees the prior year, and to the holding of public hearings to assemble information for committee consideration in the succeeding year. (Ideally, both of these activities, which are of a very public nature and which tend to attract headlines, would be scheduled in nonelection years so that the participants would not be distracted from the business at hand by the temptation to play politics at the expense of sober judgment. The distortions in the legislative process that occur while bills are voted on in the latter half of each election year are such that in all probability the best thing the Congress could do for the country would be to close down altogether between July 1 and the first Wednesday following the first Tuesday after the first Monday of November of every even-numbered year.) The alternate years would then be available for detailed consideration of new legislative proposals without arbitrary deadlines requiring hurried, patchwork approaches to important bills, and for the essential work of legislative oversight.

A system that would require committees to report out legislation one year, and to have it considered on the floor the next, would allow ample time for special-interest groups, for the public at large, and for members of individual Senatorial staffs to digest what it is that a Senator will be asked to vote upon when the legislation reaches the floor. It would also provide a period within which amendments could be introduced sufficiently in advance of debate to enable the members of the relevant committees to study them and to give the Senate as a whole the benefit of their expert assessment.

Whether the appropriation process could be placed on a biennial basis, I do not know; and, of course, any fundamental reordering of business would have to make special provision for the handling of emergencies. But if the work of the Senate could be organized in some such manner—and I see no reason why it is necessary to enact routine legislation every year instead of every other year—then the conflicts between committee hearings and markup sessions could be eliminated or greatly reduced, and the members of the Senate would be able once again to participate in floor debate of legislation they will be asked to approve or disapprove, either as advocates or as interested observers trying to assess the merits of a particular measure.

But whether or not any such sorting out of legislative activities is accomplished, there is one reform that I believe to be absolutely essential if we are to restore any vestige of the Senate's once proud claim to be a truly deliberative body. There is no excuse for a system that will permit acting on legislation under circumstances which make it impossible for the vast majority to have any understanding of what it contains. We cannot justify procedures that permit the introduction of unprinted amendments on a virtually empty floor, amendments that will profoundly affect the cost or substance of the legislation under consideration. All too often, especially when the Senate is operating under unanimous consent agreements severely limiting the time for debate on amendments, they are apt to be adopted or rejected on the basis of their emotional or political appeal without any understanding of what they will do or cost. In one heady session just before the 1972 elections, floor amendments added $4 billion, or more than 27 percent, to the cost of a welfare-Social Security bill.

I have urged in statements on the floor and in letters to the Senate leadership that new rules be adopted which would require that debate on legislation other than appropriation bills and those dealing with certified emergencies be scheduled no earlier than four weeks following the time the legislation and accompanying committee report become available, and that no amendment to such legislation be considered that has not been introduced at least two weeks prior to the commencement of debate. These simple changes in the existing rule requiring a delay of no more than three days between the issuing of a report and the commencement of debate would provide ample opportunity for the detailed examination of new legislative proposals and amendments well in advance of the time the Senate is required to act on them. Today, even the three-day rule is often observed in the breach, especially in the closing days of a session, as emphasis is placed on clearing ever more congested calendars.

Perhaps the principal benefit that would flow from the adoption of my proposal would be to allow the public adequate opportunity to examine proposed legislation in its final form. There are numbers of highly informed individuals and organizations that can quickly find the strengths and weaknesses in almost any bill. These represent a superb reservoir of knowledge that the Congress does not begin adequately to tap, especially as the legislation that public witnesses are invited to testify upon often bears little relationship to what finally emerges from the committee process.

My pleas have thus far fallen on deaf ears. It is suggested that to allow four weeks or even fourteen days to elapse between the time a bill is reported out and the time it is taken up for consideration would create substantial delays that would jam the legislative pipeline. Nonsense. With any reasonable degree of planning and cooperation, a steady stream of business could be programmed. While it is true that some bills reported out too late in the year might have to be carried over until the next, this in itself does not justify procedures that place a premium on quantity at the expense of quality. I suggest that today we have more cause to worry about too much ill-considered legislation than we have over an insufficiency of legislation.

There is another area of reform that has now been adopted in principle, and that I hope will be honored in practice. It is finally recognized that we will not soon again see the day when the Congress will adjourn its legislative work in August or September or even in October. This means that time must somehow be provided during the year for such essential matters as thought, study, and the ability to move about and talk to constituents. None of these activities can be reliably scheduled while the Congress is in session, and members ought not to be expected to devote their weekends to these purposes. Moreover, it takes more than a day or two to escape the hothouse, introverted atmosphere of Washington. We need to touch base with people where they live, and see how they live, and learn what it is they think about. It can be a liberating experience to do so.

As a result of the persistence of the newer members of the Senate, the leadership finally agreed to schedule a series of recesses in the 1975 calendar, each structured around the traditional holidays when most members visit their constituencies. Suddenly it was possible to schedule meetings and speeches with the presumed certainty that they would not have to be canceled at the last minute because of the press of business in Washington. Yet the press of business even in the initial days of a new Congress caused the Senate leadership to cancel the first of these scheduled breaks, and several score Senators had to cancel engagements they thought they could reliably make.

Press of business. It is the press of legislative business that now sets the limits to what procedural reforms can accomplish and to what the Congress can undertake with any degree of effectiveness. Reforms can have only marginal, though marginally important effects. They cannot overcome the simple fact that the Congress has now assumed to itself so vast an array of responsibilities that it can perform none with any real degree of sustained competence. The Congress today tends to react from crisis to crisis, from pressure to pressure. Far from shaping events, the Congress today is shaped by them.

But what is to be done? In the first and last analysis, only one thing, and that is to cut back on the number of responsibilities that are considered appropriate to the federal government. We must learn once again to exploit the advantages of Federalism. There is a natural hierarchy of responsibilities that determines which are best suited to each level of government, and if the Congress is to recapture the ability to do that which it does well and to match the capacity of the Executive in defining policy and seeing to it that it is implemented, it will have to redetermine what it is that the federal government uniquely should be doing, and what it is that the states are fully competent to handle. Having redefined the limits of federal responsibility, the Congress will then have to exercise the self-discipline to live within those limits without regard to the fact that this state or that may be engaged in policies of which a majority of the Congress disapproves. This will require an uncommon substitution of philosophy for impulse; but ours, after all, is a system that was founded on a coherent understanding of the limits of human institutions.

We have paid a tremendous price for the fact that Congress has expanded federal responsibility to the point where the legislative body is no longer able to do anything very well. It has stretched itself, in fact, to the point where it is now failing significantly in those areas that uniquely belong to the federal government, such as national defense, international relations, and economic policy. Finally and most importantly, the Congress has been failing to preserve and cultivate those concepts of restraint and self-reliance and self-discipline and limited governmental responsibilities on which our liberties ultimately depend.

7
A Free Economy

Were we directed from Washington when to sow and when to reap, we should soon want bread.

—THOMAS JEFFERSON
Papers, Vol. 1

THERE HAVE BEEN times during the course of Senate debate on economic issues when I have been tempted to rise and offer an amendment to the pending legislation requiring that the formula MMW = NR + HE × T be engraved on the wall above the presiding officer's chair as a perpetual reminder of certain fundamentals. The formula, printed in a publication of the American Economic Foundation, translates this way: "Man's material welfare (MMW) equals his natural resources (NR) plus the muscular and mental human energy (HE) he applies to them multiplied by the efficiency of his tools (T). Better living depends on better tools. Tools come from savings. Savings come from self-denial. Self-denial is inspired by reward." This is as succinct a statement as I have seen of how and why our economy works.

As this is being written, in mid-1975, the headlines tell of unemployment at 9 percent, of RECESSION WORST SINCE WORLD WAR TWO. At the same time, Americans continue to suffer from an inflation that brings home the truth of Thomas Mann's statement, "A severe inflation is the worst kind of revolution." The realities of economics are no longer the esoteric business of professors and statisticians; they now touch the daily lives of each of us in dramatic fashion.

151

Ours is an economic system that has produced the highest standard of living, the greatest personal opportunity, and the widest range of choice among products, jobs, and lifestyles that the world has ever seen. The prime concern of Congress ought to be to maintain an environment in which so productive a system can continue to thrive. Yet the Congress has instead contributed greatly to the paralyzing uncertainty and to the growing gap between effort and reward that underlie many of our economic woes.

There are two major reasons for Congressional failure to maintain a suitable economic climate. First, the American educational system has failed to provide an adequate understanding of the dynamics of our economic system. This is generally true for the education of the population as a whole, and for the education of those in Congress. Second, most members of Congress have had little personal involvement with those aspects of life that involve actual investment, managerial, or sales experience. They do not bring to the Congress a knowledge of the motivations and hazards that affect daily economic decisions. Yet they are called upon to make legislative decisions that have an increasingly pervasive impact on how the private sector will be allowed to operate. Moreover, Congressional life is so hectic that it is virtually impossible for members of Congress to learn the actual problems faced in business and agriculture even when they are members of the appropriate committees. It is therefore not at all mysterious that Congress should so often end up enacting laws that make productive activity more difficult, thus hurting those for whom the Congress may be most concerned.

Thus, with the best of intentions, Congress has been busily at work imposing layer upon layer of expense and regulation on producers, with the result that smaller enterprises find it increasingly hard to survive, and the cost of a myriad of products to consumers is increased.

For more than four years I have observed this regulatory mentality at close range, and it is a marvel to me that the economy still retains as much strength and resiliency as it has. A basic lack of economic understanding, combined with the inability of members of Congress to master those areas that are uniquely the responsibility of the federal government, all too often leads to the application of precisely the wrong economic medicine.

I was first exposed to these limitations in the fall of 1971 when a business downturn and an adverse international balance of payments problem caused Senator Vance Hartke of Indiana and Congressman James A. Burke of Massachusetts to introduce legislation designed primarily to curtail American investment abroad, even as the Administration urged passage of tax credits and other measures designed to encourage investments and make American products more competitive in international markets.

According to Senator Hartke, his bill

> . . . would discourage American business investment abroad and limit the flow of imports into this country. We can no longer afford to export American jobs and technology at the expense of our own industry, all in the name of "free trade." . . . To this end, this statute should be interpreted to insure that the production of goods which have historically been produced in the United States is continued and maintained.

We were treated to a festival of rhetoric about the "export of jobs" by American businesses that established subsidiaries in areas of cheap labor or in protected areas such as the European Economic Community (so that American-owned firms could get around trade barriers and compete with foreign companies on their own turf). It was apparently assumed that an act of Congress could somehow force Filipinos or Indonesians to buy all-American transistor radios at $50 rather than Japanese radios assembled in Taiwan and selling for $20. Actually, foreign assembly plants established by American businesses had become a major market for component parts, supplies, and services produced within the United States and exported to such foreign plants. Proponents of Burke-Hartke did not consider these matters, nor did they see that the alternative to "exporting" labor-intensive jobs is to make no sales at all, and to reduce to that extent employment in the United States among firms supplying foreign plants. Nor did it occur to them that our imports provide other countries with the dollars with which to buy our exports, and that real wages are higher in our export-related industries than in our import-competing industries.

This innocence of how the real world operates extended to the impact of taxation on the competitive position of businesses. Every proposal for investment tax credits or accelerated depreciation that would have had the effect of reducing business taxes, or that would bring the taxation of foreign subsidiaries more in line with the rates their foreign competitors were required to pay, encountered anguished dismay. The American consumer or worker was being raped. Big business and its notoriously affluent stockholders would reap more windfall tax benefits at the expense of the little guy, and so on.

It seemed never to occur to the Senators who voiced such complaints that under the competitive pressures then squeezing American goods out of foreign markets it was at least as likely that lower taxes would result in lower prices, greater sales, and more employment. It never seemed to occur to them that taxes are part of the cost of doing business, that business decisions are made on the basis of a calculation of the rate of return on investment after deducting all costs, including taxes. The rate of taxation will determine not only the prices at which goods can be profitably sold, but also whether or not it is worthwhile for a business firm to embark on the expansion of an existing plant, go into a new market, or develop a new product.

The Administration failed to gain all the tax adjustments it sought even though, on balance, they would have resulted in more jobs, more products, higher real wages, and lower prices. On the other hand, the Burke-Hartke bill never came to a vote, as an upturn in the economy diffused its support.

The ultimate failure of the Burke-Hartke measure was, from the point of view of economic rationality, welcome. But those of us in Congress know that there are few, if any, ultimate victories in the fight to make the policies of Congress mesh with the realities of the economic world. Nowhere has this been more clearly illustrated than in three major areas of Congressional debate in recent years: inflation, energy, and consumer "protection."

Over the past decades we have come to expect a degree of inflation as a way of life. In fact, many have come to accept the assertion that a little bit of inflation is desirable, though it has been necessary every few years to raise the rate of inflation that is thought to be conducive to optimum employment. In the early sixties, two distinguished economists theorized that a 5 percent inflation would ensure an unemployment rate of 3.5 percent, yet we have seen that even a 12 percent inflation did not bring unemployment much below 5 percent in 1973, and even that for only a short while. Nothing so discourages savings or long-term investment as the belief that the buying power of the dollar we save or invest will depreciate at a faster rate than its after-tax earnings. And savings, as we noted at the start of this chapter, provide the tools to raise productivity and real wages.

Richard Whalen, in a recent article in the Washington *Post*, had this to say about the connection between inflation and recession:

> One needn't be an economic expert to know that inflation is at the heart of our recessionary affliction. Economists may cling to the belief that inflation and recession are opposites, but it is evident to ordinary citizens that it was inflation that reduced their ability to buy, inflation which pushed the poor deeper into poverty and those on modest fixed incomes closer to becoming poor, inflation which triggered companies' sales slumps and layoffs, inflation which brought on our general economic decline. . . .

Experts may disagree about the precise relationship between inflation and recession. But, as Mr. Whalen points out, no one can doubt that there is such a relationship and that it is no coincidence that every inflationary outburst has been followed by a recession. It is therefore not only the purchasing power of the dollar that is at stake in the fight against inflation, but also the employment and real incomes of millions of Americans.

Two links between inflation and recession deserve special attention. The first is the effect of inflation in raising tax rates. The government now profits handsomely from inflation—inflating away real interest payments to holders of government bonds; taxing unreal increases in profits, capital gains, and interest income; diluting the real value of exemptions and the standard deduction; and pushing people into higher tax brackets even though their real earnings have not increased. A study prepared for the Joint Economic Committee found that the biggest increase in living costs in 1974 was not food or fuel, but taxes. An increase in taxes due to inflation is no different in its effect than an explicit tax increase—it discourages productive activity. Because such taxation is not legislated, however, it becomes nearly impossible for voters to hold individual members of Congress accountable for their part in creating the inflation-related taxation used to finance vote-buying expenditures. The benefits of more spending are obvious, at least to those receiving the money, while the costs are obscured. This creates an unwholesome incentive for politicians, and comes dangerously close to "taxation without representation." For this reason I introduced legislation to adjust or "index" the tax system to compensate for the effects of inflation. When I offered the legislation as an amendment to a tax reform bill in March, 1975, it was rejected out of hand. "It would deprive the Treasury of the 'inflation bonus,'" I was told. The phrase "inflation bonus" is a euphemism for the tax windfall which government receives from inflation, almost entirely at the expense of low- to middle-income wage earners. Congress can get pretty upset over consumer fraud—except when it is practicing it.

The second link between inflation and recession is more direct. An unexpected inflation reduces unemployment for a little while by tricking people into accepting less *real* compensation than they think they are getting. Workers get lower real wages, savers and lenders get lower real interest earnings, and these factors increase the profitability of expanding employment. Once people realize what has happened to their real incomes, however, they adjust accordingly to restore real economic relationships as they would be without the distortions induced by inflationary expectations. Then unemployment adjusts to a rate determined by such factors as real costs, supply, demand, and incentives to invest. The result is to replace stagnation with stagflation.

As the tax and price effects become more burdensome, great public pressure develops to reduce inflation quickly. With the expectation of a high rate of inflation built into long-term contracts or contractual commitments, a sudden reduction in inflation is necessarily disruptive. Businessmen have committed themselves to paying inflated prices for labor, materials, and credit. When they find they can't pass the costs along because the money just isn't there, they have no choice but to minimize losses by reducing production and employment while liquidating surplus inventories. If the monetary authorities could avoid the temptation to "reflate," the production cutbacks would eventually put downward pressure on costs, and production could resume at the lower rate of inflation that matches the slower growth in the money supply. If the monetary authorities cannot avoid the temptation, the inflation-recession cycle will start all over again, as in 1968 and 1972, both times starting from a higher rate of inflation and ending in a worse recession.

It is instructive in this connection to look back at the experience of the past few years to see what lessons we can learn. When the brief slowdown of money growth in 1970 failed to end inflation instantly, Congress enacted legislation granting the President, over his protest, standby authority to impose wage and price controls. With the authority in place, political pressures were soon brought to bear on behalf of its exercise, even though in all recorded history (including the Roman Empire and the American Revolution) price controls had never succeeded in containing inflation.

This was a classic example of buck-passing on the part of a Congress that later pretended to worry about excessive Presidential power. Delegation of unwanted authority to the President allowed the Congress to take credit for "doing something," while forcing the Executive to absorb any blame for the catastrophe that inevitably followed upon the exercise of that authority.

During the first half of 1971 there was more and more talk of the need to stimulate the economy by throwing fiscal caution to the winds and relying on economic controls. President Nixon capitulated to these pressures and tried his hand at oneupmanship when, in August, 1971, he imposed the first wage and price controls in peacetime history, announced that he too was a Keynesian, thereby giving his tacit approval to a return to large federal deficits, and slammed shut the gold window, thereby ending what remained of the fiction that the dollar was backed by gold and eliminating the constraint that a gold drain might otherwise have placed on inflationary policies.

I believe that Richard Nixon knew that wage and price controls would not prove effective for long and also knew that the stimulative spending he invited carried with it the risk of a resurgence of the inflation that his more prudent policies were in fact bringing under control (the rate of inflation in consumer prices had been reduced from over 6 percent to less than 4 percent). Yet he yielded to mounting demands for controls and spending in the hope that a quickly revived economy would facilitate his reelection. Republicans, this one included, avoided direct criticism of Mr. Nixon's failure to stand his ground and argue his case to the people because we didn't want to risk the election of a Senator McGovern, who would propose tens of billions of dollars in new spending without any thought of where the money would come from. Observing Richard Nixon yielding to political pressures, however, has persuaded me of the desirability of limiting a President to a single six-year term.

Perhaps it was my need to expiate sins of omission that caused me to take the lead in 1973 in pressing for the immediate end of wage and price controls. In November, 1973, I introduced an amendment to the National Energy Emergency Act that would have terminated controls several months before the existing authority ran out. By this time the country had experienced three and a half phases of controls, and it was easy to demonstrate that they were not even holding measured inflation down (the consumer price index was up 8.3 percent, ignoring unmeasurable reductions in product quality, delayed delivery, and other forms of concealed price increases).

In my initial try I had eight cosponsors and a total of twenty-six Senators voted for termination. A number of others expressed sympathy for the objective, but wanted to wait for a more appropriate time when conditions were less unsettled. The position of those adopting a wait and see attitude was reinforced by the Chairman of the Economic Stabilization Board, whose persuasive rhetoric reinforced my conviction that regulations are rarely relinquished without a battle, however temporary their initial intent. He too argued that we should await that elusive "appropriate time" which in the nature of things would never come. Government economic intervention tends to produce distortions that are used to justify still more intervention, and it is a rare bureaucrat who will admit, even to himself, that he is doing more harm than good.

There is an institutional reluctance in Congress to withdraw federal authority over any activity without the greatest pressures to do so. In this case the pressures were growing daily. A long and expanding list of commodities had disappeared from the market because manufacturers could not afford to produce them at controlled prices. This was creating a chain reaction in which firms were postponing expansion, curtailing production, even shutting down because of the unavailability of an essential commodity. My own mail contained urgent appeals for a relaxation or abolition of controls from a host of New York State manufacturers. Railroads, hospitals, farmers, employee groups, and meatpackers were also seeking relief. A number of firms advised me they were beginning to lay off workers because of mounting shortages.

These serious dislocations were the result of a federal government attempt to control inflation by attacking symptoms instead of causes. Worse still, by deflecting attention from the actual cause—namely, an excessive expansion of the money supply—we had allowed inflationary pressures to continue to build until they burst out everywhere violently. (The rate of money growth doubled, from 4.3 percent to 8.6 percent, from the second half of 1971 to the second half of 1972, compared to a twenty-year average growth of approximately 3.5 percent per annum.) The widespread shortages of this period were the predictable consequence of not allowing prices to bring supply into balance with inflated demand.

Our first venture in peacetime controls came to an end on April 30, 1974, not because of action to reject controls, but because of inaction. The authorizing legislation was simply allowed to expire. As was to be expected, prices continued to rise while the economic system tried to adjust to shortages and digest the $100 billion in federal deficits that had been run up in the previous five years, and the 7 to 9 percent annual increases in the money supply that resulted from the Federal Reserve buying billions of dollars of the added government debt and increasing bank reserves in payment. The rate of inflation rose to about 12 percent and then began to subside toward the end of the year. Once again, as in 1967 and 1970, efforts to bring down the rate of inflation were accompanied by an economic slowdown and rising unemployment. And once again the struggle to contain inflation was threatened by huge deficits and the attempt to spend ourselves back into prosperity.

Even though price controls had been lifted in most areas, they were retained on natural gas and oil produced from wells already in production. In the one area where there was the greatest public concern over shortages, energy, we persisted in maintaining a price control mechanism that demonstrably discouraged conservation of oil and gas as well as the development of new reserves. Artificially low prices encourage consumption and discourage production, and the resulting gap between what people want to buy at the low price and what anyone is able to produce and sell at that price is a "shortage."

In a speech to the Economic Club of New York in March, 1973, seven months before the Arab oil embargo, I noted that "we are faced with . . . a protracted period of chronic and growing deficiencies in the supply of indigenous fuels that will make our nation uncomfortably and some believe dangerously vulnerable to external economic and political pressures. This period of vulnerability will be of at least a dozen years' duration, probably more, depending on the wisdom we exhibit in establishing our energy goals, and of the policies we adopt in order to achieve them." Twenty-one months and one Arab embargo later, the Ninety-third Congress bowed into history without establishing any coherent set of energy goals or policies, let alone wise ones. The Congress treated the public to some well-televised fireworks as powerful committee chairmen hurled accusations at the surprisingly inarticulate chief executives of some of our largest corporations. After much such huffing and puffing, Congress produced a litter of legislative mice.

Legislation was passed setting up a bureaucracy to spread the misery around under virtually impossible conditions. It is not surprising that a recent American Enterprise Institute study by Richard Mancke indicates that the Federal Energy Office caused more trouble than it solved. And Congress did enact a program for research and development that may help us to meet the energy problems that we will be facing two or three decades from now. But we did precious little (other than enacting the Alaskan pipeline bill) to encourage production or conservation within the next few years. In other words, we did not do precisely what most needed to be done.

The United States and its territorial waters still contain significant quantities of oil and gas waiting to be found and developed. And while we appear to be within a few decades of exhausting our domestic sources of conventionally producible oil and gas, we do have coal resources estimated at 3.2 trillion tons, of which 150 billion tons were considered readily recoverable—enough for several centuries. Coal can be liquefied and gasified and is therefore a potential substitute for oil and natural gas. Finally, the oil shales of the West contain an estimated 1.8 trillion barrels of oil of which 54 billion are contained in zones considered to be most economically recoverable.

While some of these reserves would have to be declared out of bounds for sound environmental reasons, it was clear that we were not running out of the basic sources of energy. They were there to be found and developed—but only at prices that would justify the risks of exploration and the costs of bringing newly discovered deposits into production.

We were running into serious shortages of natural gas (which supplies about a third of our total energy needs) for the clinically demonstrable reason that the artificial wellhead prices imposed on producers by the Federal Power Commission had long ago destroyed any incentive to search for gas for commitment to interstate pipelines. This is scarcely an ideological or partisan issue, as some have portrayed it, since one of the strongest cases for deregulation of natural gas prices is contained in a Brookings Institution study coauthored by Professor Paul MacAvoy of MIT—an adviser to Senator McGovern in the 1972 campaign. The evidence is so overwhelming, in fact, that the FPC itself endorsed legislation I introduced to exempt natural gas not under contract from its control.

When it comes to energy, the ideological blinders are still firmly in place. The refusal even to consider ample evidence of the connection between price and supply was nowhere more evident than in the determination of Senate and House conferees to add an oil price rollback provision to an emergency energy bill that President Nixon had vetoed in December, 1973, and that was scheduled to be reconsidered at a joint Senate-House conference called for the following February. Earlier in 1973 price controls had been lifted from oil produced from stripper wells (those producing less than ten barrels per day) and from wells brought into production after the lifting of controls. The price for this oil had quickly risen to approximately $10 per barrel, which was somewhat lower than the landed price of imported crude.

Senator Jackson, Chairman of the Senate Interior Committee, announced that he and Congressman Staggers intended to introduce at the conference an amendment that would place a $5.25 ceiling on all domestic production, and scheduled three days of hearings on the proposal while making it clear at the outset that the only purpose to be served by the hearings was to confirm conclusions already set in concrete. Jackson's opening statement on the first day left no doubt on the matter:

> I can find no conceivable justification for current fuel price levels. By all evidence we have seen, Americans are paying unconscionable and unnecessarily high prices for essential petroleum products. . . .
> A rollback of petroleum prices to more reasonable and realistic levels is absolutely essential. That is the subject of these hearings today. . . .

The following day, Friday, February 1, 1974, the Senator announced:

> Before hearing from our witnesses this morning, I would like to announce that on Monday at 10 A.M., Chairman Staggers of the House Interstate and Foreign Commerce Committee and I will reconvene the conference on S. 2589, the Emergency Energy Act. At that time we will urge our fellow conferees to consider including in the bill in the conference report a price rollback and price ceiling provision for crude oil and petroleum products. . . .

On the third day of hearings, Saturday, February 2, a panel of petroleum economists from the academic community and industry appeared to testify on the merits of the proposed rollback. They were called at the insistence of Senator Paul Fannin of Arizona, the ranking minority member of the Interior Committee. When I asked the economists whether the time elapsing between the close of the hearings on Saturday afternoon and the opening of the Joint Conference on the Emergency Energy Act at 10:00 A.M. the following Monday morning would be sufficient to accumulate and assess the economic information necessary to make an informed judgment on the proposed rollback, each answered with an emphatic no. When I asked if they would consider it irresponsible to attempt to enact a pricing formula the following week, they answered with an equally emphatic yes.

The economists pointed out that even if the price of all uncontrolled crude oil were to be rolled back to zero, the net effect to the motorist would be a saving of no more than five cents per gallon of gasoline (and that only on the rather questionable assumption that the supply of such oil would be unaffected by a zero price). Moreover, said the economists, to hold prices below optimum levels would have the effect of encouraging consumption while discouraging the massive investment in exploration and development, in secondary and tertiary recovery, in coal liquefication and gasification, and in the recovery of oil from shale, that alone would enable us to achieve our stated goal of a reasonable degree of self-sufficiency by the mid-1980's. The consumer would ultimately pay *more* as a result of a price rollback because of increased dependency on costly imported oil and natural gas.

When the Emergency Energy Bill containing the price rollback provision came to the floor, I joined with three Senators from Western states in arguing the economic idiocy of placing artificial restraints on incentives to expand domestic supplies of oil and gas—unless, of course, the purpose of the bill was to prolong the energy emergency, and our dependence on the OPEC cartel, indefinitely. When I looked for the report of our efforts in the New York *Times* the next day, I found that all our well-honed arguments had been dismissed with the simple statement that several "oil state Senators" had spoken in opposition.

Now, I had never thought of New York as an oil state, but knowing the *Times'* reputation for accuracy, I decided to check the facts. I called the New York State Department of Mines and discovered that New York had more than 5,200 oil wells that in 1973 had produced, in the aggregate, 949,000 barrels of high-quality crude, or about half a barrel per well per day. This was the residue of what had once been a reasonably significant production of Pennsylvania-type oil. I also learned that we had 725 gas wells that were supplying somewhat less than 1 percent of New York's consumption.

The New York *Times* was vindicated. Clearly, we were an oil- and gas-producing state. Equally clearly, we had a way to go before New York could achieve any degree of independence from insecure sources of supply in Texas, Louisiana, and Oklahoma. But what intrigued me most was the speed and size of the response in New York to the lifting of controls on the price of oil the prior year. (As New York's gas is sold intrastate, it is not subject to FTC price regulation.) In less than a year, land-leasing activity had trebled, while exploratory drilling had almost doubled—from eight wildcat wells in 1972 to fourteen in 1973. Depleted fields were being reworked, and deeper targets, previously considered uneconomical, were now being tested. The incentives created in 1973 by rising prices were working their old-time magic.

I found, in short, that in New York we had a mini-oil boom in full progress, an example in microcosm of how private industry will respond when market forces are allowed to mobilize the risk capital required to increase the production of commodities in short supply.

The Congress has nonetheless persisted in the notion that the interests of energy consumers can be protected by imposing government regulations that will in fact increase or prolong the consumer's dependence on a foreign cartel. This attitude comes from a failure to understand that an uncontrolled price system reflects the consumers' own sense of priorities by letting consumers establish the relative importance of scarce commodities through the way they choose to spend their earnings, and by providing the price and profits signals that direct scarce resources and capital to uses that consumers value most highly.

It was once generally understood that the prime economic role of government was to establish a predictable legal framework to minimize conflicting claims to property, punish fraud, and ensure that the economy was truly competitive by eliminating public or private barriers to entry into industries or occupations. Now, we have redefined the rules, or rather permitted government agencies to create their own rules, and thereby greatly increased the expense and uncertainty facing those who are trying to make economic decisions in the productive sector. In recent times the new trend is especially evident in the increasing willingness of Congress to delegate virtually unlimited coercive powers to unelected bureaucrats—all in the name of consumer "protection."

Abundance, the profusion and variety of goods and services that our people produce and exchange, has offended the sensibilities of those who believe they know better than the average person what it is the average person should be allowed to have. This sort of elitism is particularly popular within the overgrown information industry (universities, foundations, and the media), which positively delights in advocating (and some say stands to profit most from controlling) a system to "plan" who shall produce what for whom. All this is not new, for like-minded bureaucrats have been trying to minimize the individual's range of choice since at least 1917, when Bernard Baruch exercised wartime powers to regulate almost everything from the style of clothes to the number of paints.

Critics of our economic system—the system in which producers do not survive unless they cater to consumer preferences at the lowest possible cost—are inclined to stress the alleged ability of large corporations to sell anything at all through advertising (a power which did not seem to help General Motors very much during the 1975-model year).

Articulate and witty men like John Kenneth Galbraith have made the best-seller lists by persuading us that persuasion is bad and that government is competent to regulate everything except the deceptive qualities of their books. Various commercial extravagances have often been unfavorably compared with an ascetic life devoted to contemplation and the fine arts by professional intellectuals who don't mind having their tastes subsidized by those whose tastes they deplore. All this is fair social comment so long as such value judgments were not buttressed by the power to prevent other people from using their own judgment about how to spend their own incomes.

With the onrush of "consumerism" the situation changed. In its quixotic attempt to shield the purchaser from every hazard, or to prevent 5 percent of the population from making fools of themselves, this movement of self-selected spokesmen for consumers (that is, for all of us) has imposed substantial costs on 100 percent of the population and greatly restricted the variety of goods available to them. Unfortunately, the public is largely unaware of the many ways in which they have been adversely affected by this expansion of arrogant paternalism. An exception was the Department of Transportation's requirement that 1974-model cars be equipped with ignition interlock seat belts to force people to strap themselves in before their car would start—even just to drive the car out of the garage. The public's resultant show of indignation was compounded by the fact that this expensive nuisance frequently malfunctioned, making it impossible for citizens to start their cars, however meekly they followed instructions.

The average driver tolerates the requirement that seat belts be made part of standard equipment. He even accepts being compelled to purchase lights reminding him that he doesn't have his seat belts connected. But the interlock system did it. The American driver understood, even if the bureaucrats did not, the important distinction between the exercise of governmental power to prevent one individual from creating a hazard to another and the exercise of that same power to prevent an individual informed of the risks from undertaking them.

When I introduced legislation to outlaw mandatory ignition interlock seat belts, I found platoons of cosponsors attracted to the cause of consumer freedom. On the other hand, a number of people in and out of Congress opposed what I was doing because they felt that any potential saving of lives justified any restrictions on freedom of choice. After noting that "approximately 40 percent of the driving public disliked the interlock enough to disconnect or circumvent it, *Consumer Reports* nonetheless concluded that "it's a pity that Congress knuckled under, for, like it or not, a lot of people were buckling up." Pursuing such logic a little further, members of Congress should presumably outlaw such voluntary risk-taking as skiing or buying houses with stairs—whether their constituents "like it or not." In any case, popular sentiment carried the day on this occasion, and on October 27, 1974, the Motor Vehicle and Schoolbus Safety Amendments of 1974 became law.

I did not, however, meet with quite the same approbation when I tried to protect the consumer, the economy, and the processes of administrative law from a far more insidious assault. I refer to legislation that came within a hair's breadth of becoming law in the fall of 1974, the Consumer Protection Agency bill.

Now, we are all consumers, and we all want to be protected, so it seems almost evil to be opposed to legislation so appealingly labeled, regardless of what lies behind the label. Moreover, we were told that the need for such an agency was obvious, that the market was a complex and confusing place, and that many or even most businessmen were in the habit of taking advantage of unwary and naive consumers.

It was acknowledged that during the last forty years or so we have created agency after agency to help the consumer by regulating business activities. But we were now told that these efforts had failed, and that many regulatory agencies, such as the Interstate Commerce Commission and the Civil Aeronautics Board, actually acted to protect established producers from competition. The consumer needed still more protection, including protection from all those other agencies that were supposed to protect him, but had failed. Instead of addressing themselves to the deficiencies of existing consumer protection legislation, the authors of the legislation proposed to create yet another government regulatory bureau, the Consumer Protection Agency, whose administrator would have been endowed with powers that were positively dazzling in their scope.

The administrator and the administrator alone would have determined what was in the interest of consumers, and his determination was not reviewable by any court of law. He could have intervened in any proceeding before any federal agency, and gone to court to reopen proceedings and appealed decisions previously considered final. The administrator, given wide discovery authority in the legislation, could release trade secrets and other private information whenever he alone deemed it "necessary to protect the health or safety of the public." Furthermore, the administrator was also authorized to undertake product comparisons, under test procedures and guidelines that he alone determined to be appropriate. In short, this administrator would have been granted unprecedented authority unchecked by any reasonable safeguards.

The authors of the Consumer Protection Agency Bill neglected to define the interests of consumers, in whose name this carte blanche authority was to be created. They failed to do so for a very good reason. There is no such thing as a single, identifiable, monolithic consumer interest. We are all consumers, but we have different and often conflicting interests at different times and under different circumstances. The variety of needs and desires among consumers forces proponents of a consumer protection agency to do little more than talk in vague generalities about the need for a governmental superman to stand up for "the" consumer.

The administrator of this agency, then, would be exercising power which had no practical limits. If there was disagreement as to just what was in the interests of "the" consumer, we would simply be told that "the administrator will decide." And he would have to decide without reference to any standards or guidelines, because the CPA bill provided none. It merely delegated the authority to declare certain acts antisocial.

The administrator could easily damage or destroy businesses for engaging in practices that had never been prohibited by law. Here the due process problem should have been obvious, because the tradition of the rule of law requires that persons who are to be held accountable for their actions must have prior-existing standards against which they can judge their performance.

Those who advocate such ever-increasing regulation sincerely believe that the net result will be beneficial—despite the damage consumers have so often suffered as a result of similar efforts in the past. Every regulatory agency was presumably intended to serve some often undefined "public interest," yet nearly all of them have had notoriously undesirable side effects. In a chapter criticizing the government's myriad regulatory agencies, the 1975 Annual Report of the Council of Economic Advisers concludes that government regulation is "imposing significant costs on the economy"—adding billions of wasted dollars to the prices consumers have to pay.

Overregulation of business has contributed substantially to our problems in a host of industries. The CPA bill would have created one more costly agency, hamstrung the operations of other agencies, and buried the American businessman under even more red tape. The added cost would necessarily have been passed on to the consumer, and the CPA bill would have reduced the individual's range of choice by substituting the opinions of an administrator for those of a broad spectrum of diverse consumers with whom he would have nothing in common. Consumerists, for example, are fond of preaching the need for improvement in the quality of consumer goods. Yet there is a legitimate place for "cheap" goods that are not inherently dangerous. Perfect products are simply not obtainable at prices that would not deprive many of their use. The CPA bill failed to pass the Senate, for the time being, only because of the sustained exertions of a handful of Senators who managed to turn back four attempts to limit debate and bring it to a vote. We succeeded through a rear-guard action in buying time to uncover the underlying issues. And we did so at some political risk, though we expected that our efforts would probably prove futile. We believed that the legislation would have ushered in a new generation of regulatory agencies, piled on top of the old, that would have moved the American economy still further under the sway of economic czars subject neither to the discipline of the marketplace nor to the procedural safeguards that define the difference between a constitutional and an arbitrary government.

The regulatory ethic, exemplified by the attempt to create a consumer czar, is only one symptom of a growing distrust in the Congress of private judgments and institutions and of a complementary faith in centralized decision-making. It is no coincidence that those who want to regulate America into their version of justice are also those who want to spend America into prosperity. When the private economy is obviously strangled by too much government, the solution is held to be more of the same—as though real resources being channeled to politically determined uses could simultaneously be devoted to market-determined—that is to say, *consumer-determined*—uses.

There are times when I despair that rational debate can even begin to convince those who are hell-bent to control every detail of the private economy. Yet it must be admitted that Congressional champions of a free economic system have yet to come up with an easily understood, easily reported formula that will sufficiently dramatize the extent to which the explosion of federal regulation, services and spending has overloaded the capacity of the American economy. The idea that American wealth can accommodate every demand placed upon it is simply not true, and we court economic disaster if the nation and its government ignore the simple truth that the growth of government spending requires corresponding reduction in private buying power, regardless of whether the government spending is financed by taxes, borrowing, or creating new money.

Richard Nixon's first significant retreat from the politically understandable position of strict fiscal responsibility took place in his 1971 State of the Union Message, when he adopted the concept of full employment budgets. Its thesis was that deficits should be calculated not in terms of monies expended in excess of monies received, but rather in terms of how the ledger would read if the economy were operating at "full employment" (rather arbitrarily defined as 4 percent unemployed at any moment). It was argued that because an economy operating at less than full employment had inbuilt slack, excessive federal expenditures would not be inflationary, and a policy of true fiscal responsibility did not require a retrenchment in federal spending merely because of the loss of revenues resulting from the economy's failure to operate at full employment.

After consulting with economists whose views I respected, I at first came to the conclusion that a fairly good theoretical case could be made for this approach. The first economist I telephoned, Professor Milton Friedman, told me that he had proposed the concept almost twenty years earlier. He argued that computing the budget on a twelve-month cycle was arbitrary, and that it made better sense to calculate total expenditures and receipts over a cycle that was more closely related to the ebb and flow of the economy.

Since 1974, however, when we managed to combine a 12 percent inflation with a 5.6 percent unemployment rate, a number of economists have begun to doubt that an unemployment rate above 4 percent provides much assurance that "expansionary" fiscal and monetary policies will not, sooner or later, be mainly reflected in prices. This is partly because women and teen-agers now constitute a majority of the labor force, and they switch jobs more frequently than married men, causing the economy to gravitate toward a higher unemployment rate even when the economy is buzzing at a hectic pace. Moreover, since unemployment has rarely been below 4 percent because of the great mobility of labor in a country as large as the United States, except when we conscripted millions of potential workers in wartime, budgeting as if employment were "full" implies literally infinite expansion of the federal debt and of the taxes required to pay interest on that debt. Another problem arises from the technical difficulty of calculating a full employment budget, and this problem is compounded when there is inflation. Tax revenues invariably rise faster than expenditures during an inflation, which greatly confuses the interpretation of deficits. A budget which is balanced by virtue of the fact that inflation pushes people into ever-higher tax brackets is hardly a noninflationary budget. Taxes themselves, after all, are a part of the cost of living—indeed as I have mentioned, the fastest-growing part in recent years. Finally, there is no reliable connection between full employment deficits and the state of the economy. If money growth remains constant, larger federal borrowing just means that there are fewer funds left for private borrowers. A sharp shift toward larger deficits did not prevent the recession of 1953-1954, for example, nor the minirecession of 1967.

In any event, I soon came to understand that political realities overrode such purely intellectual considerations. There is something starkly understandable about red ink. A clear-cut, easily understood means of determining whether or not the government is operating in the red forms its own discipline. It becomes far easier, in the political arena, to argue for restraint when it is possible to say unequivocally that a deficit is a deficit is a deficit. If the President of a "no fiscal nonsense Administration" could rationalize about a budget deficit of $11.6 billion, who could really argue that it was sinful to tack on another 2 or 6 or 8 or 10 billion dollars?

By the fall of 1972, when on a lazy afternoon a billion or two in additional expenditures could be tacked onto an appropriations bill through unprinted floor amendments nicely tailored for their election-year appeal, it became apparent that the federal spending (now estimated to have been more than 265 billion for fiscal 1973) was running dangerously out of hand. The President first urged restraint, then began holding back substantial funds that had already been appropriated. In the wake of his reelection, the President threatened massive vetoes of spending legislation.

It would have been impossible at this late stage for the Congress to retrieve the many appropriations bills already approaching the end of the legislative pipeline in order to apply Congressional judgment to the job of trimming back the excess. So Congress set out to do the next-best thing. It would adopt a ceiling for expenditures in fiscal 1973 and authorize the Executive to cut expenditures to meet that ceiling. On October 13, 1972, the Senate adopted, by a vote of 61 to 11, legislation establishing a $250 billion limit, and gave the President carefully limited authority for achieving the required cuts in spending. The House enacted the same $250 billion ceiling, but granted the President virtually unlimited discretion as to where to do the trimming. Members of the House and Senate met in conference during the hectic last days of the session, but while each side agreed that projected expenditures had to be cut by more than $15 billion, they were unable to agree on the nature of the discretion they would have to delegate to the President in order to achieve this goal. And so the Ninety-second Congress adjourned, having committed the nation to a level of spending that it acknowledged to be dangerously high. Each House had admitted that it was incapable of performing the necessary budgetary surgery, yet they could not agree on the instructions to be given to the only surgeon around, namely the President.

About this time it became fashionable to label the bulk of federal spending "uncontrollable." Most uncontrollable spending, however, is simply the result of creating legislation with automatic, open-ended financing. By fiscal year 1973 this had reached $174.6 billion, or 71 percent of total federal spending. By authorizing more-or-less permanent appropriations, such legislation escapes the annual budgetary review. A similar effect is achieved by setting up certain trust funds and off-budget agencies to provide subsidized credit. Because such spending is mandated by past legislation, there is little room to maneuver under the budget ceiling. But this spending is not really uncontrollable at all, since what Congress does, Congress can undo. It is doubtful that much of the hastily enacted social legislation of the past decade could withstand a detailed cost-benefit analysis to determine who really pays how much for what. But Congress forges ahead, piling new programs on top of old, almost never undoing those past mistakes which inevitably generate their own interest groups to oppose any fundamental reform. One way to weed out programs whose benefits do not justify their costs would be to adopt a zero-based budgeting procedure in which Congress would be required to scrutinize annually the full current and future expenditures of each program, as though starting with a clean slate. But no such fundamental reforms were even considered.

The President moved into the vacuum, and through impoundments and pocket vetoes was able to trim the projected spending by the more than $15 billion that the Congress had declared to be excessive. But since every federal program has its constituency in the Congress, in the bureaucracy, and in the thousand and one categories of recipients of federal favors and largess, the howls of anguish and outrage heard from Maine to Hawaii were entirely predictable. The President had "usurped the powers of Congress"—and never mind the fact that at one time or another Presidents Kennedy and Johnson had impounded larger proportions of appropriated funds.

By the time the Ninety-third Congress convened in January, with the Democratic ranks significantly reinforced, its leadership was determined to reenact every vetoed bill and flush out every impounded dollar, and hang the fiscal consequences. The Democrats settled on a strategy of calling up the most veto-proof measures in rapid order, beginning with the ones with the greatest political appeal. The first was a $3.5 billion bill with the appealing title of Vocational Rehabilitation Act of 1973. Who could possibly be against that? Indeed, it happens that the federal program to rehabilitate the handicapped and put them in productive jobs was one of a half dozen in the entire lexicon of federal programs that could stand the test of cost-benefit scrutiny. Over the past years it had proved enormously effective in helping thousands of persons to recapture their self-confidence and self-respect, and to become contributing members of society. The only problem was that the current offering proposed to expand the program far faster than was possible without substantial waste. It also proposed to add new functions that were wholly unrelated to the job of helping the handicapped help themselves.

Two of us had the temerity to vote against the measure, but when the bill was vetoed, the veto was sustained by the Senate by a vote of 60 to 36. As a result of this, and of the sustaining of vetoes on the next two bills trotted out, the mood in Congress changed. Chairmen of committees began to volunteer retrenchment in bills then under consideration, and there was a far more effective dialogue between Capitol Hill and the White House in negotiating acceptable limits on the cost of a wide range of legislation. The threat of a Presidential veto was given teeth by the willingness of a thin line of legislators to man the barricades of fiscal restraint. To me, this exercise was a telling vindication of the restraints on the Executive and the Congress that have been built into the Constitution.

I should note in passing that the Vocational Rehabilitation Act did not fall victim to this skirmish between the two branches of government concerned. Within a short period, a new vocational rehabilitation bill without the objectionable excesses was introduced and quickly enacted. It provided for a prudent expansion of the program, and was a measure for which I gladly voted.

One happy result of this confrontation was that it forced the Congress to develop machinery that for the first time in recent history could enable it to discharge the responsibilities it had claimed the Executive was usurping. The Congressional Budget and Impoundment Control Act of 1974, which I described in the last chapter, will for the first time require that the Congress review the budget as a whole, rather than have the total emerge from the fragmented decisions of many committees considering each part separately.

It is vitally important that the new Congressional budget machinery work, as it is the Congress and not the President which largely dictates how much we spend, and for what, and what deficits we incur. Yet, because the enabling legislation does not dictate a fiscal policy requiring restraint, and because the budgetary priorities and limits adopted by the Congress may be overturned by a simple majority vote, there are those who are highly skeptical of its success. The powers granted to the new Budget Committees, in order to be effective, will necessarily encroach on those previously exercised by other committees, and it will be interesting to see whether the Congress will be capable of the self-restraint and politically difficult choices that alone will ensure the success of this new effort at developing a coherent Congressional fiscal policy. It is one thing to establish elaborate machinery and quite another to allow it to work.

I can think of no better example of the gulf that divides precept and practice in the life of the Senate than an amendment that was adopted in the summer of 1974 by a vote of 74 to 12. We were then being confronted by a 12 percent annual rate of inflation, and the Senate declared that we would bring inflation under control by placing a ceiling of $295 billion on federal spending in fiscal 1975. Three months later, when the President urged a *specific* measure that could have saved $700 million, a measure that would not have cost a single job or interrupted a single program, but would merely have delayed for ninety days a 5.5 percent increase for a category of Americans (federal employees) who are better paid and more secure in their jobs than most, only 35 Senators were willing to support him.

As the deepening recession of 1974-1975 became the overriding economic concern, all thought of fiscal restraint seemed to go out the window. With virtually no debate, the Congress would enact a multibillion-dollar public service employment program to add still further to our already inflated public payrolls, and to the burden that this imposes on the private sector. Little or no thought was given to alternatives that would have diverted existing federal expenditures to more labor-intensive uses without adding to the whole. In January, 1975, President Ford submitted a budget for fiscal 1976 that projected a chilling deficit of more than $50 billion. By June the Congress had adopted a joint resolution providing for a budget deficit of almost $69 billion, and speculation was that the actual deficit might even reach $100 billion. It was clear that the attention span of those who had finally come to equate the cancer of inflation with chronic overspending was no longer than the time it took public concern over the recession to overtake concern over inflation in the public-opinion polls.

And so we have been drifting from crisis to crisis, each largely of our own making, without any thought to consequences beyond the next year. Because we have no clear understanding of what we are doing, we are building a cycle leading from recession to ever-higher inflation and back again to deeper recession. That can only lead to a deepening sense of frustration among the American people, and even to "devil" theories blaming the political destruction of the economy on business, labor, or the economic system.

It is clear that fiscal responsibility can only be approached from the spending side, not by tax increases. The huge and growing tax burden already threatens the roots of economic progress, namely the ability to accumulate capital and the incentives for its investment at risk. The recent increases in the tax on capital gains have already encouraged the flight of American funds abroad while restricting the sources of venture capital for investment at home. A capital gain reflects the purchaser's assessment of future income to be expected from investing in an asset such as stocks or bonds. Taxing the gain from a sale of stock, for example, is taxing the corporate income a third time—for income is taxed when it is earned by the company, is taxed again when it is paid in dividends to individuals, and since corporate earnings are reflected in the price at which the stock is sold, is taxed again in the form of capital gains when stock is transferred. This greatly increases the amount of pretax income needed to obtain any given return from the use of capital, and therefore greatly discourages productive investments.

A high level of government taxation and regulation also preempts the resources that would otherwise be in private hands, thereby concentrating economic power in government while reducing the funds available for private investment. This problem is compounded by the proliferation of off-budget federal agencies, such as the Export-Import Bank and the Postal Service monopoly, that are allowed to drain funds from capital markets on preferential terms. Money that would otherwise be spent privately in response to the needs defined by voluntary exchange is instead spent by public agencies for purposes defined by Congress to meet political rather than economic goals. Furthermore, as public agencies compete for the funds available in our capital markets (governments at all levels accounted for more than 60 percent of total capital market borrowings in 1974), twin pressures are created, the first being on interest rates, driving them up, and the second on the Federal Reserve Board to expand the money supply to reduce for a short while the pressures on interest rates. The latter is, of course, inflationary, and ultimately results in a premium being added to interest rates to compensate for the shrinking dollar. For such reasons, I cosponsored, with Senators Humphrey and Proxmire, the Senate Resolution adopted in early 1975 directing the Federal Reserve to keep the growth of the supply of money (currency and checking deposits) in line with the long-run growth of the things that money can buy. This measure should place desirable restraints on the Federal Reserve's inflationary expansion of the money supply. But this will also result in higher interest rates unless the Congress imposes on itself an equivalent restraint on federal spending.

It is estimated that over the next ten years the flow of savings will fall some $650 billion (more than a billion dollars a week) short of the sums required to finance moderate economic growth, reduce energy dependence, and clean up our air and water. The *Wall Street Journal* on February 20, 1975, reported we are currently reinvesting a much smaller proportion of our gross national product—less than 20 percent—than almost any other industrial nation. The fact is that our existing tax policies, inflation, and legal ceilings on interest payments to small savers have discouraged the habit of thrift on which our individual and collective prosperity ultimately depends. There is also some evidence that the hand-to-mouth method of financing Social Security benefits from current receipts has had the same effect. People save less because Social Security taxes leave them with less spare income and because they consider Social Security to be a substitute for saving. The trouble is that unlike any other form of saving, whether in savings banks or stocks and bonds, Social Security taxes are not available to finance, say, mortgages, oil wells, or new fertilizer plants. Whatever the exact causes, it is clear that public policies must be formed with the recognition that capitalism needs capital.

In 1929, the total of all government expenditures accounted for less than ten cents out of every dollar of national income. Today, they account for more than 40 percent, with 50 percent on the near horizon. If the growth of transfer payments (such as Social Security and welfare payments) continues at the rate of the past two decades, about 9 percent per year, half of the population will be supporting the other half by the year 2000. In 1929 one out of eleven members of the American work force was employed by government. Today the figure is almost one out of five. We are clearly reaching, if we have not already reached, a point where the overhead imposed by government will exceed the capacity of our economy to support it.

When I first came to Washington, Governor Rockefeller met with members of the New York Congressional delegation to plead the case for general revenue-sharing. He pointed out that with the cost of state and local government growing at an annual rate of 17 percent, its expenses were growing faster than the tax base—namely, property values and the incomes of those employed outside the government. As a result, he said, there was no alternative but to look to Washington. Yet Washington has no significant source of revenues other than the residents of states and localities. And there *was* an alternative—to cut back, and cut back sharply, on the rate at which government is growing. It is absurd to assume that government can grow indefinitely at three or four times the rate of the economy as a whole without destroying the productive sector in the process.

We hear much these days about compassion for the victims of poverty, of discrimination, of wars and famine. We almost never hear, however, of the victims of governmental policies deliberately designed to achieve a rate of inflation that has eaten away the savings of the tens of millions of American men and women who were encouraged to save and to place their confidence in the continuing value of the dollar. I have often thought of the suntanned, silver-haired couples who used to smile out of advertisements in American magazines in the 1940's. The caption would read, "How We Retired at Age 50 on $50 a Month." It is hard to believe that just thirty years ago Americans could be attracted by the promise of a retirement annuity of $600. Such has been the impact of inflationary policies that the American Institute for Economic Research estimates has robbed prudent Americans of more than $1.4 *trillion* in the purchasing power of their savings since 1940.

It was once understood that our economy functioned best and for the good of the greatest number when it was left to the interactions of millions of daily decisions by private investors, manufacturers, sellers, and consumers, each pursuing his own private gain and fulfillment. It was once understood that government would interfere in these decisions only when necessary to protect an overriding and clearly defined public need, and then only to the extent required to meet that need. It was understood that the primary role of government in economic affairs was not to regulate and control the private sector, but to preserve the competitive, stable environment in which that sector could operate with the greatest efficiency and confidence.

But these restraints have yielded to a new regulatory ethic that has gained acceptance on a scale broader than anyone could have conceived of just a few years ago. This new ethic takes as indisputable doctrine the desirability and even the necessity for the federal government to regulate business on an ever-larger scale. It has its own propagandists such as John Kenneth Galbraith; its own shock troops, typified by Ralph Nader; and, as is typical with all essentially ideological movements, its own slogan: The public interest.

Dr. Galbraith, the high priest of a planned economy, has written:

> . . . social pressures build up, politicians respond, so the kinds of action which are required get taken. The action may be disguised by the semantics. It will be some time before we get around to talking about planning. It will be longer, no doubt, before we get around to using so obscene a word as socialism. I sometimes use the phrase "social action," which is more benign. Even talk about income redistribution seems to many people still very odd and dangerous. But circumstances are in the saddle, not theory. . . .

Dr. Galbraith at least exhibits the virtue of candor, and what he writes should serve to remind those in public office who believe as I do that we have a special burden, a special responsibility. It is we, after all, and not a majority of those presently in Congress, who believe that we are drifting with terrible momentum in directions that threaten the political and economic bases of a free society. It is for us, therefore, to take a hand in shaping the "circumstances" of which Dr. Galbraith speaks. This requires that we do our best to inform the public by speaking frankly to the issue even when what we have to say may be unpleasant. We cannot begin to address the very real problems now confronting us unless we are willing to address them honestly and take our chances at the next election. Ultimately the public will decide what course this nation will take, but the public can only exercise its franchise intelligently to the degree that it understands the issues, and we in government must understand that we have the responsibility to cast light upon the issues, and not to sugar-coat them.

The public has become jaded with "politics as usual," and it will take an unusual willingness to speak to the point in order to reenlist the average American into the political process. There is a job of reeducation to be done, and it can't be done by talking around the issues. We need to speak out unapologetically in support of such unfashionable topics as the superiority of capitalism and the rights of private property on which both our economic and political systems depend.

The Founders of the Republic understood that a free man has to be secure in his property as well as in his life and liberty, if he is to be truly able to assert his political independence. The right to property is indispensable to that most precious of all human rights, the right to live one's life in freedom. Property is the means to all our political ends. Those who doubt it should try being an effective dissenter in a country where the sole employer is the State, and where the government "plans" who shall get the paper used in printing the news.

Most Americans still continue to be economically self-sufficient, although increasing numbers are being pushed into a position of dependency, of being wards of a paternal State. The margin of self-sufficiency is becoming dangerously thin for more and more people as it becomes harder and harder for the average wage-earner to save enough after the heavy burden of taxation to allow him to build an adequate cushion against adversity and to provide for his own retirement. Walter Lippmann understood the changes inherent in this trend almost forty years ago as he contemplated the conditions that had delivered Germany and Italy, and threatened to deliver other nations, into the hands of despots:

> The more I see of Europe, the more deeply convinced do I become that the preservation of freedom in America, or anywhere else, depends upon maintaining and restoring for the great majority of individuals the economic means to remain independent individuals. The greatest evil of the modern world is the reduction of the people to a proletarian level by destroying their savings, by depriving them of private property, by making them the helpless employees of a private monopoly or of a government monopoly. At that point they are no longer citizens. They are a mob. For when the people lose this sense of their separate and individual security . . . they are a frightened crowd ready for a master.

Because we have allowed a mentality to grow that looks to government for all the answers, because we have allowed special constituencies to plead successfully for special benefits, because we have lost sight of the root sources of our prosperity, we face major threats to our economic and political well-being. These can be averted only through a willingness to assume the political risks of saying no to new demands while working to slim down the size and authority and cost of the federal establishment. If we prize our liberties, these are risks that those of us in office must be prepared to take.

8
America and the World Outside

I
Vietnam and Its Aftermath

ON THE AFTERNOON of August 21, 1974, I stood on the floor of the Senate, listening to the clerk intone the litany of familiar names as he called the roll. Amid the usual chatter and bustle that mark the Senate Chamber during a roll-call vote, I sensed a serious mood. This vote was one that you know is different, somehow symbolic of issues larger than the specific question being voted on.

When my name was called I cast my vote against a proposed reduction in military aid to South Vietnam. As other Senators came into the chamber to answer aye or no, it soon became apparent that my negative vote was going to be one of a distinct minority. The final vote was an overwhelming 86 to 5 in favor of an appropriations bill, slashing by more than half the Administration's $1.5 billion request for military aid to South Vietnam.

The Senate had repudiated our undertaking, implicit in the Paris Accords of January, 1973, to replace "armaments, munitions and war matériel which have been destroyed . . . or used up after the ceasefire on the basis of piece-for-piece," and in the process created doubt as to the continuing ability of the South Vietnamese to repel mounting attacks by the well-equipped forces of the North.

Two months earlier the Congress had adopted an amend-

185

ment mandating a June 30, 1976, deadline for reducing the number of Americans stationed in Europe by 18,000. This had been offered as a compromise to head off another attempt by Senator Mansfield to secure agreement to an amendment that would have ordered an immediate reduction of 125,000 men. It came at a time when Europeans were expressing increased concern over the reliability of America's commitment to the NATO alliance, when the Soviets were increasing their military strength in Eastern Europe, and when East and West were engaged in negotiations for a mutual and balanced reduction of forces in Central Europe.

By the time the Ninety-third Congress adjourned in December, 1974, it had responded to the challenge to curb inflationary spending by making major cuts in the budget submitted by the Department of Defense while leaving virtually intact or increasing the funding requested by every other department. As a result the amounts available to our armed forces in fiscal 1975 for essential research, development, and procurement were at the lowest levels, in constant dollars, since 1950, and this despite the continuing buildup of Soviet power in every category of strategic and conventional arms.

This is just a sampling of the votes by which the Congress has been signaling a retreat from world responsibilities. It can be argued that these have merely reflected domestic realities. Americans have grown tired of the burdens that come with being a world power. Many long for the days of our innocence, when the security provided by two oceans and the abundance of our resources allowed us to avoid the permanent alliances against which George Washington warned us in his Farewell Address.

But times and circumstances are now profoundly changed. Two world wars have taught us that we cannot long remain uninvolved in major conflicts involving nations with which we have deep historical, cultural and commercial ties; the development of intercontinental weapons no longer allows us the luxury of disarming between major wars; and our growing dependence on foreign sources of raw materials creates a continuing need for us to work for world stability and freedom of access to resources vital to our economy.

Like it or not, we can no longer remain indifferent to developments that threaten the political independence and stability of large areas of the world in which we have significant long-term interests. And because we alone in the western world have the power to safeguard the security and integrity of the West, we have been forced to assume world responsibilities we never sought, but which we cannot avoid.

We are a great power, with all the headaches and responsibilities of one, and we cannot elect to be otherwise without the most serious consequences, not only to ourselves, but to all others who must depend on us. And as the only great power in the West, how we exercise our responsibilities, how we use or fail to use our power, will have the most far-reaching consequences. This is a fact of international life for the United States today, and it is one too few in Congress appreciate.

I will not reexamine here the old arguments as to whether we should have become actively involved in the Vietnam conflict in the first place; or having become engaged, how we ought to have conducted the war. I would only observe that there was nothing impulsive about our involvement in Vietnam. We went in, on a steadily expanding scale, as a result of decisions by three Presidents, the first a Republican, the next two Democrats. Their decisions were concurred in by the leaders of our military forces and by majorities in both houses of Congress. The critical expansion in the magnitude, though not in the essential character, of our involvement took place under the authority of the Tonkin Resolution, which was adopted by a near unanimous vote.* Although it is charged that President Johnson engaged in deception to secure approval of the resolution, the Congress nevertheless continued many years thereafter to appropriate the funds required to support our involvement in the war.

*The first critical change in the character of U.S. involvement in Vietnam took place when President Kennedy transformed what had been an essentially routine military advisory function (of the type carried out in a number of allied countries) into a full-fledged U.S. program to guide the South Vietnamese war effort. This change in function took place slowly and with Congressional approval.

The elected leaders of both parties of our government believed that the southward drive of the North Vietnamese, supported by Communist China and the Soviet Union, threatened to bring all Southeast Asia under Communist control. They were thinking not so much of Laos, Cambodia, and North and South Vietnam, as of a much larger and more significant area extending from Burma and Thailand on the west down through Malaysia and Singapore, across the Indonesian archipelago, and northward to the Philippines. This area consists of more than 1,500,000 square miles and contains one of the strategic waterways of the world, as well as immensely rich mineral resources that are important to the free economies of Asia and increasingly to our own.

Our leaders knew that if this area were to fall into Communist hands, the Communists could outflank India, control the sea routes linking the Indian and Pacific Oceans (and thus at any moment cut the flow of that important segment of world trade), and undoubtedly force withdrawal of our strategic frontier from its present forward position off the Asian Coast to the Marianas and perhaps even to Hawaii. I mention these facts because despite the fate of Indochina, it is important to remind ourselves that we have a continuing stake in the strategically located areas of Southeast Asia.

Having said this, there remains the problem of how best to look after our legitimate national interests not only in Southeast Asia but in other parts of the world, where considerations of geography, resources, and politics combine to create areas of special strategic importance. Our experiences in Korea and Vietnam have served to emphasize some of our limitations. We cannot continue to allow ourselves to be drawn into ground operations in regional conflicts. We seem unwilling to mass the power that might bring such conflicts to a speedy end, and at the same time we do not have the stomach for the attrition of a sustained war.

I believe President Nixon defined the appropriate limits on the future use of American power when he promulgated his Nixon Doctrine at Guam in July, 1969. It was the credibility of this new doctrine that was being tested by the vote to slash promised military aid to South Vietnam. What Mr. Nixon announced at Guam was a fundamental change in the character of the support the United States would henceforth provide regional alliances such as SEATO. Whereas we were once prepared to shoulder virtually the entire burden for regional security, including the commitment of ground forces, henceforward the American role would be to provide the necessary training and military hardware, while maintaining the regional naval and air power required to support indigenous forces fighting in their own defense, and to deter major aggression.

As a businessman who had spent a considerable amount of time in East and Southeast Asia during the fifteen years prior to my election, I knew at first hand the anxiety with which many of our Asian allies met the new doctrine's announcement. They feared that it would prove to be a rhetorical smokescreen designed to hide a withdrawal from the alliances we had forged. I took advantage of my last business trip to the area in June, 1970, to discuss the new developments with officials of the Philippine and Indonesian governments. They told me they fully understood the desirability of this change in American policy. The nations of Southeast Asia were now capable of organizing and fielding their own combat forces—always provided that the United States made available the weapons required to enable them to defend themselves against forces armed by the Communist powers. They left no doubt, however, about their concern over the long-term willingness of the United States to meet this lesser burden. While they declared themselves reassured by the vigor with which we were proceeding to train and equip the South Vietnamese, under the program of Vietnamization that was an integral part of the Nixon Doctrine, they nevertheless wondered whether we were really prepared to sustain the effort over the longer run.

The next development to send shock waves among our Asian allies was the startling announcement in July, 1971, that Henry Kissinger had made a secret trip to Peking, and that President Nixon would be visiting Communist China early the following year. For twenty years the United States had been the architect of a policy of economic and political isolation of the Peking regime. The weak, developing states along the periphery of China had cooperated with the United States on the understanding that we would guarantee their security. Yet, without consultation, we initiated a fundamental change in our relationship with Peking that left many of our allies feeling dangerously exposed.

We were clearly moving into new and uncertain areas of foreign policy, and I decided to revisit Southeast and East Asia, this time as a Senator, to assess how the nations in the area viewed the problems affecting their own security now that they had had a chance to see the Nixon Doctrine in action for more than two years, and to determine how they had been affected by recent significant shifts in our external policies and in the tone of our internal debates. To this end, in January, 1972, I met with senior political and military leaders, as well as private citizens, in the.Philippines, South Vietnam, Cambodia, Laos, Thailand, the Republic of China, Japan, and Korea.

In Saigon, as I spoke to President Thieu and South Vietnamese military officials, I sensed an air of confidence, a satisfaction with the progress of the Vietnamization program, although I could detect a concern as to the continued willingness of our Congress to provide the quality and quantity of military equipment essential to their survival. I recall meeting General Do Cao Tri at his headquarters north of Saigon. He was the best of a new breed of military leaders the Vietnamese were beginning to develop. He had shown a flair for dramatic personal bravery and leadership that infected his men. And he pointed out to me, in matter-of-fact terms, the practical problems he was having to face because we were supplying his forces with equipment inferior to that which the Soviets were providing the North Vietnamese.

I next visited Cambodia, whose capital, Phnom Penh, was then under sporadic attack by Communist insurgents supplied, trained, and led by the North Vietnamese. I recall my interview with President Lon Nol who, though recovering from a stroke, was still in charge of a regime that was supposed to have collapsed within days of the withdrawal of American forces a few weeks earlier from the areas we had occupied during the Cambodian incursion. He was obsessed by the prospect of what he called "cultural genocide"—the destruction of the ancient Khmer tradition—should the insurgents achieve victory. His people would continue the struggle, he said, but they could only do so with our material help.

The next day I was able to see how truly desperate the situation was as I visited Kampong Cham, a town forty-one air miles to the northeast of the capital and less than two miles across the Mekong River from the Chupp Rubber Plantation, which then harbored two North Vietnamese divisions. We had to reach the town by helicopter because Communist units had cut the road from Phnom Penh. I recall looking down on an occupied village. The Communists had constructed barriers across every road leading out of it. I was told they had commandeered its food supplies and manpower. Kampong Cham itself was protected by a ragtag army of local volunteers. I inspected one platoon comprised largely of sixteen- and seventeen-year-old boys equipped with six different types of rifles of European, American, and Chinese manufacture, some of them dating back to before the Second World War. They had had only a few hours of training by Cambodian officers who themselves were only beginning to learn the arts of war.

I knew that these ill-equipped, ill-trained villagers, and tens of thousands of others like them throughout the country, would have to absorb high losses because our Congress had not only imposed a sharp limitation on military aid, but had even forbidden American personnel to train the Cambodians on their own soil. Yet these Cambodians were supposed to stand up to well-trained insurgents equipped with some of the most modern weapons that the Soviet and Chinese arsenals could provide.

My next stop was Thailand, a country which for centuries had managed to maintain its independence through adroit accommodations, and which we have regarded as the keystone to the security of the region. The Thais were facing an increasingly serious problem of insurgency along their northern, northeastern, and southern borders. In two separate incidents during my visit, a total of forty policemen were killed in ambushes in areas where the insurgents had been increasing their control. It was no surprise that the Thais had more than an academic interest in our policies toward Laos and Cambodia, countries with which they share borders extending over 1,500 miles. Nor could they be blamed for their concern over an all-weather highway that the Chinese had by then extended across northern Laos to within thirty miles of their border. It seemed self-evident that the Thais would have to develop effective counterinsurgency forces on a major scale, especially if their eastern neighbors fell under full Communist control.

During a brief visit to Laos, our day was constantly interrupted by bulletins being delivered to Ambassador G. McMurtrie Godley on the progress of a critically important battle just seventy-five miles to the north. That evening, at a small dinner at the Ambassador's residence, Prince Souvanna Phouma spoke with anguish of the restrictions our Congress had placed on military aid and air operations in support of the beleaguered and outnumbered Laotian forces. He feared that his sparsely populated nation of 3,000,000 would eventually be absorbed by the North Vietnamese, whom he and others referred to as the Prussians of Indochina.

Throughout the region, and in South Korea and Taiwan, the concerns were the same. While the Communists continued an unrelenting drive to achieve their ends, we appeared to have become less and less certain of our own objectives, less and less willing to supply our friends with the help they needed to defend themselves against aggression. What I saw was a steady erosion of confidence in the reliability of United States that had been further shaken by President Nixon's announcement of his plans to visit Peking. Although Mr. Nixon had been able to reassure the leaders of the countries I visited that the United States would make no agreements undercutting their security, and that we would not back away from existing commitments, the seeds of doubt had been planted and it would take far more than rhetoric to root them out. There were pervasive fears that, impelled by a new mood of isolationism at home, we would in the end agree to seek accommodations with Peking that would in fact compromise the ultimate security of our allies. As one official put it, "When elephants dance, some mice will be crushed."

I returned from that trip with a far deeper understanding of the nature of the responsibilities we had undertaken, and of the extent to which the lives and fortunes of millions of men and women in remote corners of the earth depended on what we did in the United States. An unprinted amendment adopted by the Senate late in an afternoon with insufficient thought of ultimate consequences could literally mean the difference between the life or death of a country fighting for its survival.

The military aid appropriations bill that sealed the fate of the Republic of South Vietnam, the one adopted so lopsidedly on August 21, 1974, was not surreptitious. There had been sufficient advance notice to allow every member of the Senate to reach a deliberate decision on how he would vote. While the other "patron" signatories to the Paris Accords—the Soviet Union and Communist China—had violated the spirit of the accords (and in the process created still further doubts as to the utility of détente) by the exuberance with which they supplied Hanoi with the most modern weapons even as the North Vietnamese were busily building roads and airports and expanding their forces south of the demilitarized zone in direct violation of the accords, the United States Congress also violated their spirit by placing the South Vietnamese on half rations.

Barry Goldwater made a rhetorical point by proposing an amendment (which he never actually introduced) that would have eliminated military aid to Vietnam altogether. His argument was simple. South Vietnam could not possibly survive on a starvation diet. Therefore the cost of the reduced aid provided for in the Senate appropriations bill could not be justified. Senator Goldwater was, of course, correct. No matter how brave you are, it is impossible to win a battle against a well-armed enemy if your weapons and fuel are not replaced, if you have to hoard your ammunition (toward the end South Vietnamese infantrymen in the 4th Military Region were allotted two grenades per day instead of the usual ten, and twenty-five rounds of artillery ammunition per gun instead of the usual 200), and if you find you cannot concentrate your forces to meet an attack because more than 60 percent of your aircraft are grounded for lack of spare parts.

I say "no matter how brave you are" because of the prevalent myth that the South Vietnamese were unwilling to fight. The wonder is that they continued to fight so long after it became clear that our Congress had decided to abandon them. We find it oh-so-easy to overlook the fact that in the two years between January, 1973 (when the Paris Accords ushered in a "cease-fire"), and January, 1975 (when the North Vietnamese launched major attacks in the highlands in flamboyant violation of the same accords), the South Vietnamese forces had suffered more than 59,000 *killed* out of a population of less than one-tenth that of the United States.

The Republic of South Vietnam has now slipped into history, and its more than 20,000,000 people are now under the Communist rule that so many of them had fought against for more than twenty years at incalculable cost. It will always be arguable whether the South Vietnamese could in the end have maintained their independence even with unstinting material aid from the United States. What cannot be argued is the role Congress played in sealing their fate.

Whether we like it or not, the world viewed the Vietnam war as far more than a fratricidal conflict in a remote corner of Asia. It was seen as a test of wills between the United States on the one hand and the Soviet and Chinese Communists on the other—one which we ultimately failed. We can protest that we ought never have to become involved in Indochina, or that we had already expended more in blood and treasure than ought to have been expected of any outsider. But, unfortunately, the world is more interested in results than explanations, especially those parts of the world that have been asked to place their reliance on America.

The point was made with characteristic tact and clarity in a statement that caught my attention during my 1970 campaign. Abba Eban, then Foreign Minister of Israel, had this to say during the course of an interview on television:

There are two trends in American history: there is the trend toward responsibility and commitment—and there is the trend toward withdrawal and isolation. . . . Now if the argument is for withdrawal and for saying that it doesn't matter if a little country goes under, then this can become an epidemic. . . . On the other hand, if there is a line of principle which says that if there are engagements for the protection of independence of countries, these engagements must be honored to the fullest possible effective extent, then all small countries will be the beneficiaries of that approach. Now, it may be that Vietnam is not a very happy arena in which to put this principle to the test. I'm not entering that question, but I do understand those who say that if you want America to show a spirit of commitment and responsibility in one issue, then you should be careful not to take an attitude of withdrawal and folding up the tent in another. Or, if you do, you should establish the distinctions very carefully and with much logical rationality.

When the Congress decided not to honor our engagement, under the Paris Accords, to replace expended matériel on a one-to-one basis, did we make the necessary distinctions with "logical rationality"? The answer is no, or at least the rationale has proven too obscure for the leaders of the countries who must try to anticipate American intentions, as witness the following reactions to the debacle in Vietnam:

The United States does not have any morals at this point. They have already pulled out from Cambodia and South Vietnam, so we are going to have to depend on ourselves.
—THAILAND FOREIGN MINISTER CHAITICHAI CHOONHAVAN

I believe the danger of the North Korean Communist clique playing with fire is greater this year than ever before.
—SOUTH KOREAN PRESIDENT PARK CHUNG HEE

Japan, too, must rectify her position of having relied excessively on the United States.
—FOREIGN MINISTRY OFFICIAL IN TOKYO

Rather than go through the mincing machine, it makes more sense to seek political and diplomatic solutions.
—SINGAPORE PRIME MINISTER LEE KUAN YEW

Close links with the Communist states are the only ways to ensure our security and survival.
—PHILIPPINE PRESIDENT FERDINAND MARCOS

If Berlin were attacked tomorrow I am not absolutely certain that the United States would intervene.
—KURT BIEDENKOPF, SECRETARY GENERAL OF WEST GERMANY'S CHRISTIAN DEMOCRATIC UNION

These statements were made within a week or two of the fall of Saigon. But it did not take that long for the nations of Asia to begin accommodating to what they perceived to be the new realities. Thailand formally requested that the United States close down its air bases within a year, beginning with the immediate withdrawal of 7,500 men. Stating candidly that his country could no longer afford the luxury of relying on American guarantees, Philippine President Marcos ordered a renegotiation of American basing rights. Indonesia declared a policy of neutrality, while North Korea's President Kim Il Sung started rattling sabers while demanding a withdrawal of American forces stationed in South Korea. Japan sent a special delegation to the United States as part of a major reassessment that some believe could even lead to a decision by Japan to build nuclear arms, an option that the South Koreans are now rumored to have under active consideration as the one reliable means of self-defense. The rollback of American forward bases to the Marianas and Hawaii may come sooner than anticipated by the most avid advocates of the domino theory.

I do not suggest that we can never change either the form or the substance of our relationships with other nations. What I do suggest is that those changes we do make must be made deliberately with their long-range consequences well in mind, and that if we intend to continue a major role in the affairs of Asia or anywhere else, we must place a high premium on maintaining the confidence of those on whose goodwill and cooperation we must rely in our own self-interest.

We have failed a major test, and as a result we may invite others, even more difficult ones, in other areas—Korea, the Middle East, Africa, or even in our own hemisphere. It may take such a test to restore confidence in our ability as a nation to sustain a role of leadership. We may well have to redefine the engagements we are now prepared to honor. But having done so, we will have to satisfy friends and foes alike that we can be relied on to keep them. Unless we do, we will most assuredly undermine the network of alliances on which our foreign policy and world stability have so long depended.

II
The Hazards of Détente

It is in the nature of things that democratic societies will not sustain heavy expenditures for armaments year in and year out except in the face of the most clearly perceived dangers. It is also in the nature of things that self-indulgent societies are predisposed to seize upon almost any prediction of sunny times ahead as reason enough for forgoing present sacrifice. Since most of our friends in Europe are democratic as well as self-indulgent, it was hardly surprising that on a visit to England, Germany, Belgium, and France in January, 1973, I found officials so concerned over the impact on the public of President Nixon's and West German Chancellor Brandt's overtures to the East.

I recall my meeting in Bonn with Georg Leber, the West German Minister of Defense. He was deeply worried. Despite the impressive buildup of Soviet and Warsaw Pact military strength in East Europe, and despite Chancellor Brandt's insistence that the success of his *Ostpolitik* depended on a strengthened NATO alliance, opinion polls had shown an alarming decline in public support for the levels of military expenditures requested by his government. I ran across the same complaint in country after country. If a new era in

East-West relations had dawned, if we had indeed entered upon a "generation of peace," then why should the nations of Western Europe continue to support so heavy a military burden? Given the tenuous parliamentary majorities that existed in so many of the NATO nations, even minor shifts in popular opinion could produce the most profound consequences for the alliance.

I found, during my European visit, that this was not the only danger to emerge from the policy of détente. In all too many ways, in West Germany as well as in the United States, the architects of détente appeared to have become its captives. In their anxiety to protect it, and perhaps to justify themselves, they seemed prepared to make concession after concession to the Communist bloc, and at times would go to outrageous lengths to avoid ruffling Communist sensibilities.

I came across a striking example of the latter when I visited West Berlin, the city that had become a symbol of freedom because of its citizens' heroic resistance to two concerted efforts by the Soviets and the East Germans to starve them into submission.

Shortly after my arrival in the city I found myself at a window on one of the upper floors of a tall office building at the border dividing the eastern and western sectors of the city. I looked down and saw, for the first time, the obscenity that is the Berlin Wall—a broad, ugly gash separating the bustling, noisy life of the free city from the sterile, empty landscape of the Communist sector.

I don't know how many Americans have ever seen this affront to human dignity and freedom, this monument to the brutal facts of life under Communism. It is not, in the usual sense of the word, a wall at all, but a series of barriers. In some places the inner barrier is composed entirely of the fronts of buildings that stand along the line dividing the two Berlins, their doors and windows bricked in; in others, of brick or concrete-block walls topped with glass fragments or well-oiled rollers. Beyond the first barrier is a no-man's-land; beyond that, antitank devices to stop automobiles trying to crash their way through to freedom. The next obstacle consists of a line of barbed-wire and antipersonnel mines, beyond which East German soldiers patrol with dogs, always in the glare of powerful searchlights. Finally, there is the last barrier, the wall facing the West.

It is a wasteland of brutal efficiency. And yet, from time to time, men and women willing to assume any risk in order to escape life in a totalitarian state will attempt to tunnel or crash or climb their way into West Berlin.

In a building a few dozen yards from Checkpoint Charlie, the principal gateway between the Allied and Communist sectors, there is a small museum dedicated to all those who have found their way to freedom or died in the attempt. It is filled with photographs and mementos showing the thousand and one ways in which East Berliners had planned their escapes, and recording the exaltation on the faces of those who succeeded—and the bodies of those who failed. I have seen no more eloquent testimonial to man's will to freedom.

The next day I was informed that the museum at Checkpoint Charlie might have to close down. Apparently, the West Berlin authorities were considering withholding the funds needed to keep it open. I was told that some officials felt the museum presented a commentary on the reality of life under Communism that was inappropriate to the spirit of détente.

Thanks to private contributions, the museum is still there, telling its magnificent story; but now that it no longer receives official support, it has been stripped of a measure of its political symbolism. It no longer stands as testimony to West Berlin's own commitment to freedom. To that extent, East German sensibilities have been spared, but in whose interest I am by no means sure.

In this particular case, no great interest was at stake, but the story does reflect a one-sided preoccupation with détente that time and again has led us to be overanxious to please and overwilling to yield. Time and again, as in the Berlin treaty and in our trade relationships, we have granted the Soviets concrete advantages in return for intangible benefits that have proven ephemeral or promises that are unenforceable. In the case of Berlin, the West made specific concessions differentiating the political status of West Berlin from that of West Germany. This is something the Soviets and the East Germans have long sought as a prelude to the eventual incorporation of West Berlin into the East. Among the benefits won by the Western negotiators was recognition of mutual rights of visitation between the two Berlins, a concession that the East German government promptly rendered meaningless through its power to intimidate. East Germans have the right to visit West Berlin, but virtually none dare exercise it.

Whereas the United States was once pressuring other Western industrialized nations to refrain from trade in items that could strengthen the Soviet Union's military capabilities, today the United States has been taking the lead in urging the removal of items from the proscribed list. While the Soviets will meet the slightest provocation with threats to pick up their marbles and return to the status quo ante détente, we have not, to my knowledge, applied or even threatened any countermeasures despite the most serious breaches of explicit agreements considered central to the policy of détente.

Here I cite the experience of the Yom Kippur War, in October, 1973. Under the terms of an agreement signed by Brezhnev and Nixon in Washington the prior June, each party undertook (a) to advise the other if it had any advance warning of the outbreak of a local war, (b) to try to contain the same, and (c) to cooperate with the other in defusing the conflict before it got out of hand. When Egypt and Syria launched their attacks on Israel just four months later, Brezhnev (a) neglected to inform the United States that he knew an attack was imminent, (b) urged the other Arab states to join in, and (c) immediately shipped huge quantities of arms to Egypt. Did we telegraph our displeasure by embargoing a shipment or two of wheat, or by canceling the Soviet-American space docking program, or by halting the transfer of some item of advanced technology? Absolutely not. To have done so might have upset the Russians and thereby threatened the policy of détente, one of whose primary purposes was to assure the cooperation of the superpowers in keeping local conflagrations from getting out of hand.

The policy of détente, of course, has another larger purpose, and that is to achieve a relaxation of tensions between the superpowers and encourage them to reach for their telephones instead of their missiles anytime they have a serious disagreement. This is a goal most devoutly to be sought, but it begs the question as to whether it is one capable of being sustained over the longer run when one is dealing with a closed, totalitarian society such as the Soviet Union.

I hadn't given the question serious thought until my European trip in January, 1973. But in discussing the forthcoming Conference on Security and Cooperation in Europe with officials in London, Bonn, Brussels, and Paris, I found that they all were making the point that the West's prime objective at the conference should be to open up channels of communication between the *peoples* of Europe and not just their governments. They maintained that only through a freer movement of ideas, information, and people among all the nations of Europe could a common understanding be developed that might place some measure of restraint on even the most authoritarian of governments.

They felt that the forthcoming conference offered the West an unusual opportunity to open a few windows in the Iron Curtain because the Soviets had been so anxious that it be held. It was no secret that the Soviets had two major political objectives they wished to pursue at the CSCE. The first was to achieve formal Western acceptance of the status quo in Eastern Europe, including de facto recognition of a special Soviet sphere of influence. The second was to establish a pan-European entity dominated by the Soviet Union that would exclude the United States and allow the Soviets to apply future pressures for the dismantling of the NATO alliance.

It goes without saying that the Western powers were less than enthusiastic about this particular conference, but because it was the price the Soviets insisted on as a condition for their participation in the negotiations we were seeking for the mutual and balanced reduction of forces in Central Europe, the Western nations decided to go forward with it. At the same time they were determined to exact their pound of political flesh. Specifically, when the Foreign Ministers of the participating nations met in Helsinki to discuss the specific agenda for the CSCE, the Western nations united behind a demand that any agreement include the requirement that the Communist nations loosen their restrictions on the free movement of people, information, and ideas.

Because of the tenacity of the Western bloc, the final recommendations adopted at Helsinki for the conference agenda included a Title III, commonly referred to as "Basket Three," Cooperation in Humanitarian and Other Fields, calling for an expansion of human contacts and for the freer and wider dissemination of information of all kinds—books, newspapers, journals, and, most particularly, radio broadcasts.

Time alone will tell whether the Soviets will accede in any meaningful way to these demands. As of this writing, the nations of Western Europe are holding firm, although I am advised that they are doing so with less than enthusiastic support from the United States.

The effort launched by the West European Foreign Ministers at Helsinki in 1973 makes a point of fundamental importance. Anytime the Soviet Union seeks important concessions from the West that it cannot pay for in tangible coin of comparable value, the West must insist on meaningful political concessions in return. From the point of view of the long-term interests of peace and tranquillity, the most important political concessions the West can seek will be a liberalization of the Soviet structure. Otherwise, the concessions sought by the Soviets will in all likelihood serve only to strengthen their economic or political position, to tighten their grip on their own citizens, and to increase the long-term dangers to the free world. I am not hopeful of a large degree of success in any efforts on our part to liberalize the Soviet system. By the same token, I am not so anxious to accommodate Moscow as to be willing to grant important advantages unless the considerations to be received can be measured in the most tangible terms.

It was, of course, a significant political price that the Congress intended to exact in the fall of 1974 when it enacted long-pending trade legislation linking the grant of most-favored nation status and trade credits to a liberalization of Communist bloc emigration policies. The condition was the outgrowth of an amendment introduced by Senator Jackson in October, 1972, prohibiting preferential treatment to any non-market-economy nation that denied its citizens the right to emigrate. Because it tells us a great deal about the Nixon Administration's single-minded preoccupation with its policy of détente, I believe it worthwhile to elaborate on the history of this amendment.

In 1970 and 1971, while we were preoccupied with the Vietnam war and were suffering from a mild recession, a not-so-mild inflation, and a series of international monetary crises, we badly neglected our relationships with our European trading partners. There were growing pressures for protectionism on both sides of the Atlantic. Congressman James A. Burke of Massachusetts and Senator Vance Hartke of Indiana introduced the legislation I have previously mentioned that would have placed severe restrictions on U.S. investment abroad under the simplistic slogan of stopping the export of jobs. In debates on the Senate floor on almost any economic topic it was commonplace to hear Senators confirm their dedication to the concept of freedom of trade while threatening retaliation against the "nontariff barriers" that Japan and the leading European industrial nations had erected against American goods. (In pointing accusatory fingers overseas, members of Congress conveniently overlooked the host of nontariff barriers that over the years the Congress had legislated against foreign goods.)

Officials in the Nixon Administration and the Common Market expressed concern that the mounting protectionist pressures on both sides of the Atlantic could result in serious setbacks in the liberalization of international trade at a time when there was a growing interdependence of the world's economies. It was considered imperative that a new trade conference be held between the members of the Common Market and the United States. The trade legislation introduced in 1972 would have provided the President with the negotiating authority he needed in order to be able to reach agreement with our trading partners on a great variety of issues. Not only was this legislation important to us economically, but it would permit the elimination of a number of mutual irritants that left unattended could lead to a new wave of protectionism in Western Europe as well as in the United States.

But unfortunately this measure (whose first objective was to improve commercial relationships within the Atlantic community) became embroiled in the politics of détente. Among the several agreements that Richard Nixon and Leonid Brezhnev signed in June, 1972 was one providing for an elimination of special barriers to Soviet-American trade. The Jackson Amendment flew in its teeth by stipulating conditions for their elimination that the Soviets declared to be an unwarranted intrusion into their internal affairs. As the Jackson Amendment ultimately acquired seventy-eight cosponsors, the Administration was faced with an impasse.

President Nixon made it clear that a trade bill that discriminated against the Soviets was unacceptable in light of détente, and the Senate made it equally clear that it would stand fast in its insistence that the Soviets liberalize their emigration policy as a condition for preferential treatment under a new trade bill. And so matters stood for the next two years.

What finally broke the deadlock was a compromise negotiated between Senator Jackson and Secretary of State Kissinger. The terms of the compromise were revealed in two celebrated letters released in October, 1974. In exchange for assurances cited by Secretary Kissinger that the Soviets would allow freedom of emigration and call a halt to their practice of harassing those applying for exit permits, Senator Jackson agreed to modify his amendment so as to permit the extension of credits and most-favored-nation status to the Soviet Union subject to termination within eighteen months if the President could not certify that harassment had ceased and the doors to emigration had been opened.

I was in Moscow the following month, November, 1974, and met with leading dissidents and leaders of the Jewish community. They were deeply worried about how the Jackson compromise would work in practice. Even though only three weeks had elapsed since the release of the Jackson-Kissinger letters, harassment had already been intensified. Telephones had been disconnected, job permits revoked, and individuals arrested for questioning on the most spurious grounds. Every form of intimidation was being employed. What the dissidents feared was that the Soviets would bring such overwhelming pressures to bear on those applying for exit permits that they would dry up the supply of candidates for emigration before the eighteen-month probation period had expired. In the meantime the Soviets would be enjoying all the advantages they sought under the trade bill. The dissidents warned me that we could expect the Soviets to ignore the unwritten understandings on which Secretary Kissinger relied when he made his assurances to Senator Jackson. The Soviets would claim compliance with their unacknowledged undertakings by allowing token emigration while intensifying their internal repression. It was clear that compliance with the conditions imposed by the modified Jackson Amendment would require the most careful monitoring.

On my last day in Moscow I met the man who would be responsible for implementing the "unwritten understandings" on which Secretary Kissinger was relying. He was Minister of the Interior Nikolai Shchelokov, who was in charge not only of Soviet emigration policies, but of the vast network of prison camps described by Aleksandr Solzhenitsyn in *The Gulag Archipelago* and its sequel.

I told the minister that I had sought the interview for several reasons. First, I had been asked to intercede on behalf of a number of Lithuanians and Ukrainians within the Soviet Union who were trying to join relatives now living in the United States. Second, I had been asked to seek the release, on humanitarian grounds, of two political prisoners who were reported to be on the verge of death. Third, I wanted to report the great concern in the United States over reports of intensified religious persecution throughout the Soviet Union. Finally, I wanted the opportunity to convey some idea of how serious the Congress was in its determination to condition trade benefits on a lifting of barriers to emigration. I noted that while he might consider the last-mentioned an internal matter of no concern to outsiders, he would have to concede that it was uniquely our business to stipulate the conditions under which we would ask our taxpayers to finance, on preferential terms, the trade the Soviets were so anxious to have.

Mr. Shchelokov said he would look into the matter of the Lithuanians and Ukrainians seeking to rejoin their families, advised me that all criminals in Soviet prisons received the very best of medical help, and dismissed my concern over religious persecution with the expression, "more dead cats." The Soviet Constitution guaranteed full freedom of religion. Soviet authorities enforced the law. Ergo, the talk about persecution was a lot of nonsense.* When he came to the matter of emigration, the minister looked me in the eye and stated that I must have been talking to malcontents because (a) Soviet law guaranteed the right of emigration and (b) anyone seeking to emigrate is in fact free to do so unless he happens to be in possession of State secrets, in which case a five-year quarantine period must first elapse.† He then asked me to assure members of the Senate that "Soviet leaders are as good as their words."

---

*A few days earlier Dr. Sakharov had given me a grim example of the zeal with which the authorities enforced their laws. Soviet parents are required by statute to encourage in their children the highest regard for socialist ethical and moral standards. Such ethical and moral standards do not permit a belief in the deity. Therefore, parents who teach their children about God are in violation of the law. The Soviets used to enforce this law by jailing a delinquent parent here and there. This is a risk that a deeply religious person is willing to take. In recent days, however, the authorities have adopted another enforcement technique. They remove the children from the offending parents and place them in State orphanages, there to be inculcated in socialist values. This is something that very few parents are prepared to risk.

†The alleged possession of "State secrets" is a reason the authorities commonly give for denying an application for an exit permit. One gutsy "refusenik" (the slang term used in Moscow for those who have been denied permission to leave), a brilliant biochemist by the name of Aleksandr Goldfarb, told me that after his application had been denied for this reason, he had arranged to have his "secret" papers smuggled to the Weisman Institute in Israel. He then wrote the authorities telling them what he had done and demanding that they either try him for treason or let him leave. Six months later I had the great pleasure of seeing a suntanned Aleksandr Goldfarb in Israel. He told me the publicity I had given to this story had helped win him his release.

Now it happens that at the time of the interview I was in possession of a list containing the signatures of 6,000 heads of ethnic German households (representing more than 25,000 men, women, and children) who had been trying to emigrate to West Germany. As most of those listed were farmers and miners living in the Soviet Central Asian Republic of Kazakhstan, it was not likely that they were in possession of many State secrets. Furthermore, just four days earlier I had spoken to dozens of Jews outside the Moscow synagogue who described in detail the harassment to which they had been subjected after applying for permission to emigrate to Israel. They had said there were hundreds of thousands of Jews in Moscow alone who would leave at the first opportunity.

It is a fascinating experience to talk with a man when you know that he knows that you know that what he is telling you is not the truth. It was an instructive exposure to the mentality of our partners in détente.

A few weeks later, when the Jackson Amendment in revised form was finally being debated, I raised the problems of verification, and Senator Jackson agreed to have his Senate Permanent Subcommittee on Investigations undertake responsibility for monitoring on a day-by-day basis independently of the State Department the actual experience of individuals seeking to leave the Soviet Union after enactment of the trade bill. This would be done by maintaining contact with dissident groups in Moscow who, I had been assured, would be able to provide Congress with reasonably accurate estimates of the numbers seeking to emigrate and the treatment accorded those applying for exit permits. When I expressed concern that the Soviets might end up enjoying the benefits of preferential treatment for a period of eighteen months without in any way relaxing their emigration policies, Senator Jackson stated for the record that he had received assurances from President Ford that any benefits extended would be terminated immediately on evidence of bad faith—the kind the Subcommittee on Investigations would be in a position to provide. As I knew these assurances would help dispel some of the fears that had been expressed during my Moscow visit, I immediately contacted the Voice of

America, and a report of the safeguards was broadcast to the Soviet Union.

The response to the adoption of the Jackson Amendment was immediate. The Soviet news agency Tass denied the existence of any understanding on the matter of emigration and made public a letter that Gromyko had handed Kissinger shortly after his exchange of letters with Jackson had been released—a letter, incidentally, that Kissinger neglected to mention in testimony before the Senate Finance Committee in early December when he was describing the nature of the assurances he had received.

A few weeks later, amid rumblings about the precarious state of détente, Moscow repudiated the Nixon-Brezhnev trade agreement on the not unreasonable grounds that it had been scuttled by the Congress. Whether the villain of the piece was the Jackson Amendment or a $300,000,000 limit that had been placed on the credits that could be extended to the Soviet Union, I do not know. What is obvious is that the Congress was treading on extremely sensitive ground, and that the Kremlin has an enormous interest in gaining greater access to American technology.

It is widely recognized that the economic benefits to be derived from expanded Soviet-American trade are not symmetrical, especially when financed with credits unilaterally extended by the United States. While the American economy has relatively little to gain from even a dramatic expansion of Soviet-American trade, the Soviet economy would be immeasurably strengthened by it. The Soviets are in desperate need of our agricultural and consumer goods, but most especially of our agricultural, industrial, and computer technologies. The *Economist* of London has described the contemplated expansion of Western and, in particular, American trade with the Eastern bloc as a "rescue service" to deliver the Soviets and their allies from decades of economic mismanagement. Soviet technology, with the exception of some specialized military areas and a few research-oriented specialties, is primitive in comparison with our own.

That is why the Kremlin is seeking a wholesale transfer of American technology and manufacturing know-how. They don't want to buy our trucks. They instead want us to build them a truck manufacturing facility incorporating our most advanced mass production techniques. And this is precisely what we are doing today, at the mammoth Kama River plant. The Ford Motor Company and other foreign contractors are pooling their engineering, production, and managerial knowledge to create a vast facility that will be able to produce more trucks than all American factories combined, far more than Russia itself can utilize—which suggests that we are helping the Soviets not only to meet their own needs, but to compete with American business and labor for international markets.

So it is in other areas. The Soviets are seeking our help in transferring to their soil the capacity to make quantum jumps in the production of computer components, agricultural equipment, refineries, conventional and atomic power plants, aircraft, and a host of other goods. The Kremlin is under immense pressure to provide the Russian people with a greater variety and quality of consumer goods, but rather than divert any considerable portion of their engineering and scientific and manufacturing resources from the deadly business of developing and producing ever-more sophisticated weapons, they are turning to the West. Under all the circumstances, it is not unreasonable to ask in whose interest it is for us to cooperate with the Russians in meeting their growing consumer demands and in modernizing and strengthening their economy.

The fact is, of course, that irrespective of what we may decide to be the appropriate policy, the Soviets will continue to have access to advanced technology through trade with other Western nations; and to the extent that we are dealing in technologies that are widely held, there is no reason why American firms should not compete for the business. Nor should we adopt so narrow an approach to commercial dealings as to deny the Russians some of the amenities that are a byproduct of the American system—Pepsi-Cola, for example. On the other hand, there are areas in which the United States retains a clear advantage in economically and strategically important technology—advanced computers, agriculture, wide-bodied aircraft, to name a few. Moreover, because it caters to a mass market, American business has developed techniques for manufacturing a host of goods in quantities that other nations cannot match with equivalent efficiency and quality controls. More than any other advanced industrial nation, the United States has been successful in integrating complex systems of technologies into effective functioning units. This is the aspect of American industrial know-how that Soviet planners are most anxious to acquire.

These are important technologies and techniques that we alone are in a position to provide the Soviet Union. After culling out those that have potential military application (an issue in itself with which I will not deal here), we need to ask ourselves on what terms we should be willing to part with them—or, for that matter, the vast quantities of grain that in due course the Soviets will once again require in order to make up for the inherent inefficiences of collectivized farming. I suggest that the stakes are such that we cannot settle for cash or trade alone. We must insist on some form of political coin that can take a variety of forms—anything from a cessation of the jamming of American-supported radio broadcasts (a measure I have recommended in the past), to a lifting of restraints on the free movement of American newsmen within the Soviet Union, to a withdrawal of Soviet submarine tenders from Cuban waters. I concede that in all probability the Soviets would balk at paying the political price asked. What they might be prepared to do, of course, would depend on the value they attach to the technology and goods we are in a position to sell them. But even if we should fail to strike a bargain, we would at least have the satisfaction of putting the lie to Lenin's prediction that when there are only two capitalists left in the world, one of them will sell the rope with which to hang the other.

It is argued that any major expansion of commerce with the Soviet Union will in itself produce important political advantages. By multiplying the areas of collaboration between our countries—commercial, scientific, political, cultural—expanded trade will create incentives to stability. The Soviet

Union will have too many advantageous relationships with the United States to risk upsetting them. I find this reasoning less than compelling. Hitler did not hesitate to risk war with his major trading partners when he felt strong enough to do so. I therefore question the prudence of a policy that would strengthen a known adversary in exchange for intangibles of such unproven value.

It is no doubt because of such statements on my part that *Pravda* has taken to branding me as one of the foremost enemies of détente. It is flattering to be so singled out. I am not sure, however, that I deserve the honor, as I am not at all unsympathetic with the policy—as pursued in Moscow. The Soviets perceive détente (or "coexistence" as they usually call it) as a new phase in the continuing struggle between two competing systems, one that is removed from the arena of potential military confrontation, although they are continuing to prepare for such a contingency. I cannot fault the following statement on the nature of détente that appeared in *Pravda* in May, 1973: "Only naïve people can expect that recognition of the principles of coexistence by the capitalists can weaken the main contradiction of our times between capitalism and socialism, or that the ideological struggle will be weakened." The Russians are obviously serious people with serious objectives, and we owe it to ourselves to understand and respect their view of the "principles of coexistence."

My problem with détente is not so much how it is perceived in Moscow as how it is perceived and pursued in the United States. The Soviet view is consistent with the realities that Communist doctrine and power have imposed on the world scene. Our view, on the other hand, has tended to obscure those realities. We have hailed détente as heralding a generation of peace, a new era in which the superpowers will reason together in their common search for harmony. By making such extravagant claims for détente, we have blinded ourselves to the fact that the ongoing conflict has only been shifted to other arenas. The Cold War may be dead, but the Communist struggle against the "imperialist" world continues. It is one thing to establish useful lines of communication with the major Communist powers. It is something else to proclaim the millennium.

Time has given us a more realistic perspective on détente. The Communist leopards have amply demonstrated that they are not yet prepared to change their spots. We learned this the hard way in the Yom Kippur War which the Soviets did their best to widen; and again in Indochina, where Peking and Moscow refused to use their leverage on Hanoi to exact compliance with the Paris Accords. The euphoria is gone and we are the better for it.

The Nixon-Kissinger policy of détente involved, of course, far more than the opening of doors to the East. It was an exercise in balance-of-power diplomacy that however brilliantly conceived and executed could never provide a base for a long-term, dependable American foreign policy. The reasons for this have nothing to do either with the soundness of their basic concepts or the manner in which they attempted to carry them out. The problem is that balance-of-power diplomacy is inherently unsuited to our political institutions and alien to the American psyche. Such a diplomacy, with its necessary reliance on maneuver and pragmatism, requires a certainty of execution we cannot deliver and a moral neutrality that destroys the basis for continuity.

For better or worse, Americans tend to see things in terms of black and white, whereas the diplomacy of détente, as practiced by its authors, involves a kaleidoscope of grays which by turning and twisting can be formed into patterns that meet immediate goals without any intelligible thread of objective consistency. This is not to say that Nixon and Kissinger did not have long-term strategies, intelligently conceived, for meeting goals to which all Americans would subscribe. Their problem was an excess of subtleties that our system cannot accommodate, given the need for Congressional cooperation and the hazards of Presidential elections. To speak in elementary terms, we Americans need to know who are the good guys, and who are the bad guys. Then, having identified and allied ourselves with the former, we can be reasonably reliable friends and reasonably formidable opponents.

In the post-World War II years, Communism has provided the great divide by which we have decided whom we will work with or against, without being sidetracked by such niceties as to whether this or that regime on *our* side of the divide is democratic or authoritarian, or meets a standard of purity higher than that of the Hague machine in Jersey City. Given the historical record of international troublemaking during the past thirty years or so, it is hard to fault this formulation. Unfortunately, when with an excess of exuberance Richard Nixon rushed to Peking and raised his glass in extravagant toasts to the high priests of Communist China, and then went on to Moscow to pay the same honors to the Soviet leaders in the Kremlin, he undercut the perceived moral basis of a foreign policy which Americans could understand and support, and for which in times of test they were willing to sacrifice.

We are now without a compass of the sort we need to chart a reliable course in international affairs. There is something very unsettling for most Americans, this one included, about a policy that will go to great extremes to confer economic benefits on governments that in turn encourage and supply our opponents in a costly, bloody, undeclared war.

Yes, we need to be able to communicate with all who can have a decisive influence on the shaping of world events. But this does not require that we pretend that those who intend to bury us are our friends or that we pursue policies so morally ambiguous that it becomes impossible to generate the popular and political support that alone can give American foreign policy the coherence and credibility that friend and foe will rely upon and respect.

This is why I declare myself to be a friend of détente—Soviet style.

III
Power and Peace

One of the predictable political effects of Richard Nixon's policy of détente was to undercut further the willingness of Congress to maintain the level of military power that the

President held essential to its success. Time and again, he stressed the fact that he had been able to undertake effective negotiations in Peking and Moscow only because he spoke from a position of unquestioned strength. Only if we maintained that position could we expect to make real progress in the forthcoming negotiations for a mutual and balanced reduction of forces in Central Europe and for prudent limitations on strategic arms. But the exalted expectations that the President himself encouraged with his constant talk about a generation of peace merely gave new ammunition to those who in recent years had been working to cut back almost every area of military spending. When I suggested this at a private meeting with Henry Kissinger, he expressed astonishment that Congress should fail to see the connection between a credible military posture and effective diplomacy; and in so doing, he confirmed my long-held suspicion that one of Kissinger's major weaknesses is his inability to understand the political currents within Congress.

It was his and the President's bad fortune that they had launched a new direction in American foreign policy at a time when we were caught up in a mood of antimilitarism triggered by the growing disenchantment with the Vietnam war. The battle cry of the antimilitarists was the need to "reorder our priorities," by which they meant the need to slash military expenditures so that we might have more money to spend on a vast array of social programs.

When I was first elected to the Senate, it never occurred to me that I would be spending any substantial time on military matters. My interests lay in other directions, and I had assumed (along with most other Americans) that America continued to maintain a comfortable superiority in every category of military power. I was aware, of course, that the Congress had imposed substantial cuts in this or that area of military spending and had long since abandoned its habit of rubber-stamping every request that emanated from the Pentagon. The reassertion of Congressional responsibility was long overdue.

I did question, however, whether the Congress might not be overdoing some of the cutting in substantial part because much of the rhetoric that accompanied it had overtones of a willingness to engage in unilateral disarmament at a time when I did not perceive the world to have grown appreciably safer. Because of these misgivings, and as a result of prodding by the late Frank Meyer of *National Review* and others whose judgment I respected, I decided to look into the facts. This in turn required a course of self-instruction in such exquisitely esoteric fields as nuclear arms and strategy.

What I soon learned was that the very high military budgets of the Vietnam years had gone largely to train, pay, and equip our fighting forces, and to purchase the huge quantities of weapons and munitions that were soon consumed on the battlefield. This had disguised the fact that we had long since reached the limit of our deployment of intercontinental ballistic missiles, had drastically reduced the scope of research and development required to increase the effectiveness of our weapons, had postponed the deployment of more modern arms, and had permitted a serious deterioration in the capacity of our active fleet.

Furthermore, because of the attrition caused by inflation, these cutbacks had been more severe than appeared on the basis of dollar figures alone. We had not simply cut the fat out of military budgets; we had been hacking away at the sinews and muscles as well.

This process of attrition has been allowed to continue to the point where despite the record dollar amount we are now spending for defense we were able to purchase 50 percent less military research and hardware than we did ten years earlier before we became actively involved in the Vietnam war. Over the same period, we reduced the number of our Navy carrier wings from twenty-four to fourteen and reduced the number of our active Navy vessels from 932 to 490.

During this same ten-year period the Soviets had expanded their active naval forces to more than 1,500 combatants (or more than three times ours), outstripped us in both the size and numbers of intercontinental ballistic missiles, overtaken us in the number of submarine-launched ballistic missiles and missile-launching submarines, and outspent us in research and development. They were developing a formidable edge in almost every area of conventional weaponry ranging from tanks to artillery to antiaircraft capability to various classes of short- and medium-range surface-to-surface and surface-to-air missiles.

Now, admittedly, there is no inherent virtue in maintaining a large and costly military establishment or in developing increasingly sophisticated weapons. But the adequacy or inadequacy of a nation's defenses is determined not by considerations of domestic priorities, but by the power relationships within which that nation must operate. And we must keep in mind that in the real world, no country can conduct an effective foreign policy without a military capability which is appropriate to its responsibilities.

In the case of the United States, those responsibilities, since World War II, have been global in scope as they were concerned primarily with the need to contain the outward thrust of the Communist powers. These were responsibilities we did not seek, but which we could not escape, as the only free-world power capable of facing up to the Soviet challenge. In the past we succeeded time and again—witness, for example, the Berlin and Cuban crises—in causing the Soviets to back away from confrontations which might have ignited a major war precisely because we had the overwhelming military power with which to back our positions. The Soviets simply could not risk a test of strength.

For most of the postwar period, the effectiveness of our foreign policy ultimately rested on our so-called nuclear umbrella—our ability to absorb a first strike and still lash out with a nuclear attack that would inflict unacceptable losses on any aggressor. This is what our policy of nuclear deterrence was all about. This is what was called the balance of terror.

The only problem with this thinking is that the Soviets have not been playing the game by our rules. Instead, they have persisted in building land-based and submarine-launched ballistic missiles in sizes and numbers far beyond the requirements of Mr. McNamara's neat formulation of mutual assured destruction, and they have developed a program of evacuation and civil defense that would limit their potential losses to less than 6 percent of their population—a lesser percentage, one should note, than Stalin liquidated in order to consolidate Communist control over the Soviet people.*

Since 1965 the Soviet Union has launched and sustained a truly extraordinary drive to increase and modernize every element of her strategic forces, to the point that when we signed the first-round SALT Accords in May, 1972, they had achieved a momentum that enabled them to bargain for interim limitations that granted them an advantage of roughly 50 percent in the number of intercontinental ballistic missiles (ICBM's), submarine-launched ballistic missiles (SLBM's), and missile-launching submarines. Moreover, as their missiles were significantly larger than our own, and as the accords froze the sizes as well as the numbers of the respective missiles, the Soviets were assured a "throw weight" capacity several times larger than our own.

The conventional wisdom that has dominated strategic debate in the United States for too many years holds that any development of nuclear warheads beyond a certain point, whether by the United States or the Soviet Union, is simply superfluous, representing merely an overkill capacity that is an expensive folly. Yet, the buildup in Soviet capability, at extraordinary cost to the Soviet economy, so far exceeds any plausible requirement for a policy of deterrence that we can only conclude that the Soviet Union has some other purpose in mind.

For an insight into what the Soviets may be thinking about let us assume, as we must, that the Soviets will soon achieve on a production-line basis a level of warhead guidance technology equivalent to what we now have. Because of the very large size of their warheads, this means that they would have the capacity to destroy specific fixed targets. Let us further assume that they were to launch a preemptive strike against our ICBM silos, strategic bomber airfields, and submarine bases. Such a strike would spare most of our population and indus-

*By way of contrast, we might lose upward of 40 percent of our population in a major nuclear strike aimed at our cities.

trial centers and would still leave us with 5 to 10 percent of our ICBM's, perhaps up to half of our strategic bombers, and up to two-thirds of our missile-launching submarines.

What would be our options under such a scenario? Under our doctrine of mutual assured destruction, we have deliberately denied ourselves the accuracy that would enable our missiles, with their smaller warheads, to destroy such military targets as missile silos. We are limited in our response to striking out at cities and industrial centers. If the main Soviet thrust were against France or Japan, is it really plausible that an American President would respond to a counterforce strike that killed relatively few Americans by ordering the destruction of Soviet cities in the certain knowledge that he would be inviting the annihilation of sixty or seventy million Americans and much of our industrial base? It was in order to provide a President with broader options that I introduced, in October, 1971, amendments to a defense bill that would have authorized the research required to improve the accuracy of our strategic missiles so that we could go after military and military-support targets rather than civilian populations. The suggestion that we develop a more discriminate nuclear capability was anathema at the time, and my amendments were handily defeated. In 1974, however, Secretary of Defense Schlesinger requested, and the Congress approved, funding for the kind of research I had earlier proposed.

I do not believe it probable that either the Soviet Union or the United States will ever launch a strategic strike against the other. But this does not diminish in the least the necessity of our having appropriate nuclear weapons in appropriate numbers until such time as we can negotiate realistic and enforceable agreements that will assure genuine parity and enable us to begin mutual reductions in our nuclear stockpiles. Until this is accomplished, what is critically important, and this the Soviets appear to understand, is the perception of the relative strength of the major powers. If we are perceived to be weaker, if our deterrent capacity loses its credibility because it becomes unlikely that we would ever launch a retaliatory strike, then we will see some subtle but important shifts in existing power relationships. This will not only affect our own perception and that of the Soviets as to when and where we will be willing to stand our ground on matters of vital importance. It will also determine the political alignments of other nations. Over the course of the past twenty-five years we have been able to hold together a NATO alliance in reasonable unity of purpose only because our allies could place their confidence in our ability and willingness to provide credible protection against Communist adventurism.

This fact underscores what ought to be our understanding of the principal function of a military establishment, rightly conceived. The prime reason for a strong defense is not so much to be able to win a war as it is to prevent war, especially one of major dimensions. But nuclear warfare becomes unthinkable only insofar as we maintain the conventional strength essential to our needs. Here again, while we have allowed our position to deteriorate, the Soviets have been overtaking us with astonishing determination and speed.

In the field of air defense, for example, the Soviets have deployed several thousand highly effective surface-to-air missile launchers while we have allowed our own air defenses to deteriorate to a point which the *Armed Forces Journal* has described as their weakest condition since 1942.

In Europe the Soviet Union is now capable of fielding over 45,000 modern tanks west of the Ural Mountains, while less than one-fifth that number is available to the NATO forces. While the Soviets have a production capacity of 3,000 tanks per year, ours is down to 460, and we are currently 1,500 short of our own requirements.

In still another area, the Russians have unveiled a whole new series of aircraft, such as the MIG-23 Flogger and the MIG-25 Foxbat, that are eroding the once unchallengeable superiority of American tactical air power.

But the most dramatic advance the Soviet Union has made has been in the expansion of her navy from a small coastal defense force in 1965 to what is today a deep-water navy with a capability for worldwide military action. Furthermore, this modern, rapidly expanding fleet is being serviced by an ever-larger structure of bases that have been established along the west, north, and east coasts of Africa, in the Caribbean and, more recently, in the Indian Ocean. This is a development of profound significance. It has catapulted the Soviet Union for the first time into the position of a truly global power capable of challenging the American Navy in every ocean and of applying diplomatic and military pressures anywhere it chooses.

Thus, while we have been allowing our relative military strength to decline, the Russians have been moving rapidly to establish a position from which they will be able to challenge the West in areas that are of central importance to us.

Let me illustrate the dangers posed by these developments by focusing on just one area in which the superiority of our aircraft and naval forces has played a decisive role in protecting our strategic interests. I speak of the Mediterranean.

In years past we have relied on our European air bases and on the Sixth Fleet to protect the southern flank of NATO and to safeguard our vital interests in the Middle East. The presence of these forces gave the United States unquestioned control over the entire Mediterranean basin, guaranteed our ability to supply Israel with the weapons required for its survival, and dissuaded the Russians from the kind of adventurism that might escalate an Arab-Israeli conflict into a Soviet-American confrontation.

In recent years, however, the balance of forces within the Mediterranean has been shifting dramatically. The Soviet Union has provided the Arab states with a wide variety of the most modern military equipment, some of it superior to anything we have been able to supply the Israelis. Furthermore, while the Sixth Fleet is suffering from growing obsolescence and from the abandonment of American, British, and French bases along northern Africa, the Soviets have been rapidly expanding their own naval forces in the Mediterranean and have been deploying fighter-bomber, and reconnaissance squadrons at air bases in Libya and Algeria. As a result, our margin of superiority in the Mediterranean is being reduced to the vanishing point and with it the effectiveness of the Sixth Fleet as an instrument of American policy.

To complicate matters further, we are now facing the strong possibility of losing the basing rights in Portugal and the Azores that have been essential to our ability to move matériel into the Middle East in times of crisis.

Our concern for the survival of Israel involves far more than a history of friendship between our two countries. It reflects an understanding that the United States' national self-interest is directly involved in Israel's continued ability to protect its own existence. The Middle East remains a strategic crossroads of the first importance. It is the gateway to the enormous oil resources on which the economies of the industrialized nations of the Western world now depend. It is an area that we cannot afford to see fall under the domination of a power hostile to the West; and a strong, independent Israel remains our best guarantee that the Soviet Union will not achieve its ambition of hegemony over the Middle East. Israel, however, cannot survive without an America that remains militarily capable of facing up to the growing Soviet challenge in the eastern Mediterranean.*

The inescapable fact is that unless we modernize and reinforce the Sixth Fleet, and develop weapons that can challenge the increasingly sophisticated arms that the Soviets are able to provide the Arab states, we will find that American foreign policy objectives in the Middle East have become irrelevant because we will be without the means of implementing them.

And once we begin backing down under pressure here and there around the globe, we will court the disaster of a third World War, because aggressor nations seem inevitably to overestimate the readiness of free men to retreat. This was the lesson of the First and Second World Wars, a lesson which we forget at our peril.

Military forces are not a luxury but a necessity. So long as we live in a world in which some nations feel a compulsion to dominate others, we have no choice but to maintain those

*This is something that is lost on too many in Congress who will sign any and every petition reaffirming America's commitment to Israel's survival while routinely voting against the military appropriations that alone will enable the United States to carry out that commitment.

levels of defense that are essential to our survival. We can find no escape in isolationism because great nations are not allowed the luxury of retiring from the world. For great nations, there can be no peace unless they have the power and the will to defend it.

IV
Politics and the Water's Edge

We used to have a saying in this country that "politics stops at the water's edge." Unfortunately this has been forgotten in recent years, perhaps unavoidably so, given the complexity of our involvements in the affairs of the world beyond the water's edge, but I think we ought at least to try to revive it.

Politics stops at the water's edge. What this means is that we, as citizens, ought to judge issues of foreign policy not as political partisans but as Americans. In foreign affairs, the President should act, and be understood as acting, not as the leader of his party but as the leader of the nation. In his intercourse with foreign powers he should be seen as serving the common defense and the common interest and not the defense and interest of his own section, class, or party

This does not mean that there is no room for differences of opinion about issues of foreign policy. In a free country there will always be differences about governmental policy, and to the degree that our involvement in the affairs of the world beyond the water's edge has become complex, it is to be expected that we will rarely find the degree of consensus that we once took for granted.

What we cannot long afford is the sharp divisions on matters of fundamental foreign policy between the Executive and the Congress that have emerged from our Vietnamese experience. The United States must be able to speak to the world with one voice, credibly and consistently, and that voice must necessarily be the President's. But as foreign policy nowadays involves a host of areas requiring Congressional concurrence—military and economic aid, to name the most important—it is necessary that some basis be found for making sure we are at least in accord as to the goals that our foreign policy should seek.

A President, especially if he is of a different political party from that in control of the Congress, ought to have some means of informal consultation with the Congress that would enable him to formulate policy and secure agreement to overall objectives with some assurance that he will not be undercut.

It is the unfortunate fact that today there is virtually no way in which a President can enter into the kind of dialogue that will assure him the support required in the conduct of foreign policy. The Congressional leadership is no longer in a position to speak for the membership, and the Foreign Relations and Armed Services Committees neither represent their respective houses as a whole nor are they effective instruments for the dissemination or transmission of views.

Once again we are caught up by the fact that most members of the House and Senate are too distracted by a thousand and one concerns to be able to concentrate on the handful of areas of truly national concern, of which America's relationships with the outside world are among the most important. And so, while each member of the Congress will have his opinion and cast his vote, only a few, by virtue of committee assignment or personal interest, will have within their grasp the breadth of view and information that can make their opinions and votes truly informed. Somehow we must restore the kind of informed consensus that will enable the United States to resume the role of world leadership that the times require.

Perhaps we can move toward the reestablishment of a common ground if we will focus on certain fundamental goals that in themselves ought not to be controversial.

What are those goals? There is nothing really mysterious about them. The two basic goals of foreign policy are, or surely ought to be, obvious. The first is to protect and defend the nation's security—"to provide for the common defense," to use the words of the Preamble to the Constitution. The second, to defend and promote the national interest and the interests of the citizens. This doesn't mean that we are against the security interests of other nations. On the contrary. Those of us who have confidence in America believe that the security, peace, and well-being of America are bound up with the security, peace, and well-being of all mankind.

Now, it is self-evident—or, at least, it ought to be—that we cannot provide for the nation's defense and interest unless we have the strength to do so. If we do not have military force adequate to meet any possible threat, we will have to yield to those who do. It cannot be otherwise. Unfortunately, in recent years we have allowed this elementary fact to be obscured by talk about national priorities, as if any society has a higher priority than to assure its own survival.

We are told by those who are urging drastic cutbacks in defense spending, the apostles of unilateral disarmament, that we can afford to relax militarily now, because Communism has grown benign, has split into a half dozen pieces. I will not try to analyze here the very complicated historical question of so-called Communist pluralism. But I will call attention to the following fact:

When the chips are down, *every* Communist government lines up against us. Whether the issue is Korea, Taiwan, Cuba, the Dominican Republic, Israel, or Vietnam, every Communist government and every Communist party, beginning with our own, supports the anti-American side. Whatever their differences among themselves, all the Communist states and parties, Leninist, Stalinist, Maoist, Castroite and what-not, are united against us. Those who tell us that the threat from Communism has disappeared prefer to close their eyes to it.

In determining our foreign policy and the military program on which it must rest in the last analysis, we cannot rely on the kind intentions we hope the leaders of other nations will have toward us. We must take into account what other nations are capable of doing to us.

With thousands of nuclear weapons in the hands of a few men in the Soviet Politburo, we cannot afford to assume that there will be no change in policy or in the makeup of the Politburo. The history of U.S.-Soviet relations, in fact, has been remarkable for its lack of stability rather than for its stability, alternating as it has between periods of hostility and accommodation.

But if we are to look for a common thread in Soviet actions and reactions, it is prudence. In crisis after crisis the Soviet Union has generally behaved in a highly prudent manner, exerting force only when confident that its moves would not be challenged. The Soviets felt free to invade Czechoslovakia when assured that the Western powers would take no action to prevent them from doing so. But when faced with the U.S. strategic nuclear alert during the Arab-Israeli conflict in October, 1973, they backed away from their plan to deploy Soviet airborne divisions in the Middle East. What this suggests is that strength begets prudence, and that for the United States, the prudent course is to maintain, now and in the future, sufficient military power to meet any foreseeable threat.

Having agreed on first goals, we can then proceed to work for our other foreign policy objectives—whether they be negotiations for truly symmetrical reductions in strategic arms based on a concept of parity or for a permanent settlement of the tensions in the Middle East—from what Dean Acheson was fond of calling a "position of strength." That phrase, I fear, is unfashionable today. But it seems to me only common sense that any sort of policy, program, or negotiation has a better chance of succeeding if conducted from a position of strength. Certainly you don't get very far when you try to operate from a position of weakness—which is really the point of view of those who still believe it is possible to operate in reliance on the good word of a totalitarian regime.

To summarize, I believe that all of us—political officials, members of Congress, all citizens—should try to deal with issues of foreign policy as Americans, not as political partisans. I believe that the first and basic aim of American foreign policy should be to defend America's security and interests, and that by so doing we will also be making our best contribution to global peace and well-being. I believe that the Communist states continue to be a major and indeed a growing threat to

America. I believe, finally, that an American foreign policy can be successful only if backed up by military strength capable of meeting any present or foreseeable military threat.

These principles are not going to give us an automatic answer to every question of foreign policy that comes along, but they suggest where to look for answers and they give guidelines for testing the answers we come up with.

But perhaps even more important is the underlying attitude and outlook from which we view our country and its place in the world. In foreign affairs, as in our critical domestic problems, I feel that our worst troubles have been self-made. Too many of our citizens, especially too many of our leading citizens, seem to have lost their confidence in America.

Our country is the most powerful, the most dynamic, and, for all its faults and troubles, the most free in the world. It is still, as it has been since its foundation, the symbol for men everywhere of their hope for a freer and better life. If our country fails, that failure will be a disaster for men and women everywhere. They will be left to face the then unchecked global power of the Communist totalitarian state.

This is the measure of the challenge now facing us—a challenge we cannot escape and dare not fail to meet.

9
Who Defines Compassion?

AMONG MY MOST treasured memories of the days immediately following my election are the cries of anguish that emanated from certain quarters at the thought that someone labeled conservative had actually been elected to represent New York State, of all states, in the United States Senate.

The New York *Times*' editors, through gritted teeth, told the world:

> The election of James L. Buckley to the United States Senate is a step backward for New York and a possibly misleading one for the country. . . .
>
> It must be recognized that Mr. Buckley's victory was built on a frank appeal to the frustrations and fears of New Yorkers unhappy about the disordered state of current society and yearning for pat solutions. . . .

The reaction that delights me most, however, one that I have framed in purple and hung on my office wall, appeared in a column in the Long Island newspaper *Newsday* under the title "The Shame of New York."

> It crept in during the night. It was hanging over the city when we awoke yesterday, gray and imponderable, like the fog. Morning became afternoon and still it would not go away, the shame, the burden, the thorny crown of collective guilt. We sat in darkened apartments, Dostoyevskyan, vaguely aware of gray light filtering in through the windows, unable to stir outside, unwilling to face our neighbors, eyes cast down, unseeing. New York! New York had come to this.

227

James Buckley had kept his first campaign promise. He had pledged that the world would not end on the morning after he was elected, and it hadn't. The pushers were still out there near the school kids. The murderers and the rapists were still walking the streets. The public schools were still a scandal. The cost of living was still outrageous. None of the candidates could have changed this. . . . But the Buckley victory added something new, a heavy patina of shame that covered it all; the knowledge that New York voted to turn its back on the afflicted, had voted for bombs instead of bread. . . .

On one dark day New York removed Allard Lowenstein from the House, and placed James Buckley in the Senate. That is enough dirty work for a decade. . . .

Such has been the burden of the label "conservative," at least as it is defined by certified liberals who lay claim to having cornered the market on compassion. Because the liberal gentry so dominate the national media, they have created a set of presumptions of virtue for their positions which force self-confessed conservatives to bear the burden of proof that they are really reasonably decent types who really do care, who don't eat babies.

Consider an article in *Time* magazine immediately following President Ford's nomination of Nelson Rockefeller to the Vice Presidency. After reporting that in his last term as New York's Governor, Rockefeller had made "a calculated shift toward conservatism," the writer proceeded to reassure his readers as follows: "But in his last months in office, Rockefeller demonstrated that his humanitarian instincts were not permanently interred. In succession, he vetoed bills that would have repealed New York's liberal abortion law, prevented busing to achieve racial balance in schools, and prohibited low-cost housing in comfortable Forest Hills."

Now, *Time* notwithstanding, I like to think of myself as both conservative and humanitarian; moreover, in the two years prior to Mr. Rockefeller's nomination, I demonstrated my concern for my fellow man by (a) introducing a constitutional amendment that would prevent the killing of unborn children; (b) publicly siding with the predominantly black teachers and parents of the Mark Twain Junior High School in Coney Island, New York, in expressing my opposition to a court order that would have led to the busing of black children out of their neighborhood school in order to achieve racial balance; and (c) seeking a reconsideration of a large low-cost housing project in Forest Hills that even the New York *Times* considered ill-advised. I believe it is time that political discourse moved from reliance on stereotypes to a more thoughtful and productive level where it is mutually understood that most Americans are in fact humane, and that their disagreements are not so much over broadly stated social goals as they are over the means by which these are to be achieved.

In this connection I believe it useful to recount some of my own experiences, if only to illustrate the difficulties one encounters when one runs against the grain of the prevailing orthodoxies.

I first attracted substantial attention for being allegedly insensitive to human needs, especially those of the poor, when I led the opposition on the Senate floor to the proposal that the federal government institute a wide-ranging child-development program, complete with a national network of day-care centers, that would eventually reach all children in the United States irrespective of the financial status of their parents. I was portrayed by some as a latter-day W. C. Fields, a man who thought that anyone who hated children and small dogs couldn't be all bad.

This "child-development bill" is a classic example of how the most far-reaching and expensive programs can be enacted into law with little or no Congressional understanding of what they are really all about. This new proposal was incorporated into a bill innocently titled A Bill to Provide for the Continuation of Programs Authorized Under the Economic Opportunities Act of 1964, and Other Purposes. It was reported out the day before the Senate recessed in 1971 for its August vacation, and was scheduled for debate immediately upon our return. One of those "other purposes" was Title V, the proposed establishment of so-called comprehensive child-development programs nationwide at a "tune-up" cost of $100,000,000 for the first year, rising to $2 billion the year after, and doubling every two years thereafter to an estimated $20 billion by 1980.

Thanks to an alert "little old lady in tennis shoes" who had followed Title V on its progress through committee, I got wind of what the innocuous-sounding bill contained. My staff and I did the necessary homework during the recess and we were prepared to take it up on the day we returned.

The phrase "comprehensive child-development" may seem innocuous enough. In fact, most members of the Senate assumed it to be little more than a modest extension of existing Head Start programs for the children of the disadvantaged. What was actually proposed, however, was anything but modest. Nor was it limited to the poor. As the name implies, it was truly comprehensive—both as to the number of people to be covered and as to the range of services sought to be provided. As to eligibility, the bill would have covered, immediately, better than 32 percent of the population. And for the future, it proposed to include every child in the nation, without regard to income. Section 501(a) of the bill put it this way:

> The Congress finds that (1) millions of children in the nation are suffering unnecessary harm from the lack of adequate child-development services, particularly during early childhood years;* (2) comprehensive child-development programs, including a full range of health, education, and social services, are essential to the achievement of the nation's children and should be available as a matter of right to all children regardless of economic, social, and family background.

I can best convey the extraordinary sweep of what "full range of health, education, and social services" was intended to include by quoting from the report of the Senate Commit-

---

*On examination, the factual basis for this "finding" evaporated into the vaguest assumptions.

tee on Labor and Public Welfare, which stated that the bill would, among other things, authorize the federal government to establish

> . . . comprehensive physical and mental health, social and cognitive developmental services; food and nutritional services (including family consultation); special programs for minority groups, Indians, and bilingual children; specially designed programs (including after school, summer, weekend, and overnight programs); identification and treatment of physical, mental, and emotional problems, including programs for emotionally disturbed children; prenatal services to reduce malnutrition, infant and maternal mortality, and the incidence of mental retardation; special activities for physically, mentally, and emotionally handicapped children and children with special learning disabilities; training in the fundamentals of child development for family members and prospective parents; use of child advocates to assist children and parents in securing full access to other services; and [as if the foregoing omitted any conceivable area of activity] other activities.

Let there be no mistake about it: This federal comprehensive child-development program would have established the federal government as the most significant arbiter of child-rearing practices in the United States. Moreover, there were certain Orwellian overtones to the proposal that at the very least ought to have sent out warning signals recommending a cautious approach to a program that one of its supporters, Dr. Edward F. Zigler, Director of the U.S. Office of Child Development, candidly described as "a concept quite alien to the American ethos."

My own apprehensions were hardly set at rest when I came across the following words by Dr. Reginald Lourie, a former Director of the Joint Commission on the Mental Health of Children, who testified in favor of the bill during the Senate hearings. Comprehensive child development, he said, should begin as early as possible because, "in the first 18 months of life, the brain is growing faster than it ever will again. It is then also more plastic and most available for appropriate experience and corrective interventions."

I don't know how other parents may react to such a statement, but I am made uneasy, to say the very least, by the thought of government functionaries making "corrective interventions" in the brains of my own children.

An occasional news story confirmed that it was anything but irrational to worry about the "other purposes" that had been tacked on to the extension of the Equal Opportunities Act. One article reported that Dr. Humberto Magera of the Children's Psychiatric Hospital of the University of Michigan warned that such services could become

> . . . dumping places for children who have proven burdensome to some of the new generation of parents. . . . Many young mothers are, of course, totally unaware of the potentially damaging effects of such practices to their children's emotional growth. . . . Such babies . . . as will grow up under inappropriate conditions in the new day-care services will in due time become adolescents. I fear that many of them will be damaged to the point of becoming irretrievable casualties during their own adolescent revolt.

The general impression created by the testimony and by the committee reports of both Houses was that experts were in unanimous agreement as to the desirability of comprehensive child-development. One can read the entire corpus of testimony and the committee reports without once discovering the slightest suggestion of the substantial controversy among professionals over the need for the kind of child-development program for which the bill provided. One would have concluded from the report that experts on early childhood education had risen up as a man to proclaim the virtues of the bill. Yet, the professional literature was and is chock-full of warnings that permanent harm can be done to younger children placed in the impersonal environment of the kind of day-care facility that was apt to result from the legislation.

The silent assumption behind most of the bill's child-development provisions was that mothers were somehow inadequate to the task of caring for their own children, that it was in fact *desirable* for professionals to take over many of the traditional functions of the family. This flew in the face of such carefully researched conclusions as that of John Bowlby, a distinguished British doctor, on the effects of maternal deprivation analyzed in a well-known monograph entitled "Maternal Care and Mental Health." After revealing the extensive research performed by many child specialists, he concluded from the evidence:

> It is plain that, when deprived of maternal care, the child's development is almost always retarded—physically, intellectually, and socially—and that symptoms of physical and mental illness may appear. Such evidence is disquieting, but skeptics may question whether the retardation is permanent and whether the symptoms of illness may not easily be overcome. The retrospective and follow-up studies make it clear that such optimism is not always justified and that some children are gravely damaged for life.

This general conclusion is succinctly corroborated by Dr. Jack Raskin, Director of Seattle's Children's Orthopedic Hospital Psychiatry Service: "There is no good substitute for a mother's presence. The best day-care center in the world cannot begin to compete in this regard with even the average mother."

Another authority in the field, Dr. Dale Meers, child psychoanalyst at Children's Hospital in Washington, D.C., and an authority on international day-care, in testimony before a Senate subcommittee the following year, warned: "There are so many real and significant dangers we know of in institutional type care . . . that this proposal entails a potential and very real danger. To establish day-care centers across the country, without having empirical, psychiatric assessments over some time, is an undue and foolhardy risk."

Meers explained that developmental day-care did have potential value as a *remedial* measure for those children who had been socially deprived, neglected, or handicapped, in order to circumvent developmental decline; but he stated that "in failing to designate that day-care is remedial in its intent, the legislation infers that intact families can securely use such facilities."

It cannot be emphasized enough that Title V was not an antipoverty measure as such, although I happen to believe the children of the poor should be entitled to as much protection from well-intentioned meddling as those of anyone else. The authors of Title V intended that it eventually be universal in its coverage.

It seemed to me that this bill ought to have been recognized as among the most controversial ever presented in the Congress. And, controversy being the lifeblood of electronic journalism, one would have expected extensive coverage of the issues involved. Yet, except for an article here and there, in journals of limited circulation and influence, the discussion of the bill never rose above the assumption that it involved little more than a proposal for day-care centers that would enable poor mothers to find jobs, while providing something akin to Head Start programs to give their children an equal break in life. Those who opposed the measure were generally branded as being against women, the poor, and disadvantaged children.

Fortunately, the bill was vetoed and the veto sustained, primarily on the grounds I have outlined. I was later able to arrange for witnesses to testify at a subcommittee hearing conducted by Senator Walter Mondale in connection with legislation that was more modest in its objectives. Apparently for the first time, Senator Mondale heard authorities with impeccable credentials declare that programs of the kind that the Congress proposed to adopt could do lasting and wide-scale damage to infants "warehoused" under the wrong conditions. As a result, Senator Mondale and I (who occupy the opposite ends of the acceptable political spectrum) have collaborated on a number of provisions now adopted into law that are designed to require minimum safeguards for day-care facilities supported with federal funding.

From time to time a vigilant feminist reminds me that I have still failed to make my humanitarian's case for the most careful scrutiny of all proposals for federal intervention in the field of child development. There is another area in which I have challenged the accepted orthodoxies and in which I think I will fare better. In this case I do not have to rest my argument on findings published in journals on child psychiatry, for my views, I believe, are reinforced by the experience of increasing numbers of Americans who have to face the federal government's headlong pursuit of what can only be described as "reverse discrimination." Department of Labor and HEW zealots call it "affirmative action," but by whatever name, its effect is to turn the civil rights concept of equality of opportunity on its head. It is an issue that is apt to remain with us until the Supreme Court (ideally in a case involving a charge of discrimination against a white, Anglo-Saxon Protestant male) rules squarely on the question.

As is so often the case, the concept of affirmative action was developed with the very highest of motivations as a means by which some people would make sure that other people did right by their fellow men and women. College professors, news commentators, and editorial writers complained increasingly about the fact that we were not achieving our goals of nondiscrimination in hiring practices and job promotions at a fast enough rate, pointing to cases of discrimination in various industries and unions. And, in fact, it remained true that either by virtue of thoughtlessness, or indifference, or custom, or downright conscious discrimination, too many Americans were being denied equal access to economic opportunities.

And so, out of the demands that the majestic powers of the federal government be enlisted to put an end to job discrimination in fact as well as in theory, there developed an enforcement device known as affirmative action. Simply stated, any parties receiving funds under contract with the federal government would be required to do more than just demonstrate that no one had been denied a job or promotion by virtue of race, ethnic origin, or sex. Henceforward they would be required to adopt a program in which they would take affirmative action to make sure, for example, that all qualified black men and women within a given employment market received reasonable notice of job openings and that they had the opportunity to secure those jobs in fair competition on the basis of ability alone.

Setting aside latent fears as to what seems inevitably to happen when federal bureaucrats become too intimately involved in essentially private matters, who could complain about this positive approach to correcting a continuing social wrong? Well, I was soon to find from my mail that a great many people could and did complain. They were complaining not about the principle of affirmative action, but about the way it was being applied. What intrigued me was that, at least initially, the letters came not from the managers of construction firms or factories, but almost exclusively from professors and university administrators. Each letter told of some outrage perpetrated by an HEW bureaucrat, all in the name of affirmative action. I was told in angry and dismayed tones that what we had was not a system that would ensure that qualified men and women, whether they be black, or Mexican-American, or Indian, or Oriental, would be accorded a full opportunity, based on training and ability, to qualify for teaching or administrative posts. Rather, I was told, colleges and universities receiving federal funds under contract were being required to adopt programs that imposed a system of employment quotas on them.

A *quota* system? Surely there must have been a mistake. Quota systems were things out of the dark ages of the American past, when only a specified number of Jews would be allowed in medical schools or a certain percentage of Catholics hired at a given institution. Surely, in these enlightened times, anything remotely approaching quotas would be rejected out of hand as anathema.

I asked the Office for Civil Rights (OCR) of the Department of Health, Education and Welfare to comment on these complaints, as OCR had been assigned the major responsibility for implementing affirmative action programs in the schools. I was referred to a statement by Mr. J. Stanley Pottinger, former Director of OCR, who had been primarily responsible for developing its policy. Mr. Pottinger was, everyone concedes, the most forceful and eloquent proponent of the affirmative action strategy as it was applied to Academe.

Here is how he described it:

> The concept of Affirmative Action requires more than mere neutrality on race and sex. It requires the university to determine whether it has failed to recruit, employ and promote women and minorities commensurate with their availability, even if this failure cannot be traced to specific acts of discrimination by university officials. . . . There must be some form of positive action, along with a schedule for how such actions are to take place, and an honest appraisal of what the plan is likely to yield—an appraisal that the regulations call a "goal."

The charges that affirmative action is a quota system and a form of reverse discrimination are, according to the bureaucracy, unfounded. Or, in Mr. Pottinger's words:

> Every crusade must have its simplistic side—a galvanizing symbol, a bogeyman, a rallying cry. The word "quotas" serves these rhetorical purposes in the present case. Since quotas are not required or permitted by Executive order, they are for the most part a phony issue, but very much an issue nevertheless.

I note in passing that everyone appears to concede that the setting of employment quotas on the basis of sex or ethnic origin or religion cannot be condoned. In speaking for the Office for Civil Rights, Mr. Pottinger in fact suggested that anyone who raises the quota issue is either deliberately misleading the public or does not understand what the government is requiring.

The real issue, of course, was not what we were to call what was happening in our colleges and universities and businesses because of affirmative action directives, but the fact of what was happening. What was happening, no matter what name it may be given, was wrong. It was wrong from the point of view of civil liberties, wrong from the point of view of academic freedom, wrong from the point of view of elementary justice.

Letters written by chairmen of academic departments in colleges and universities were quite clear: *De facto,* if not *de jure,* the effect, if not the stated purpose, of affirmative action programs was to impose employment quotas on universities on the basis of sex, race, and ethnic origin. What else could account for letters containing passages such as these:

> The Faculty of Arts and Sciences of Washington University desires to increase the number of Faculty members who are either women or members of minority groups. . . .

> Your prompt response to my letter of May 12 with four candidates, all of whom seem qualified for our vacancy, is greatly appreciated. Since there is no indication that any of them belongs to one of the minority groups listed, I will be unable to contact them at present.

> Claremont Men's College has a vacancy in its economics department as a result of retirement. We desire to appoint a Black or Chicano, preferably female. . . .

It seemed to me that such letters in and of themselves demonstrated that something was drastically wrong with the idea of affirmative action. Its effect on employment practices was so apparent that any attempt to make a distinction between "goals" and "quotas" became a patent absurdity.

Apologists for the affirmative action system nevertheless persisted in trying to make the distinction by stating that (to quote a White House official during the Nixon Administration) "affirmative action goals are usually arrived at through collaboration between government and private parties, while quotas are imposed arbitrarily upon the employer." This use of the word "collaboration" is an exercise in poetic license exceeding anything since Humpty Dumpty told Alice that words meant what he alone chose them to mean, "neither more nor less." If what was going on (and, at this writing, still is) between the universities and the OCR is "collaboration," then God help them if duress is ever tried. The plain fact is that universities were being bludgeoned into compliance with the OCR's notion of what constitutes an appropriate plan by the threat of withholding federal funds.

I did my best to help New York educational institutions overcome specific impasses created by the OCR's almost fanatic pursuit of its mathematical goal of forcing faculties to reflect the exact ethnic mix of the communities in which they operated—goals whose achievement was made more difficult to assess by New York's civil rights laws making it illegal to list race, religion, or national origin on employment records. (OCR agents were reduced to relying on surnames and visual assessments to determine the degree to which an institution currently matched the ideal.) I helped where I could, and in May, 1973, I took to the floor of the Senate to speak out publicly (I believe it was the first such speech in the Senate), defending colleges and universities against a form of harassment that I believed did violence to the entire concept of individual rights and equality. In so doing, I did far more than those institutions have yet done in their own defense; and this, frankly, has irritated me, for they were asking me to fight their fight without showing the courage to fight it on their own behalf.

Why was this? Because to have done so would have required them to challenge an orthodoxy that was to a large degree the creation of the intellectual community. Professors and social commentators had issued the call for government action to force fair employment goals on mortals less purely motivated than themselves, and they had given birth to governmental excesses that had come home to roost.

And so, despite its unhappy experience, the academic community continues to give basic support to a madness that has perverted the basic meaning of civil rights from a passionate concern over the dignity and rights of individual men and women irrespective of the accident of birth to a preoccupation with individuals as members of groups—groups that are to be given preferences over other groups in a game designed to redress historic wrongs with present ones. In their zeal to catalog the groups to be granted governmental preference, bureaucrats are creating what amounts to a market premium on the ability of individuals to lay claim to membership in one or another of a historically discriminated-against minority.

The Higher Education Guidelines, originally issued by the Department of Health, Education and Welfare, designate the beneficiaries of affirmative action programs as "Negroes, Spanish-surnamed, American Indians and Orientals." Then, in January, 1973, in a Department of Labor proposed regulation entitled Guidelines on Discrimination Because of Religion or National Origin, members of "various religious and ethnic groups, primarily but not exclusively of Eastern, Middle, and Southern European ancestry, such as Jews, Catholics, Italians, Greeks and Slavic groups . . ." were officially designated as victims of discrimination. It is surely only a matter of time before spokesmen for these groups will seek formal inclusion under affirmative action plans.

This pursuit of abstractions beyond the point of absurdity, needless to say, has gone wildly beyond anything the Congress intended when it enacted the Civil Rights Act of 1964, the legislation on which the Department of Labor and HEW claim to base their affirmative action programs. That these departments have indeed twisted the intent of the 1964 Act is testified to by one of its authors, former Congresswoman Edith Green of Oregon, herself a longtime and eloquent champion of equal rights. Here is what Mrs. Green had to say about this bureaucratic mischief:

> In drafting the language of Title IX I never intended it to be interpreted as establishing a quota system. I consider the rhetoric of some in saying, "We don't require quotas, we require goals," as nothing more than a game of semantics. . . .
>
> One of the most damaging things about prejudice, in my view, is that it gives primary value to a group characteristic rather than recognizing the unique individuality of each human being. It does not matter whether this discrimination works in the person's favor or against him. What he or she still loses is the irreplaceable privilege of being looked upon as an individual rather than an anonymous face in the crowd.

As I see it, only genuinely equal opportunity, containing neither advantage nor disadvantage, can provide this. . . .

I made much the same point at a hearing in September, 1974, before the House Special Subcommittee on Education, which was then investigating complaints made by victims of affirmative action. In so doing I made it clear that I drew no distinction between the application of employment quotas to colleges and universities and their application to any other category of employers. All applicants for a given job had an equal right to be judged on the basis of individual qualifications and merit without reference to a computer printout of the racial-ethnic-religious mix represented by the prospective employer's existing payroll.

My testimony produced no plaudits from civil rights activists, but it did result in a stream of letters, telegrams, and signed petitions, all but one expressing agreement with my view that affirmative action programs were discriminatory in practice if not in theory. I was not entirely surprised that none of these communications had come from a college or university, as I had phrased my arguments in terms of human rights rather than academic rights. They came, rather, from men and women employed in what are usually termed the blue collar and white collar fields. Members of unions wrote to me citing specific examples in which they felt they had been discriminated against in terms of employment or advancement because of these programs. They all saw in affirmative action quotas not a system to guarantee equality to compete, but a guarantee of preferential treatment, and they asked why Americans of Spanish ancestry should be granted preference over Americans of Polish, Italian, Irish, or Greek ancestry.

I mention all this to underscore the uncritical nature of so much that passes for compassion these days. Why should official government policy discriminate against the twenty-two-year-old son of a Polish immigrant just because someone else's great-grandfather had discriminated against the great-grandfather of a young black man or woman who has had equal educational opportunities and an equal chance to compete? Is this compassion? I think not, and I know that many Americans agree with me.

Having said all that, I must add that a sense of justice and reality also requires us to acknowledge that a history of past discrimination has had its continuing impact on Americans today. Certain groups, notably black Americans, suffer from the effects of generations of paternalism and dependency. As a result, too many of them are handicapped by a deficiency of certain traditions and skills and self-confidence in commercial and business matters that other minority groups have had and which has enabled them to take full advantage of the dynamics of the American system and to integrate themselves into the economic life of the nation.

I believe that these deficiencies can and ought to be addressed, and for three years I have been working for the adoption of a new approach to government programs to facilitate the financing of certain minority enterprises that will result in a significant expansion of the reservoir of business skills and experience and self-confidence. My proposal would broaden current investment guarantees to cover equity or stock investments as well as loans. An excessive reliance on debt financing (as is currently the case) too often saddles a new enterprise with debt-service costs that can kill the best-conceived venture. Moreover, as a banker is concerned primarily with the security of his loan, he does not have the continuing interest in a new venture that will bring to it the special managerial help that can often save a foundering business. By encouraging equity financing as an alternative to loans, my proposal would open up the normal sources of venture capital, and because the investor acquires a continuing interest in the business, he has every incentive to work with management to ensure its success.

This kind of targeted approach can do much to complete the job of spiritual emancipation and economic integration essential to the achievement of full equality among Americans. There are things that can and ought to be done to enhance the ability of Americans to compete on equal terms. I believe that the kind of assistance I have proposed, which helps individuals acquire the experience to become competitive, is a far cry from protecting them against the consequences of competition which, when stripped of the pieties, is what lies at the heart of affirmative action as it has been put into practice.

I will mention just one other example where my understanding of compassion has flown in the face of conventional orthodoxy.

Shortly after my election, after a campaign when it was routinely assumed that conservatives do not care about human beings, I made a resolve to demonstrate that we do in fact care, are in fact concerned with, the well-being of the least privileged members of American society. During the turbulent period of 1968–1970 we witnessed the extent of the frustration and anger of young Americans, particularly members of minority groups, who could not find employment. Their massive frustration provided kindling for the violence that flared up in our streets. A genuine feeling of despair caused increasing numbers to turn to drugs for escape or as an act of defiance and a means of survival.

In 1972 I voted for those young Americans by voting against a bill to raise the minimum wage for the explicit reason that no provision had been made in the law for teenagers seeking to enter the work force for the first time. In so doing I committed a cardinal political sin. I had voted against a "living wage" for the American working man and woman. That statutory minimum wage levels focused on the statistical needs of the proverbial family of four, and had too often frozen marginal workers out of employment on terms (a) that are socially acceptable and (b) for which they are more than willing to work, was irrelevant.

Armed with the massive evidence that academic economists had compiled, I joined with Senators Peter Dominick and Robert A. Taft, Jr., of the Senate Labor and Public Welfare Committee in insisting that any proposal for raising the minimum wage that did not make special provisions for untrained, inexperienced teen-agers would in fact prove to be antiyoung, antipoor, and antiblack. The evidence was clear. Young people, particularly those from disadvantaged backgrounds, have the greatest difficulty in finding jobs and are among the first to be let go when an employer finds that he must trim his payroll.

There is nothing especially surprising about this. Teenagers who have received no vocational training in school and who are entering the job market for the first time have the least to offer a potential employer. Moreover, many teenagers, especially those who drop out of school, are not attuned to the disciplines that holding a steady job requires. These disciplines include the motivation and ability to get to work on time every day, to take and follow instructions, and to adjust to the other workers and to the routines of business. To those who have been working for many years, these disciplines tend to be taken for granted as natural habits. For a young person who has never worked, they are part of a work ethic that must often be acquired with experience.

This experience, of course, is best acquired under conditions of actual work. Yet, if an arbitrary minimum wage requires an employer to pay an inexperienced worker more than that individual can contribute to the enterprise, that individual simply will not be hired in the first instance.

It was for these reasons that Senators Dominick, Taft, and I urged adoption of a "youth differential" that would have permitted the employment of teen-agers, for limited periods, at rates lower than those that the law itself would adopt as a standard. What we proposed could hardly have been considered as condemning these young men and women to subhuman standards of existence. Sixteen- to eighteen-year-olds, after all, are generally single and live with their families. The effect of requiring them to earn, as a minimum condition of employment, an amount required to keep a family of four above the poverty level was to require them either to be able to earn (under the conditions prevailing in 1972) $1,200 per year more than the poverty level for a single person living in a city or not to work at all.

I have rarely felt so frustrated at having to present my arguments to an empty chamber. I had well-documented facts. Rising minimum wage rates have had the effect of preventing even larger numbers of teen-agers, especially nonwhites, from being able to cross the threshold into the labor force. I pointed out to the three or four Senators on hand to hear me that in the prior year, 1971, general unemployment was at 5.9 percent while the rate among teen-agers was 16.9 percent. This did not tell the entire story, for unemployment rates for minority teen-agers were much higher than for their white contemporaries. In 1971 nonwhites sixteen to nineteen years of age had a 31.7 percent unemployment rate while that of their white contemporaries was 15.5 percent.

Even these statistics understated the real extent of minority youth unemployment. Government unemployment statistics include only those who are actively seeking jobs. There were, however, large numbers of minority youths who were so discouraged over the prospects for work that they did not even bother to look for employment. Indeed, one study estimated that in addition to those listed as officially unemployed, at least another 20 percent of the minority teen-agers in large urban areas desired work but were not actively seeking it.

The situation for minority-group teen-agers reflected a fact that ought to have been self-evident: the more disadvantaged the individual's background, the less apt he was to have at the outset those skills that contribute to productivity. And the statistics bore this out. Economists Sar A. Levitan and Robert Taggart reported: ". . . the employment status of black youths [has] deteriorated significantly relative to that of other groups in the labor force. In 1960 the unemployment rate of nonwhites aged 16 to 24 was 1.6 times that for all youths; by 1970 it was 1.8 times as high. Over the same period the rate of black youth unemployment increased from 3 to 6 times that for all labor-force participants aged 25 years and over." This trend exhibited a gradual increase in the disparity between teen-age unemployment and general unemployment; and within the ranks of teen-agers, between whites and nonwhites it had widened steadily with each increase in minimum wage rates since 1955.

The social implications of these figures ought to have been of the greatest concern. Yet the youth differential amendments we offered were voted down; and because it did not contain such a provision, the 1972 minimum wage bill was vetoed.

The following year, after a youth differential amendment that I had introduced to a new bill had been rejected, I once again voted for black and other teen-agers by voting against a new minimum wage bill. On this occasion I exhausted the patience of the New York *Post*, which has always had a low level of tolerance for what it perceives to be my idiosyncratic ways. In commenting on the fact that the Senate had voted by a margin of 57 to 40 for an increase in the minimum wage, and that five of the six Senators of the tristate area— New York, New Jersey, and Connecticut—had voted with the majority, the *Post* was moved to note editorially that "one did not. Sen. James L. Buckley (C.-R., N.Y.) once again distinguished himself by standing fast for mean-spiritedness." I replied by writing a letter to the *Post* in which I quoted Harvard economist and Nobel Laureate Paul Samuelson: "What good does it do a black youth to know that an employer must pay him $1.60 an hour if the fact that he must be paid that much keeps him from getting a job?" Out of the mouths of liberal economists sometimes comes sense, but the New York *Post*, secure in its righteousness, didn't condescend to try to answer Samuelson's question.

So much for some of my own travails at the hands of those who claim a corner on the humanitarian market. There is, however, one aspect of our tendency to make instant and uncritical assessments on what is right, just, and proper that has profoundly important implications for the process of responsible self-government. It was said of the missionaries who first traveled to Hawaii that they went there to do good and ended up doing well. In quite another sense, too many people in public life today find they can do well politically in direct proportion to their pursuit of the "good" as measured in the most superficial terms. The tragedy of it is that the press does not insist on bringing a truly critical light to bear on the easy assumptions as to what in fact constitutes the good.

Part and parcel of the political art must be to understand

the limitations of the political process. In this context the massive intrusion of the federal government into areas of social services previously considered the exclusive provinces of state and local governments or private organizations has been to create virtually irresistible pressures to sweeten the pot of social services at least every even-numbered year.

The perceptive student of the contemporary American scene Irving Kristol made this point in a *Wall Street Journal* essay:

> This intimate association [of the Congress] with popular opinion is its source of strength in a Constitutional crisis, but it is a source of weakness when it comes to the business of governing. . . . This normal condition has been much aggravated, in recent years, by the development of what David Stockman calls "the social pork barrel." As the federal government has sponsored more and more programs which deliver goods and services for more and more people, each Congressman finds himself more firmly the captive of the particular constituency created by each program. His votes, then, become a series of discrete appeasements, and what they add up to he will not reckon.

With the launching of Lyndon Johnson's War on Poverty, the last barriers to federal intervention were effectively destroyed. There is now no conceivable area of social concern that is considered out-of-bounds to Washington. In the Senate, I have yet to see constitutional objections to a new program seriously considered. Thus, there is no longer any constitutional restraint on the imagination of members of the Congress in proposing still other areas in which the government can "do good."

These factors, in addition to the genuine social concerns that erupted in the 1960's, have resulted in an extraordinary growth in the amount of federal funds that have been devoted to "human resources." And this in turn has created a wholly new, well-financed, and articulate constituency that has sprung into being in order to supply and service these new programs.

A quick glance at the charts in the Ford Administration's *The United States Budget in Brief* for fiscal year 1976 reveals the astonishing rate of growth of federal services that were virtually nonexistent twenty years ago. In the ten years from fiscal 1966 through 1975, aggregate outlays for education, manpower and social services, health, and public assistance rose from $11 billion to almost $60 billion. These have become, quite clearly, the fastest-growing areas within the federal budget—with the honors going to the food stamp program, over half of whose current beneficiaries have incomes above the poverty line. Launched in 1964 at a cost of $26 million, expenditures for the program reached $2.3 billion in 1974 and will cost an estimated $4.3 billion in 1975.

These programs support armies of well-paid bureaucrats, and a whole new multibillion-dollar industry of corporations and consulting firms that supply and service them. We have, in short, developed what might be called a "welfare-industrial complex" that has an enormous financial stake in their growth and proliferation. If we add in the growth of federal contributions to education generally (from $868 million in 1960 to $6.9 billion in fiscal 1975), we have some measure of the extent of the "knowledge and services" economy's vested interest in expanded federal budgets in the areas of welfare and education.

Therefore, in assessing the strength and influence of the political constituencies of each new social program created by the Congress, we must count not just the numbers of intended beneficiaries, but the enormous influence and wealth of the interests that are their indirect beneficiaries—interests that can play an extraordinarily persuasive role in defining the areas of "compassion" they are called upon to service.

This phenomenon must be understood, because it is the virtually uncontrolled growth of social and educational programs that has placed the ultimate strain on fiscal prudence and that has invaded the last areas that have been reserved to the states. The runaway growth of these new areas of federal activity has become a major threat both to the concept of Federalism and to economic stability.

Unfortunately it will be anything but easy to bring this situation under control. We will not be able to initiate the necessary reforms until we develop a clearer understanding of what is actually being done in the name of compassion, and until we begin developing a little compassion for the hardpressed men and women whose earnings are taxed, and savings depreciated, in order to pay the skyrocketing costs of social services.

If we are to maintain the long-term fiscal solvency required to meet essential humanitarian needs, and if we are not to jeopardize that political system that has provided us with such great individual freedom and opportunity, we will have to muster up the courage to review the whole spectrum of federal social programs. There is something patently wrong about a food stamp program so loosely structured that 25 percent of the population of the world's most affluent society are entitled to participate in it; something manifestly unjust about a federal welfare system that enables some families on public assistance to live better than others who are earning their own way.

To reassess the federal role does not mean that we intend to condemn the elderly, the sick, the handicapped, those with dependent children, and those who cannot find work to lives of helpless penury. It does mean that we must rediscover the fact that other levels of government, and a whole host of private charitable institutions, can and do fill their needs, and that in most instances they can do so satisfactorily at a lower cost to society as a whole. This was nowhere better demonstrated than in California where, as I have described elsewhere, a determined Governor was able to secure exemption from federal regulations and guidelines and was thereby able to reduce dramatically the cost of welfare and reverse the growth in welfare rolls while increasing individual benefits to the needy.

We must reject the slander that the average American cannot be trusted to look after the less fortunate, and that we must, in effect, circumvent the democratic process by referring humanitarian matters to the level of government that is the least subject to the control of the electorate. The whole history of our nation argues to the contrary. In time, however, this slander can take on the coloration of truth. A natural consequence of a transfer of increasing responsibility to Washington for every area of social concern is to relieve our-selves individually and as communities of any feeling of residual responsibility for the manner in which these concerns are met. We will encourage a retreat from individual involvement in the problems and needs of others that must inevitably reflect itself in the quality of services delivered at every level and in our own quality as human beings.

Who defines compassion? I will not presume to do so. Nor will I impugn the motives or humanity of those who disagree with me on how we can best meet the needs of those who are unable to care for themselves. My concern is that we not lose sight of the fact that while man has many needs—for food, shelter, and clothing—he also has a need for freedom and self-fulfillment. I hope this is a proposition with which all men of goodwill can agree.

10
Federalism: The Problems of Reform

EVERYONE, IT SEEMS, agrees on the need to restore the vigor of our federal system. But few do anything about it, perhaps because a substantial number of those who routinely make their offerings at the altar of American Federalism are also among those who for more than a generation have been chipping away at its foundations.

The Congress as now constituted will do little more than pay Fourth of July lip-service to the idea that the states ought to have wider real responsibilities restored to them. Old attitudes die hard; and I had never assumed, when elected in 1970, that it would be an easy matter to persuade a majority of the Congress that they had been wrong, wrong, wrong these many years. Rather, I had hoped to help form part of a coalition that would fight rearguard actions here, and possibly make small advances there, while waiting for our ranks to be reinforced in succeeding elections.

But I have discovered over the past few years, even without the setbacks of the 1974 Congressional elections, that the road to reform of the federal system is far rockier than I had ever imagined. We have created over the years a web of dependency on Washington that makes impossible any sudden withdrawal of the federal presence. As a practical matter, there simply is no way to legislate a quick return to square one in those areas from which we need to extricate Washington.

In 1974, when there was widespread support, at least in the abstract, for holding the line on federal expenditures in

251

order to bring inflation under some sort of control, minor cutbacks were instituted in a number of federal programs. Almost overnight, platoons of amateur lobbyists descended on every Congressional office in Washington. It seemed that there was not a library, or theater, or private hospital, or research program, or sewer, or minipark, or program for the handicapped, or drug rehabilitation center, or school for guide dogs for the blind, that was not about to be put out of business because of unexpected reductions in federal funding.

The practical problems these groups faced were real and the work most of them were engaged in was clearly worthwhile. Many of them had, during most of their existences, gone about their good works without any assistance from Uncle Sam. Eventually, however, the Congress had enacted programs in which they could qualify for funding; and like good, resourceful Americans, qualify they did. They began to tailor their financing and budgets to the expectation of federal largess; and when, for economic and political reasons wholly unrelated to the merits of their particular programs, Washington decided to restrict their funding, they were faced with genuine emergencies.

Each of the recipient groups—many public, many others private—had traded off some measure of their autonomy in exchange for federal favors. Many of the programs in which they were participating ought never to have been initiated. But all of this was now irrelevant. They faced financial crises. And this underscored something I hadn't sufficiently appreciated. In recent years an extraordinarily large segment of American life had been brought within the net of federal financing. It isn't just the mayors and county executives and school boards who now have an important financial stake in federal programs. There is a vast private constituency as well, and these private organizations tend to draw as their directors and trustees some of the most influential citizens in their respective communities. They may abhor in principle the extension of federal power, but they panic at the prospect of any curtailment of federal help in their own particular cases. It is clear, then, that there is no easy cure to this relatively new dependency on Washington. A cure, however, must be found before the withdrawal symptoms become too difficult to face.

I recall my delight when, in attending my first State of the Union address, on January 22, 1971, I heard Richard Nixon's call to ". . . reverse the flow of power and resources from the states and communities to Washington, and start power and resources flowing back from Washington to the states and communities and, more important, to the people all across America. . . ."

This was a historic moment. For the first time in half a century a President of the United States had recognized that we had centralized power to a dangerous degree. President Nixon had adopted as explicit policy the need to restore the authority, responsibility, and vigor of state and local governments. I rejoiced in his announced purpose while disagreeing with some of his specific proposals for achieving a redistribution of governmental responsibilities.

Programmatically, Nixon proposed to implement his New American Revolution through twin programs whose very distinct character was obscured through the use of the common term "revenue-sharing." Under the *general* revenue-sharing proposal, tax dollars collected by the federal government would be recycled back to state and local governments for use at their discretion with a minimum of federal strings attached. Under a package of *special* revenue-sharing proposals funds currently being distributed to state and local governments under more than 100 different programs would continue to be disbursed, but without the attendant federal regulations, directives, and limitations so long as the funds were spent for broadly defined objectives such as housing, urban development, and education.

The revenue-sharing proposals were designed, each in its own way, to short-circuit the kinds of bureaucratic interference and frustrations and costs of which state and local authorities had long been complaining. I found myself an enthusiastic advocate of special revenue-sharing but highly skeptical of general revenue-sharing, which was proposed as an emergency measure in response to the acute financial squeeze then being undergone by local governments throughout the country. Because emergency measures tend to become permanent, the longer view had to be taken in considering this measure.

In my maiden speech on the Senate floor I expressed my misgivings over the Administration proposal and submitted an alternative. The good intentions of general revenue-sharing didn't alter the fact that in practice it violated an important principle of responsible government: the requirement that those who authorize a spending program justify the level of taxation needed to finance it. While this restraint is somewhat theoretical at the national level, it is real at levels of government closer to the taxpayer. It was on this basis that the first attempt at revenue-sharing was defeated more than 140 years ago, when President Jackson vetoed a bill that would have distributed a federal surplus to the states. In his veto message he stated:

> I am quite sure that the intelligent people of our several states will be satisfied, on a little reflection, that it is neither wise nor safe to release the members of their local legislatures from the responsibility of levying the taxes necessary to support their state governments and vest it in Congress, over most of whose members they have no control.

If the general revenue-sharing proposal were to be adopted as a permanent feature of the federal landscape, we would institutionalize a permanent division in the responsibility for the collection of revenues and the responsibility for their expenditure. We would establish a precedent that would encourage state and local officials, at little or no political cost to themselves, to mobilize pressures to pass on to the Congress the responsibility for financing an ever-larger share of their own budgets. In time, this could only lead to an erosion of fiscal restraint while helping to perpetuate the myth that monies dispensed by Washington come from sources other than the pockets of the people who had elected those same state and local officials. In the case of New York, this kind of program was bound to be a losing proposition. New Yorkers were bound to pay more in federal taxes than they would receive back under any scheme of distribution that was likely to be adopted.

The alternative I proposed, which went by the rather clumsy title of revenue-shifting, would have substituted a mechanism that could have provided the financial relief being sought by local governments in the wake of the 1970–1971 recession without incurring the dangers that I described. It recognized that about the only area where the federal government can justifiably claim to be efficient is in the collection of taxes. My proposal would have achieved the Administration's principal objective by reducing federal tax receipts by the $5 billion per annum intended to be returned to the states through a cut in personal income tax rates, while simultaneously authorizing the Internal Revenue Service to collect on behalf of each state the savings in federal income taxes which were realized by its citizens. It would be up to each state to decide whether to allow its citizens to enjoy the benefit of the reduction in federal income taxes or to require that part or all of the savings be paid to the state. In this manner each state would have retained ultimate responsibility for the amount of the taxes collected from its citizens for state purposes. In effect, my proposal would have allowed the states to "piggyback" on the highly efficient federal tax-collection system in much the same way that Canadian provincial governments do today.

I had introduced my bill on April 20, 1971, three months after being sworn in. Because of the reservations I expressed over the general revenue-sharing concept, I soon received a thorough course of study in the fiscal problems being faced by every city, county, and hamlet in New York State. In meetings with delegation after delegation of worried officials from every part of the state I learned for the first time the full dimensions of the practical difficulties they faced.

The problem was simply this: Over the years, both the federal government in Washington and the state government in Albany had developed a habit of mandating expenditures to lower levels of government without bothering to ask where they would get the funds with which to meet their new responsibilities. Yet, by state law, the counties and municipalities had a highly restricted tax base on which to draw. With some exceptions, such as New York City, these were largely limited to real property taxes. Whereas this was a sufficient base to support such services as education and police, it was proving totally inadequate to meet the added demands imposed by such programs as medicaid and welfare. The result was that the cost of local government had expanded far more rapidly than had the property, sales, and other non-income-tax bases on which local governments had traditionally depended. As a consequence many counties and municipalities found themselves at the practical limits of their taxing capabilities while having no power to control the rise in the costs that had been mandated to them, principally by the federal government.

Ultimately, and with great misgivings, I decided that the practical problems faced by these governments through no fault of their own justified the relief contained in the general revenue-sharing bill that was adopted as an emergency program in September, 1972. I voted for the bill at the urging of virtually every responsible official of the cities, counties, and municipalities of New York State. I pointed out, however, that I opposed the permanent adoption of general revenue-sharing. The bill was an expensive way for New Yorkers to overcome their institutional difficulties, because over the five-year life of the program they would be contributing to Washington $460 million more in taxes than they would receive back.

I reasoned that the time bought at this expense could be used to achieve a more rational distribution of governmental responsibilities and taxing powers within the state. Unfortunately, as of this writing, pressures to transform this "emergency" program into a permanent fixture are mounting, and no concerted effort has been made to bring the taxing powers and spending obligations of local governments into better balance. In the meantime pressures are also mounting to attach more substantial strings to the expenditures of funds distributed under any future extension of general revenue-sharing.

The Nixon Administration's special revenue-sharing proposals had a purpose quite different from that of injecting funds into the fiscal bloodstreams of state and local governments without any apparent cost to their taxpayers. They were intended, instead, to do away with 108 federal grant-in-aid programs in six general areas while continuing the flow of funds that state and local governments have been receiving under them. All that would be required of the recipient governments is that the monies distributed to them be expended to advance the broadly stated objectives of the respective special revenue-sharing programs. This approach would allow an immediate substitution of local judgments and priorities for those previously imposed by federal functionaries in charge of the programs that were being discontinued. It would begin the job of dismantling segments of the existing national bureaucracy without inviting the fiscal traumas that would result from an abrupt cutting off of the federal funds that state and local governments had come to depend upon.

I enthusiastically supported these special revenue-sharing programs as being essential first steps toward what could be developed into a long-term, conscious plan to disengage the federal government from unwarranted intrusions into areas more appropriately left to state and local governments.

But the special revenue-sharing proposals were never enacted. They were early casualties of the Watergate affair. The necessary attention had not been devoted to thinking through the mechanical problems involved in their implementation, and the mere invocation of the principle that "government closest to the people is best" was not a substitute for a detailed analysis of the practical difficulties to be faced.

When I studied the details of the Nixon Administration's Better Communities Act (which was to take the place of a number of grant-in-aid programs designed to meet urban problems), I found that no thought had been given to the problems of transition. For one thing, our state and local officials have no clear idea of how much federal money is flowing into their respective jurisdictions, and for what purposes. Thus when faced with a specific proposal, such as the

Better Communities Act, calling for the abrupt termination of a number of existing programs, the mayors of our cities had no way of anticipating the specific consequences of its adoption. Even though they were assured that the flow of gross funding would be continued, they had no quick way of determining whether they could be prepared in time to take over the necessary responsibilities. The practical difficulties to be overcome in any special revenue-sharing plan are illustrated by a statement made by Major Robert K. Walker of Chattanooga, Tennessee:

> Right after I took office in March 1971, I asked for a list of all categorical grant-in-aid programs. No such list was available. Then I asked for a list of what categorical grant-in-aid programs were operating in Chattanooga. No such list was available. Then I asked for information on the exact federal dollar input into Chattanooga. That wasn't available either. Then I asked for an outline of the Chattanooga review process through which our grant applications and funds passed. That wasn't available and our people here said it was handled on an ad hoc basis, if at all.

It should have been obvious that before special revenue-sharing programs were put into effect, a period of time would have to be assigned in which an inventory could be made of all the programs that would be affected by a termination of federal funding within each jurisdiction. Time would also have to be allowed for local machinery to be established with the capacity of first assessing the relative merit of individual programs and then taking over the supervision of those that were to be continued after Washington bowed out.

This inattention to detail cost the Administration much of the support it should have had from state and local officials, who while approving of special revenue-sharing in principle were reluctant to commit themselves to any specific proposal. Furthermore, by allowing the Better Communities Act to become embroiled in its highly controversial attempt to exterminate the Office of Economic Opportunity and its Community Action Agency by executive fiat, the Nixon Administration generated unnecessary opposition to one of the most important mechanisms for reversing the flow of authority to Washington.

General and special revenue-sharing—these proposals illustrate the problems we now face in trying to restore a healthy Federalism in which each level of government is allowed to discharge its own responsibilities without dictation from "higher" and often less competent levels of government. If and when the necessary Congressional majorities are mobilized behind a comprehensive effort to restore a vigorous federal system, an essential first step will be to reexamine which levels of government ought to be doing what. I say "reexamine" because the Supreme Court has long since dismantled the traditional constitutional barriers limiting the scope of federal responsibility.

We will therefore have to start essentially anew in assigning areas of governmental responsibility, and this could be for the best. The nation, our technology, and the habits of our people have developed in ways that those who authored the Constitution could not possibly have anticipated. A new Federalism would be built on the firmest ground if it were based on a contemporary appraisal of which responsibilities a national government is uniquely competent to handle, and which lie within the competence of the states. Once the areas of respective responsibility have been redefined, however, all hands would have to be required to take blood oaths, binding on their successors, to resist a natural impulse on the one hand for the federal government to intrude into the business of the states as redefined, and, on the other, for the states to go panhandling to Washington every time they run into financial problems or find it politically expedient to pass the buck.

What I am basically proposing is that we consciously apply to a reassessment of government at all levels an ancient doctrine known as the Rule of Subsidiarity. It states, in effect, that each governmental responsibility should be relegated to the lowest level of government competent to handle it. There will always be argument as to where the line of competence is to be drawn with respect to any particular function, but as a general proposition it not only provides useful guidance as to how to go about assigning responsibilities, but it does so in a manner consistent with our own historic practices. The doctrine's conscious application would ensure that the greatest number of responsibilities are exercised by the levels of government that are the closest to the governed.

The Rule of Subsidiarity acknowledges a natural hierarchy of responsibilities, private as well as governmental, that we would do well to keep in mind if we should ever become serious about restoring a more healthy distribution of governmental power within the country while reducing its overall size and cost. I can think of no area of reform that is more important to the future welfare of the American Republic. The kind of reassessment that is needed will not occur, however, unless we see a return of confidence in Congress in both the ability of state and local governments to do their jobs in a relatively efficient way and in the inherent merits and strengths of a federal system. After four years in Washington I have yet to see any hard evidence of exceptional competence that flows from centralized direction at the federal level, but I have seen ample evidence—some of it detailed in this book—of the problems created in the attempt. However, the value of Federalism rests on far more than an assessment of relative efficiency.

The Spring, 1974, issue of the quarterly *The Public Interest* contained an article by Daniel J. Elazar, "The New Federalism: Can the States Be Trusted?" that made the following compelling case for localism:

> There are those who assert that, since the national government is in many respects as close to the people as local government, there is no need to sacrifice the virtues of national uniformity for the will-o'-the-wisp of local control. Given the ease of nationwide communications today, it is reasonable to argue that national political figures can reach out to their constituents in ways that make them better known than their state and local counterparts. At the same time, however, one-way communication through the media is not the only

—or even the best—measure of closeness. Granted that more people watch the President on television than the mayor, it is still questionable whether sheer visibility without the possibilities of interaction constitutes "closeness" in the sense that a democracy requires. Moreover, the sheer size of the national bureaucracy creates a degree of remoteness, inefficiency, and waste that rivals that of the least professionalized state government.

But efficiency is by no means the only value involved here. Part of the strength of the American political system derives from our understanding that where men are free it is not always necessary to use direct national action to achieve national goals. Often, they can be as effectively achieved through local or state action, and in such cases the results are almost certain to be more enduring because the decisions are more solidly rooted in public opinion. The history of the great innovations in the American Federal System affirms the truth of this proposition. . . .

Increasingly, it would seem, we are rediscovering the special virtues of local self-government which the Founding Fathers understood so well. . . .

If such a rediscovery is to result in a return to local responsibility, we will also have to explode the myth that money is generated in Washington at no expense to the taxpayers of the several states. There is, in fact, no source of revenue available to the federal government, other than tariffs, that is not also available to state governments. All states are the losers when tax funds are recycled in the form of federal grants-in-aid that are accompanied by a tangle of regulations that distort priorities, encourage waste, and reduce state and local governments to the status of clerks for the federal establishment. On a purely cash basis, even those states that receive a larger percentage of federal grants than their citizens contribute as a percentage of total federal revenues are apt to be net worse off. Too much is consumed in overhead expenses in Washington in processing applications and superintending the redistribution of funds, and at the state and local levels in lobbying and qualifying for federal grants. Quite clearly it is to the net financial advantage of the taxpayers of a majority of the states to have the federal government cut back on the funding of those programs the states are competent to handle on their own, if the retrenchment in the size of the federal operation is translated into a reduction in federal tax collections.

Let me use my own state of New York as an example of something that is becoming increasingly typical. Whereas New York was once among the "havingest" of the have states, a combination of factors, including New York's increasing skill in hustling the federal dollar, has resulted in the state's receipt of approximately the same overall percentage of the funds distributed by federal programs as it contributes to federal revenues. In 1973 New York State taxpayers contributed 10.54 percent of the taxes collected by the federal Treasury while the state received back 10.8 percent of the $43.9 billion distributed under the eighty-four federal grant-in-aid or categorical grant programs in which it participated. If we assume the federal overhead costs of these programs to have been 10 percent (and the figure is on the low side), then it cost New York State taxpayers almost $500,000,000 net for the dubious privilege of being told by federal bureaucrats how to go about spending their own money in the delivery of a variety of services a great majority of which New Yorkers are far more competent to handle on their own, and at a lower cost. This, of course, is the "trace-the-dollar" logic that suggests why even special revenue-sharing should be regarded as no more than a halfway station in the achievement of a new Federalism.

When I advance these self-serving (from a New York taxpayer's point of view) arguments against federal grants as a form of financial assistance to the states, I am invariably asked, "But what about the poor states? What about those that cannot afford the services now financed in large or small part by the federal government? What about the benighted states that will not look after the basic needs of the poor or of the victims of discrimination?"

The first of these complaints addresses the fact that some states may not be able to afford the minimum social services that we as a society believe ought to be the birthright of every American. This need can be met through the device of spe-, cial revenue-sharing programs that would, in effect, identify the have-not states, measure the extent to which they are less able than the average state to meet the cost of such services as education or welfare, and then have the federal government (acting in the role of Robin Hood) contribute the difference. Such an approach would constitute an honest, above-board redistribution of funds within the Union for socially justifiable purposes. It would in no way encourage the fiscal shell game in which the citizens of the richer states are somehow persuaded that the money the federal government returns to them is someone else's.

An objection that is raised against this or any other proposal that falls short of a federal preemption of a given social field is that it does nothing to protect a state that is more generous than the average from suffering the consequences of its generosity. Those in need of public assistance will tend to gravitate to the states with the highest level of benefits, thereby compounding the burden on their taxpayers.

The Supreme Court, of course, has gone a long way toward "nationalizing" the welfare problem through its rulings striking out the attempts of some states (New York included) to protect themselves from swelling welfare rolls by requiring a minimum period of residence within the state as a qualification for the receipt of benefits. Because of this ruling and the mobility of even the poorest Americans, I was at one time tempted to conclude that this particular problem had escalated beyond the abilities of states to handle until I began to hear of the success that Governor Ronald Reagan was achieving in his massive and heavily resisted program of welfare reform in California.

When his program was put into operation in the spring of 1971, California had the fastest-growing welfare rolls in the country, adding new cases at the rate of between 25,000 and 40,000 per month. Within thirty days of the time that his reforms were put into effect, the welfare caseload began to level off, and then to decline. By 1975, there were 400,000 fewer persons on the California welfare rolls than there had been less than four years earlier, even though those remaining on welfare had received an initial 30 percent increase in benefits plus a cost of living adjustment that has protected welfare recipients from the effects of inflation.

What I found particularly intriguing about Governor Reagan's experience was that many of his principal battles were fought with an entrenched welfare bureaucracy and that bureaucracy's arbitrary rules and regulations and red tape. What he first had to do was to lobby to have the entire State of California exempted from the application of HEW regulations by having it classified as an experimental area. Having achieved this, he proceeded to put into effect a series of reforms that among other things banished from the rolls tens of thousands of cheaters who either were not qualified for welfare or had qualified to receive checks from too many states at one time; required able-bodied recipients to work for their keep; and pursued energetically the fathers of children on welfare and required them to contribute to their offspring's support.

The California experience is instructive in several respects. It illustrates the counterproductive effect of trying to handle social problems of a vast and complex nation from a command post on the Potomac; it points up the tendency of those manning our federal bureaucracies to become adversaries of state and local officials who are trying to do something sensible about problems they understand; and it demonstrates that state governments are competent to meet their responsibilities when emancipated from federal guidance and direction.

But we are still left with the argument that, all things being equal, the state that pays the highest benefits is apt to draw an out-of-state clientele against which, thanks to the Supreme Court, it is helpless to protect itself. This still doesn't make the case for having the federal government take over the full burden of welfare and the attendant responsibility for its administration. First of all, there is no reason to assume that national standards would be set at as high a level as those maintained by the most generous states. This would still leave those states with the problem of immigration, unless the law required them to reduce their level of payments. But if a reduction of payments is mandated by Washington in order to protect New York against the consequences of its own generosity, why shouldn't it be possible for New York to do the same in its own protection? The fact is that too many of those who argue for federal preemption want Washington to pick up the tab without ordering any diminution in current levels of welfare benefits.

Welfare isn't the only area in which states or localities find themselves in competition. New York City's policy of free tuition in its colleges and universities undoubtedly attracts a significant number of students from outside the city and state. Should New York be protected from the consequences by having the federal government pay the tuition of students in other less enlightened cities? A number of states now offer special tax inducements in order to attract industry that might otherwise settle elsewhere. Is this a form of unfair competition that should require the federal government to preempt the field of state business taxation?

I acknowledge that there are strong arguments for having the federal government assume full responsibility for the welfare system, especially because of the mobility of our poor. But before we conclude there is no alternative to such a takeover by the national government, I would first like to see New York freed of the federal laws and rules and regulations that have frustrated the state's attempts to emulate the California example rather than see the system made still more unmanageable by turning over the whole responsibility to Washington.*

Now let us look at the other end of the spectrum. What about those states that are indifferent to the basic needs of their own citizens? Here it is important that we first cull out the question of civil rights. Harold Hammett, in a prizewin-

---

*In 1971, the New York State Legislature adopted welfare reform measures that were in significant part based on the California experience. Unfortunately, as New York could not also qualify for exemption as an experimental area, these reforms had to run the gauntlet of the welfare bureaucracy's resistance and court tests that declared a number of them invalid because they ran counter to federal laws or regulations.

ning article on the role of the states that appeared in the November, 1972, issue of the *American Bar Association Journal*, approaches the question this way:

> . . . one of the major premises of federalism is the protection of freedom. But, in view of the contemporary association of "states' rights" with racial segregation, the question arises: Does federalism really protect freedom? . . .
>
> The answer to this . . . is that Lord Acton has not become obsolete. If absolute power tends to corrupt absolutely, over the long term the chances of maintaining individual freedom are increased if the source of power is dispersed. Diversity increases the probability of disagreement. In a country as diverse as the United States, the risk of local discrimination is worth bearing when one considers how much more difficult improvement would be if discrimination were imposed at a national level as a uniform policy. And lest we forget this can happen, recall the plight of Japanese-Americans during World War II (and of school bus drivers anywhere today). . . .

I would add a further point, and that is that civil rights are constitutionally protected. This basic principle has been reinforced in a series of Supreme Court decisions that leave no question as to the jurisdiction of federal courts in cases involving discrimination by virtue of race and, more recently, by virtue of sex. The question of discrimination, therefore, should no longer be allowed to muddy the assessment of the concept of states' rights, which has a life and logic of its own.

Setting aside, then, the matter of civil rights, and even setting aside the overriding considerations of freedom to which Mr. Hammett addressed himself, we are left with the proposition that some states are less concerned than others with the levels of education, housing, food, and health that their people enjoy. I would offer the following observations:

If we really believe in the competence of Americans to govern themselves, if we really believe that our people, whether they be located in the East, or in the South, or in the Midwest, or in the middle of the Pacific, are part and parcel of

Homo americanus, we must be willing to accept a diversity in judgments as to what constitutes acceptable minimum standards under all sorts of diverse conditions. It is easy to justify the imposition of federal standards under the claim that this state or that is dominated by a bigoted or complacent electorate. Even when the evidence supports the charge, we ought to be slow to accept this as reason enough to jeopardize what is left of our federal system and all it means for the protection of our liberties.

There are other, safer ways to achieve reform than by empowering the federal government to impose its judgment on the whole spectrum of American life. Social progress can and has been made state by state through the processes of education and example and through well-organized political action. Moreover, this organic approach is more likely to achieve true reform and right real wrongs than the attempt to shortcut the process by imposing centralized solutions that on the record can create as many problems as they attempt to solve, while making it all but impossible for even the best-motivated states to cope with them.

I am quite willing to grant that when all is said and done, when all the educational effort has been made, when all the indignation is mobilized, there will still be injustices. We live in an imperfect world and we deceive ourselves if we try to claim that there is any ordering of society that will restore the Garden of Eden. At least we have the satisfaction of knowing that the kind of injustices apt to be perpetrated by a county government will not be so damaging or difficult to uproot as those imposed by a federal regulation with ideological fervor on an entire society of more than 200,000,000 souls.

The case for Federalism is not efficiency but freedom. Those of us who are concerned for its state of health do not claim that it holds the key to a perfect society. Rather, we see in it the only ultimate guarantee that Utopians in control of the national government will never be able to impose on us, as individuals, their own concept of the perfect society.

Throughout our early history the rights and prerogatives of the several states were jealously protected in the implicit understanding that this was the best protection against the concentration and consolidation of power that in other societies had ultimately destroyed their people's liberties. Nevertheless, by imperceptible degrees at first, and in recent years by ever-larger ones, we have been emasculating the states and turning them into mere administrative agencies of a national government. We can now see the giant distance we have gone in destroying the ability of our constituent states to perform their original functions. We are also beginning to see the practical and political difficulties that must now be overcome in any effort to restore the federal system as originally conceived. It is, however, an effort that must be sustained even if we can do no more than hold the present line, since the historical and human impulses are to concentrate authority.

11
A Summing Up

Richard Nixon's celebrated trip to Peking in February, 1972, did more than open channels of communication with the Communist regime. It gave us an unsettling insight into the relative value that some Americans now seem prepared to place on individual freedom.

I still recall my dismay as I read the stories about life in Mainland China written by American journalists, scholars, and tourists in the wake of Mr. Nixon's visit. There was reflected in so many of them a fascination with the tidiness and order to be found everywhere. No litter in the streets, no flies, nothing one-half inch out of place as the millions of human ants went about their programmed lives. The authors' seeming obsession with order for the sake of order suggested a deep tiredness with the risks and challenges of a free society. Never mind the fact that none of the ants dared rise up and express an independent thought, or wander an inch from the path that had been charted for him.

And now we are beginning to read the same kinds of reports out of Castro's Cuba, accounts marveling at the organization and hard work and cooperation everywhere in evidence, with never a mention of the terrible cost in terms of human liberty and freedom of expression that the Cuban people have been required to pay.

When reading such articles I need to remind myself that their authors are not representative of American society and that the great majority of Americans have not yet lost their taste for liberty or their understanding of the unstructured life essential to it.

Over the years, however, we have seen some subtle

changes in what Americans perceive to be the relationship between freedom and government and the individual. Originally, Americans viewed liberty as derived not from government or a written Constitution, but from God ("that God, who gave us life, gave us liberty at the same time," to use Jefferson's words). Man's inherent right to liberty was held to be his ultimate protection against the predations of government. In a famous case in colonial New York, in which the rights of a free press were first litigated, the lawyer for the publisher of the New York *Weekly Journal* argued that wise men must use their "utmost care to support liberty, the only bulwark against lawless power." He also stated that "the question before the court . . . is not of small nor private concern; it is not the cause of the poor printer, nor New York, alone . . . it is the cause of liberty . . . the liberty both of exposing and opposing arbitrary power by speaking and writing Truth."

Fifty years later Thomas Jefferson wrote to James Monroe: "Equal and exact justice to all men . . . freedom of religion, freedom of the press, freedom of person under the protection of the habeas corpus: and trial by juries impartially selected—these principles form the bright constellation which has gone before us."

The freedoms cited by Jefferson were written into the Constitution by a Bill of Rights designed to protect the citizens of the new Republic against the abuses of governmental power that its architects knew to be the ultimate enemy of individual liberties.

In significant contrast, the catalog of freedoms that Franklin D. Roosevelt and Winston Churchill proclaimed in the Atlantic Charter contained two new ones: freedom from want and freedom from fear. These, together with the traditional freedoms of speech and religion, constituted the celebrated Four Freedoms.

The substantive difference between the freedoms itemized in Jefferson's "bright constellation" and those contained in the Atlantic Charter is best summarized by one commentator who suggested that the Roosevelt-Churchill formulation fell somewhat short of a ringing affirmation of what the war was all about, as their Four Freedoms were enjoyed by the animals in any first-class zoo. This was somewhat of an exaggeration, perhaps, but the comment does highlight a governmental role that was alien to the thinking of the Founding Fathers. For what did freedom from want imply but an affirmative government role as ultimate provider?

The inclusion of the newly proclaimed freedoms reflected a change in basic political perceptions. Whereas government was once seen by most Americans as a necessary evil, it was now beginning to be perceived in the role of benevolent provider. Thus, the freedoms enumerated in the Atlantic Charter include not merely those protecting individuals from government, but an assertion of rights that could flow only from government. And so government has come to take a place beside the Creator as the author and source of our blessings, just as individual security has come to claim parity with individual freedom in the hierarchy of those blessings.

There is no doubt but that Roosevelt and Churchill spoke to the most basic of human needs. Men and women have sought throughout the ages to be free of want and of fear, and it has been to achieve these ends that they have organized their own activities, and societies as well. It is only right and natural that they should do so. It was nonetheless novel, and a reflection of the present age, to see these age-old concerns added to the traditional litany of our freedoms.

Freedom from want—an understandable goal for all mankind, but one with inherent dangers when expressed as an explicit governmental responsibility in a democratic society that is subject to excessive political demands. But it is not the ability of the Congress to say no to a growing number of special interest groups asserting special claims on the public treasury that should concern us so much as the fact that so many claimants now exist. For they are, after all, only the manifestations of an evolving doctrine that would impose on government the obligation to cushion and protect its citizens from every vicissitude of life.

As I see this willing retreat from self-reliance, I begin to worry. There are times when I am haunted by a passage that Edward Gibbon wrote about the ancient Athenians:

In the end, more than they wanted freedom, they wanted security. They wanted a comfortable life and they lost it all—security, comfort and freedom. When the Athenians finally wanted not to give to society, but for society to give to them, when the freedom they wished for was freedom from responsibility, then Athens ceased to be free and never was free again.

I do not suggest that Gibbon has written an epitaph to the American Republic as well. But he has defined the choice that Americans must be prepared to make, and make consciously. It is a choice, fundamentally, between security and freedom as their first political goal. If faced squarely with the alternative, I believe the American people would today, as did their ancestors 200 years ago, choose freedom. Moreover, in making that choice, the American people would understand perhaps better than their representatives in Congress that in choosing freedom they will have the best of both worlds. Our experience has demonstrated, as did that of West Germany as it recovered from the destruction of World War II, that truly free societies—free economically as well as politically—are the most productive ones. They unleash the human energy and creativity that can lift the standard of living of an entire people while generating the surplus wealth that will enable society to provide its neediest members with a decent level of care.

It is a commonplace today that there has been a tidal shift in American attitudes toward the federal government, its role and its capabilities. A new perception of the limitations of government has emerged from the shambles of the Kennedy and Johnson programs that were to have solved all our problems. The American people have been able to observe their excesses and failures, and they are ready for fundamental changes in our current approaches to government.

This analysis finds support in a dozen recent surveys and studies, of which I will cite only one. I refer to a study commissioned in 1973 by the Senate Subcommittee on Intergovernmental Relations which was designed to assess public attitudes toward government, and which, unfortunately, has yet to have any effect on Congressional attitudes. The subcommittee report on the study summarized its principal findings as follows:

> The public underscores its belief in shared governmental responsibilities with an overwhelming endorsement of two policy propositions:
> (1) State and local governments should be strengthened, and
> (2) The Federal Government should have power taken away from it.
> Public support (61%) for reinforcing the structure and authority of local government almost precisely matches the percentage (59%) by which it advocates strengthening state government. In contrast, only 32% of the public feel the federal government needs added power, while 42% recommend diminishing its clout. . . .

What is equally interesting, the study found that substantial majorities believed that such areas as health and the care of the aged should be the province of state and local governments or private institutions, with less than 20 percent of those polled suggesting that the federal government ought to assume prime responsibility.

There is a growing resentment among Americans who earn too much to qualify for one form or another of public assistance, but who do not earn enough to protect themselves against inflation or aggressive bureaucrats, over what they see as public policies that discriminate against them. They resent having their taxes used to provide the children of others with levels of education they cannot afford to provide their own, and they bridle at the injustice of welfare and food stamp regulations that will allow some families to enjoy a higher standard of living at public expense than their self-supporting neighbors.

More and more Americans—parents, small-business men and women, farmers, state and local officials, college administrators, consumers—are experiencing the frustrations of being told what to do or what is good for them by federal bureaucrats over whose often arbitrary action they can exercise little or no control. Even when convinced they are in the right, few citizens or businesses can afford the delays and high costs of defending themselves against regulators who are under no pressure to act and who can mobilize batteries of full-time lawyers.

Even in the academic world, which in the past spearheaded so much of the movement to concentrate and expand governmental responsibilities, there is a new awareness of the adverse consequences of federal regulation. Study after study is now beginning to document the ways in which the Interstate Commerce Commission and other regulatory agencies have limited competition and consumer choice and imposed unnecessary costs that have increased the price of virtually every item purchased by the American public. In the area of transportation alone, the costs imposed by limitations on competition have been estimated at $100 billion. Articles in such scholarly journals as *Public Interest* and *Commentary* are beginning to reflect a retreat from the Utopianism that was the hallmark of so much of the social legislation of the 1960's.

Under the circumstances it is not entirely romantic to believe it possible to achieve a fundamental redirection of our public affairs, one that will restore the vigor and integrity of our political institutions. But while the public may be receptive to the need to reverse our drift into a centralized state and regulated economy, it will take a formidable marshaling of political forces to bring this about.

Only through the political process will it be possible to consolidate a majority mandate to restore the necessary authority to state and local governments or to begin dismantling the layers of regulations that are sapping the vitality of our economy. To accomplish these ends, we will need to encourage the process of political realignment now going on so that our national parties can present the people with coherent alternative views on what ought to be the role of government in American life.

It is no secret that our political parties are in a state of disarray. Large numbers of traditional Democrats find themselves increasingly alienated by the leftward drift of their party's leadership. There are factions within the Democratic ranks that in time may prove too antagonistic to be held together by the glue of political power and patronage. And so it is not unthinkable that the coalition stitched together during the days of the Great Depression may split into its component parts, ready to be reassembled along more rational lines.

The Republican Party faces challenges of a different sort. Its ranks have dwindled to a point where it must accomplish a major reconstruction or fade into history. It is self-evident that most Americans no longer see any compelling reason to commit themselves to the Republican Party. It is equally clear that the party must broaden its base. The well-advertised discussion within Republican ranks revolves over how this is to be accomplished. I believe it is fatuous to say that the Republican Party can command the allegiance of disillusioned Democrats and large numbers of voters who today prefer to remain unaffiliated by pursuing a policy of talking about Republican principles while studiously avoiding any meaningful attempt at defining them.

Today's public is wary of politics and politicians. It feels cut adrift, and millions of Americans are seeking something to believe in once again, a cause to which they can commit themselves. A political party that seeks to be all things to all men will attract none.

In this climate, and especially as it offers the least plausible stepping-stone to political success and power, it is more important than ever that the Republican Party identify itself with a coherent view of what is the proper role of government in a free society, and of the proper relationship between government and free men and women. I believe the view of government, society, and the individual that comes most naturally to the Republican Party also offers it the best chance to broaden its electoral appeal, and that is the view which today is most commonly described as "conservative."

The Republican Party cannot plausibly begin to outbid the liberal wing of the Democratic Party. But if it will stand up and affirm in unambiguous terms the principles that are in fact shared by the great majority of those who identify themselves as Republicans, the party can offer a hospitable harbor to tens of millions of Democrats and independents of the kind who in 1972 voted for the Republican Presidential ticket.

This is not a plea for the polarization of American politics. It is a plea for its rationalization. Ours is a two-party system and it is apt to remain one so long as we resist the temptation to abandon the constitutional device of the electoral college in favor of the direct election of Presidents.* Under the American system, neither party can survive if it becomes identified with a narrow, brittle ideology; nor can either long survive if it ceases to have any point of view at all. Each must be able to accommodate a broad range of opinion in order to stay in business; but if a party is to have long-term relevance and appeal, those opinions must have a common philosophical denominator.

Generally speaking, responsible Americans find themselves divided on the issues into one or another of two camps representing a reasonably consistent political perspective. This is nowhere more apparent than in the Congress of the United States. A substantial majority of those who vote together on issues A, B, and C today are apt to be voting together on issues D, E, and F tomorrow. This is so because they share common premises and common goals. If they find themselves in the minority, they are there not because they enjoy that status but because they believe their views coincide with the larger public interest and because they hope that in time they will be able to consolidate majority support. This is what the political process is, or at least ought to be, all about.

Most Republicans in and out of Congress will find themselves with great consistency on the same side of the major issues, while a majority of Democrats will find themselves on

---

*As the winner in each state (whether by a majority or plurality) is awarded all of that state's electoral votes, Presidential candidates must compete nationally through parties that have a broad national base. It is therefore virtually impossible for candidates or parties with a purely regional appeal, however strong, to compete successfully in a Presidential campaign. It is this institutional peculiarity of the American system rather than any unique character trait that has been largely responsible for the essentially stable two-party system we have enjoyed since the ratification of our Constitution.

the other. Moreover, if the opinion surveys are to be believed, most Republicans find themselves on the same side of the issues as tens of millions of Democrats and independents who find little in common with the current leadership of the Democratic Party. The fact is that while the Republican Party represents a diminishing political minority, it also represents a latent popular majority—one that it has been able to mobilize in the last two national elections.

Under the circumstances, it is foolish at best, and suicidal at worst, for Republicans to try to cultivate the other side of the political fence. The Democrats may be able to afford the luxury of playing both sides of the field, especially in the South, but the Republicans cannot. The Democrats are now in charge of most of the power centers. They are riding the crest, and political power provides its own rationale. But Republicans need to provide the uncommitted with convincing reasons for identifying themselves with what is currently the losing side, and this can only be done if their party is seen as standing for something more meaningful than a set of platitudes.

If the Republican Party is to recapture its old place in the sun, it must move to preempt its logical constituency; and this it can do only by identifying its principles, and positions, and priorities with those of its natural allies. This will require more than talking about principles and the fact that Republicans really do care about people. It will require *defining* those principles and explaining plausibly why Republicans can be trusted to apply them in building the kind of society most Americans still want.

What are these principles? What is the underlying philosophical thread that defines the Republican Party's natural constituency? Without attempting a definitive catalog, I would suggest a few propositions on which most Republicans could agree:

(1) The basic purpose of government in a free society is to protect the lives, liberty, and property of its citizens. This means that government has the duty (a) to bring crime under effective control, and (b) to pursue political and economic policies that will prevent a concentration of public or private

power at the expense of the individual and will enable most individuals to maintain their economic independence of government.

(2) The United States Constitution, with its principle of Federalism (to protect the states against encroachment by the national government), its checks and balances (to prevent a concentration of power within the national government), and its Bill of Rights (to protect the individual against the national government), remains the best blueprint for the protection of those liberties.

(3) Our system of free, competitive enterprise is not only essential to the preservation of individual liberty, but is the one best calculated to guarantee the highest standard of living for the greatest numbers.

(4) Citizens have the right to expect the value of their income and savings to be protected. This means that government has the duty to protect the value of its currency by avoiding fiscal and monetary policies that create inflation. In short, government must learn to live within its income.

(5) Ours is a society dedicated to the proposition that all men are created equal. This means that we cannot accept the proposition that an individual can have rights derived from membership in an arbitrary class. To do so would be to deny equal treatment under the law to those not members of that class.

(6) The federal government has no right to play social engineer, or to use its taxing powers for purposes of social manipulation. Whenever it attempts to do so the inevitable results will be for the government to dispense political favors at the expense of an increasingly hard-pressed middle class.

(7) The United States cannot afford to spend less on defense than is required to enable it to meet any plausible threat to its security and legitimate national interests. In today's world, that means that the United States cannot allow itself to become militarily weaker than the Soviet Union.

(8) Our great strength lies not in government, but in the responsibility and industry of free men and women. In Lincoln's words, "In all that the people can individually do as

well for themselves, government ought not to interfere. . . ."

(9) In a free society, the role of government is to serve, not to rule.

These propositions are broad enough to permit wide areas of disagreement as to how they should be applied in any given situation, or the circumstances under which exceptions might be made to them, but they do suggest certain underlying principles: the primacy of liberty in the political life of America; confidence in private initiatives; hostility to any concentration of power; distrust of government planning and regulation; a commitment to the traditional fiscal virtues; a belief in our system of free enterprise; a subordination of government to the individual; and a rejection of government as an instrument of social manipulation. While they provide a basis for the development of consistent policies and programs, they do not dictate their shape. They will accommodate, in short, the wide range of opinion to be found today, for example, in the Senate among the great majority of Republicans who on important issues vote together more often than not, and among the Southern Democrats who but for the accident of history might list themselves as Republicans.*

For the Republican Party to adopt a statement of principles reflected in these propositions would not only affirm in positive terms what it is that the party stands for, but would provide a coherent basis for developing specific programs for putting them to work. These could cover the spectrum ranging from a concerted campaign to restore a vigorous Federalism (beginning with Richard Nixon's special revenue-sharing proposals), to a call for a systematic review of existing regulatory agencies, to a reappraisal of public assistance programs, to calls for a return to fiscal prudence.

I fully recognize the institutional difficulties that the Republican Party would face in affirming any set of principles

---

*In the Ninety-third Congress, 39 Senators (31 Republicans, 7 Democrats, and 1 Independent) voted with the majority of Republicans against a majority of Democrats more than 55 percent of the time. *Congressional Quarterly,* January 23, 1975.

sufficiently meaningful to attract others to the Republican banner. The fact is that any statement that would distinguish the Republican Party from the Democratic Party would necessarily prove uncomfortable for a number of prominent Republicans who on the majority of controversial issues find themselves most at home with the position taken by a majority of Democrats. It is simply not possible to draft a meaningful statement of political principles that can accommodate every point of view. The fact that each party has its mavericks, however, should not dissuade either from affirming a broad set of beliefs that will distinguish one from the other in the public mind, and define its missionary territory. The Democrats, at least, found no such inhibition when they adopted their policy resolutions at their Kansas City "miniconvention" in December, 1974.

The one course that the Republican Party cannot afford is to allow itself to be perceived as standing for nothing. To the extent that it fails to identify itself with one or the other of the two camps in which most Americans find themselves divided on political issues, to the extent that it tries to keep its feet planted in both, it will dilute to the vanishing point its ability to attract new recruits and in time it will fall victim to its own irrelevance.

For better or worse, we are in a period of great political mobility. There are organic forces at work today that are seeking to bring about realignments that will cause our parties more accurately to reflect the natural division that exists within American political thought. Although ours is a two-party system, it is by no means static. If the existing national parties fail to reflect the kind of alternatives the public seeks, it is not at all impossible that the Democratic Party will find itself splintered, or the Republican Party drifting into oblivion, as their old constituencies reassemble into more natural coalitions under new political labels.

However it is brought about, it is essential that our existing political structure be rationalized if the current drift toward a centralized, socialized society is to be reversed, and if new goals are to be defined and translated into public policy. Nor can we afford to concentrate too much of our political effort on Presidential politics. We should know by now that it takes more than Presidential leadership to achieve major reforms, as a President is powerless to implement them without the concurrence of the Congress.

We should also understand by now that at any given time Congress is at best an imperfect reflection of the electorate. There is a kind of cultural lag built into the system that reflects the average length of incumbency. In the usual Congressional district, incumbents of more than a half dozen years in office are almost impossible to unseat. Even in 1974, only 40 out of 383 incumbents seeking reelection were defeated, all but four of them Republicans. Incumbents become known and are apt to be supported more for what they have been able to do to help their constituents with specific problems than for how they have voted on legislation that can have the most devastating impact on their constituents' lives. Thus, any fundamental change in national policy will require a significant change in the makeup of the Congress that it will take more than one election to accomplish.

Only such a shift in the Congress, together with strong Presidential leadership, can check and reverse the consolidation of governmental authority in Washington. And only if this is done can we begin to reduce federal responsibilities to a manageable number and return the Congress to a position where it can once again deal thoughtfully and effectively with matters that are uniquely national in character—defense, economic policy, the Social Security system, trade, the environment, foreign policy, and those other areas that clearly lie beyond the competence of state and local governments.

All these things *can* come to pass, but will they? Are Americans in sufficient numbers really so concerned over the growing size of government that they are willing to forgo those special programs and advantages that happen to benefit them? Do Americans still prize their liberties above their comfort and security? Will elected officials really assume the political risks necessarily associated with the curtailment of any program that has developed a large constituency? This is the measure of the challenge this generation of Americans is called upon to meet.

When I told some of my more experienced friends that I had undertaken to write this book, they stressed the need to end it on an upbeat note. I will confess that I find it hard these days to maintain an upbeat mood. A catastrophe of incredible proportions has overwhelmed the people of Cambodia and South Vietnam, and allies around the globe are reassessing the worth of American commitments. In reaction to the current recession, Congress seems determined to repeat all the mistakes and policies that in the recent past have moved us from inflation to recession, then back again, in a cycle of increasing severity that unless broken is destined to break the back of the American middle class.

In order to cure the inflation, unemployment, and high interest rates produced by more than $150 billion in deficits over the past five years, the Congress has adopted a budget that *boasts* a "stimulative" deficit of almost $70 billion for fiscal year 1976. The Congress has demonstrated, however, that it does have the ability to cut back on spending—so long as those cuts are made in military aid promised to an ally desperately fighting for its survival or in budget requests for the weapons research, development, and procurement that are essential if we are to continue to provide a credible match to Soviet power in the years ahead.

At one point I was sorely tempted to end this chapter shortly after quoting Gibbon's epitaph to the ancient Athenians. I had in mind writing something along the following lines:

Will this be written of the present generation in America? I don't know. I do know that we are rushing hell-bent for the edge of the precipice, but I also believe that with an extraordinary effort, and the intercession of the Lord to boot, catastrophe can be averted, and a new, stronger, and chastened America can emerge. If so, it will be a tribute to the profound good sense and sound instincts of the American public, and not to the kind of leadership we find today in government or to the self-anointed elite who presume to lecture Americans on what is good and beautiful and right and just.

The mood, however, has passed. If strapped to a lie detector, I would still have to confess to being deeply worried, intellectually, about the future of freedom in the United States. But I am also an optimist by nature, and it is because of this optimism and my belief in the worth and beauty of the American experience and the essential decency and intelligence of its people that I have joined the battle. It is for this reason that I have been digging in my heels, working with others to gain the time in which a clearer vision and a better understanding of what is truly at stake can turn the tide.

Our Bicentennial celebrations may well prove to be the catalyst that will convert the present widespread discontent over the scope and role of government in the United States into a sustained determination to renew our commitment to individual liberties and to restore the safeguards essential to their preservation.

The day-by-day retelling of the events and beliefs that gained us our independence and formed our political institutions will cause tens of millions of Americans to pause, to reexamine their roots, and to ask themselves what it is that has made our country so uniquely free and strong and prosperous. If they do, they will see that it is not government that has given us these blessings, but rather free men and women who have been able to risk, to work, to plan their own destinies and achieve the best within them without undue interference from government. And if they seek the sources of their freedom, again, they will find them not in government, but in the safeguards written into the Constitution to protect the individual *from* government.

They will note the care with which the Founders sought to prevent a destructive concentration of governmental power, to provide limited delegation of responsibilities to the new national government, and to create the other safeguards that were designed to protect individual liberties against the abuse of authority. But as Americans think back on their political origins, they may also gain a new appreciation of the interdependence between individual liberties and individual responsibility.

The American experiment is, after all, an informed act of faith in the ability of free men and women to act responsibly, to govern themselves. The Founders knew that the nation they were launching with such high hopes would remain free and would prosper only so long as its people remained willing to assume responsibility for their own lives and to exercise a responsible concern for the health of their political institutions. This last may well be the most important lesson to be learned from the insights that gave rise to the American nation: the need for self-reliance on the one hand and a willingness to assume the responsibilities of self-government on the other.

It is this, no doubt, that Benjamin Franklin had in mind when, in Philadelphia in 1789, he presented the challenge that has come down to us through the generations: "You have a Republic, if you can keep it." For almost 200 years we have kept it; we have kept faith with Benjamin Franklin and the other extraordinary men who together gave us this great and free nation.

If we will just focus on what it is we need to do, we of the present generation can continue to keep it and hand it on to the next generation with its best traditions reasonably intact as we enter our third century as a free society. With a display of faith and understanding and drawing on the enormous reservoir of American good sense and good humor and optimism, we can emerge from these troubling times with a greater strength and with our institutions revitalized, and safeguard "the blessings of liberty" to which this nation was dedicated in 1776.

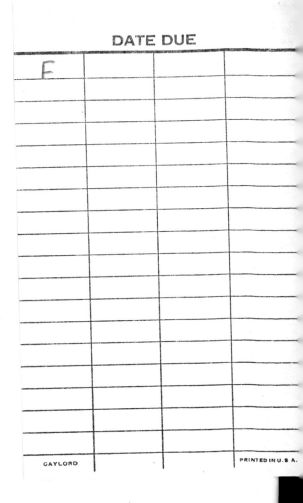

DATE DUE

GAYLORD

PRINTED IN U.S.A.